August 12th 1991.

To you, my brother Jack, a present on your 70th Birthday, to bring back pleasant memories (I hope) of your life on the footplate, and of Dad's, especially over the C. K. & P. with the "Cauliflowers".

Happy reading

Audrey.

RAILS Through LAKELAND

**An Illustrated History of the Workington-Cockermouth-Keswick-Penrith Railway
1847-1972**

by

HAROLD D. BOWTELL

Silver Link Publishing Ltd
The Trundle, Ringstead Road, Great Addington, Kettering, Northamptonshire NN14 4BW

CONTENTS

FRONT COVER (MAIN PICTURE): A classic image of Keswick road passenger traffic in the years before 1948. A London & North Western Railway '18in goods' engine (of a class popularly known as 'Cauliflowers') climbs away from Penrith with a Workington-bound train. *Eric Treacy/Courtesy Millbrook House Ltd.*

FRONT COVER (INSET): Peter Thompson, Secretary and General Manager of the Cockermouth Keswick & Penrith Railway. *Author's Collection.*

BACK COVER (UPPER): A fascinating pre-Grouping glimpse at Brigham station, as a Maryport & Carlisle Railway train awaits the rightaway for Cockermouth, after arriving from Bullgill. *J.D. Hinde Collection.*

BACK COVER (LOWER): The 'Lakes & Fells' railtour (organised by the Stephenson Locomotive Society and the Manchester Locomotive Society) stands at Keswick on April 2 1966, the year in which the Keswick-Workington closed. *Derek Cross.*

TITLE PAGE: The beauty of the CKPR; on Whit Monday 1963, a Carlisle-Keswick train approaches Keswick hauled by a pair of Ivatt Class 2MT 2-6-0s. *Stephen Crook.*

FACING PAGE: On August 7 1950, '18in goods' 0-6-0 No. 58389 is seen standing in the Up platform at Threlkeld with the 11.50am ex-Workington train. This is the eastern end of the station; note the distinctive and most unusual signalbox at the western end of the island platform buildings. *E.S. Russell.*

Copyright © Harold D. Bowtell

First published in the United Kingdom June 1989, reprinted June 1991

All rights reserved. No part of this publication may be reproduced, stored in a retrieval system, transmitted in any form, by any means electronic or mechanical, or photocopied, or recorded by any other information storage and retrieval system without prior permission in writing from the Publisher.

Printed in Great Britain by Woolnough Bookbinding Ltd, Irthlingborough, Northants, and bound by The Bath Press, Bath

British Library Cataloguing in Publication Data
Bowtell, Harold D.
    Rails through Lakeland: Workington, Cockermouth,
Keswick and Penrith Railway, 1847-1972
    1. Cumbria. Railway services, to 1979
I. Title
385'.09427'8
ISBN 0-947971-26-2

RAILS THROUGH LAKELAND
WORKINGTON-COCKERMOUTH-KESWICK-PENRITH, 1847-1972
AUTHOR'S PREFACE

Every railway has its own unique character. This is created not only by impressive features, such as a Kilsby tunnel, bridges by Brunel, or engineering works of the kind found between Settle and Carlisle. Character is the sum of a complex recipe: the country and the towns, and the traffics conveyed, all contribute – but above all it is the *people* who create character. The families and folk who ran the Keswick line were quietly dedicated and I have sought to give them a little more individual attention than is usually possible in histories of 'grander' railways. An effort is also made to indicate how the local company Directors and also those nominated by the London & North Western and North Eastern Railways were caring figures in the railway and the communities it served.

Other notables from the earlier years who come into the story include William Wordsworth and his son, the Reverend John Wordsworth, and, from the middle period, Canon Rawnsley of Crosthwaite (Keswick) and the National Trust. The Canon was at Carlisle Cathedral when he received a telegram from the Editor of the *Daily News* telling of the death of Scott of the Antarctic - and he composed a suitable sonnet while returning to Keswick by train that afternoon. It was duly carried by the CKPR, LNWR and the Post Office in time to be published in the newspaper in London, next day.

Rather less confidence was shown by the writer of the message on a picture postcard from Lakeland: "I will come (to Manchester) tomorrow by the train leaving Keswick at 3.50. The trains on this line are very late...all the trains on this line are very late today, they are not particular about time on this line. It is very wet tonight.' Nevertheless, the Post Office (with the Railways' assistance) was relied on to deliver this card, postmarked at Keswick at 7.00 am on August 16 1906, to a Manchester suburban address the same afternoon, and doubtless did so.

Rural aspects also come through. There is William Boyd's memory of his schooldays trip from Edinburgh to Keswick in August 1920. Leaving Penrith, a swishing sound not evident on the 'Caley' or Lancaster & Carlisle main lines was evident - and it proved to be that of the CKPR train passing through the long grass! Again, in the 1930s, a certain station-master became cross with engine drivers who repeatedly stopped to pick mushrooms in the fields near his station. So, he picked them himself and substituted empty eggshells; after a few abortive halts, the drivers had their suspicions, but desisted.

Concerning the setting of the railway and touching on just one aspect, H.H. Symonds (*Walking in the Lake District*, 1933) wrote "...Saddleback...many look at it from carriage windows, as the train from Penrith comes first in sight of it at Penruddock, then warms to it by Troutbeck, and at last is smothered under the glory of it all the way to Threlkeld and on into the woods and cuttings towards Keswick. These are six miles of 'parly third' which leave the World's Best Permanent Way, the Royal Scot, the thunders of Shap Summit, nowhere."

The general map, in two overlapping sections (see page 10) sets the route of our railway (and its junctions and stations) in perspective amid the rivers, lakes and mountains. Original siding diagrams of 1874 and 1915-17 are reproduced (with a little extraneous detail removed, for clarity) to expand details of the once-industrial western end of the route. Where available in suitable form, LMS engineering and estate department plans of the 1930s form the basis of station plans, notably depicting Cockermouth and Keswick stations, but also part of Brigham, Penruddock and Blencow. Cockermouth's elongated junction and goods yard, also plans of the station layouts at Bassenthwaite Lake and Troutbeck, are provided. Richard Foster has made available his reconstruction, basically illustrating the 1920s-1930s period, of Threlkeld, which provides an emphasis on signalling, and is complemented by his architectural presentation and various photographs.

The reader may ask: why is the line not described westward, from Penrith to Workington? This is because the railway began life in the west, between Workington and Cockermouth (in 1847) and following its opening throughout in 1864-65 the emphasis was on working the coal pits in the west and carrying coke from Durham to West Cumberland's ironworks. The pattern became, in time, one of primarily passenger and tourist travel, chiefly on the Keswick section, and the last part to operate (until 1972) was between Keswick and Penrith. The story is therefore taken from Workington to Cockermouth, to Keswick and finally to Penrith.

Regrettably, the railway is no more. Why did it disappear? The study in this work of the multitude of bridges - mainly designed in the first place by (Sir) Thomas Bouch - hints at one of the economic reasons. Then, there is the total disappearance of the basic traffic in coke westward, along with the decline of the collieries and shipment of their output; after all, these were the traffics which the railway was built to carry. Also, by the early 1960s, there was pressure by the Ministry of Transport to build a virtually new road between Penrith and West Cumberland. There was pressure too to provide such a link as impetus to the establishment of a bus-building factory near Workington. For many miles, the railway's route provided a tempting right of way, which in the event was taken over for long stretches and greatly widened for the new road. A parallel local bus service survived the railway but, from November 1985, this all but disappeared between Penrith and Keswick, with only two daily workings each way advertised.

The railway is long gone, but there are still many reminders of its presence to be viewed and explored. I hope that this account, in words, pictures and plans will enable the residents of Lakeland, railway enthusiasts and historians and many other visitors to locate and interpret the scenes and surviving structures.

Harold D. Bowtell,
Kendal,
Westmorland.

January 1989

Chapter 1

SETTING THE SCENE

THE COCKERMOUTH & WORKINGTON RAILWAY

Authorised by an initial Act of July 23 1845, this essentially single track link of some 8 1/2 miles extended from a terminal station at the west end of Cockermouth, to Workington Harbour. It was designed primarily to carry coals from pits (to be connected to it) for shipment from Workington. Opening for all traffic was on April 28 1847. From a convergence at Derwent Junction with the Whitehaven Junction Railway, the CWR's passenger train – the Company had an engine and carriages for but a single train – crossed the river and ran south to reach the WJR's nearly new, but scarcely grandiose Workington station. This was remote from the town (to eastward) and the sea (to the west). Workington was at this time newly connected with Carlisle, following completion of the of the Maryport & Carlisle Railway (February 10 1845) and the WJR, Maryport-Workington (January 19 1846), which was extended from Workington to Whitehaven Bransty (March 19 1847). Not until 1857 was there a through connection southwards (via the coastal line) to Carnforth and thereby the London & North Western Railway's Anglo-Scottish main line from Euston to Scotland.

The CWR's route, features, local industries and traffics are separately described in *Chapter 2*. Its 19 years of independence were conducted with surprisingly little cognisance of

Above: A delightful and characteristic scene looking west at Cockermouth, in the early 1900s. The permanent way lengthmen take a break from their work as an unidentified LNWR 'Cauliflower' 0-6-0 coasts into the platform with a four-coach Up passenger service, for which a group of smartly-attired ladies and gentlemen are waiting, outside the station's refreshment room. The hot summer weather is clearly apparent: note the ladies' sunhats and the gents' straw 'boaters!' On the right, cattle wagons (with their lower planking 'limed' to prevent the spread of disease) are awaiting their next turn of duty, probably in connection with Cockermouth's Monday market. The Sankey Collection.

its coastal neighbours - and it never persevered with, or supported, the early project for an extension eastward, following the northern shore of Bassenthwaite Lake, to Keswick.

THE KESWICK COMPANY AND ITS RAILWAY NEIGHBOURS, LARGE AND SMALL

The Cockermouth, Keswick & Penrith Railway was constituted under an Act of Parliament of August 1 1861, with authorised capital of £200,000, accompanied by the authority to raise £66,000 by loans; a modest increase in capital was made in 1876-77. The undertaking was a more substantial affair, in both aims and achievement, than the purely local CWR. What the CKPR lacked in direct associa-

Right: The splendid setting of the Penrith-Workington route is amply illustrated by this view from Latrigg, circa 1895-96. Keswick station and the impressive hotel are visible in the foreground, backed to southward by the town, Derwentwater and the mountains of central lakeland.
Author's Collection.

tion with industry, it compensated for it in its cross-country linkage of industrial interests, and its superb setting in northern Lakeland. Construction (discussed on pp 7-8), was put in hand, leading to opening of its entire route - some 31 miles - for mineral traffic on November 4 1864 and subsequently to passengers on January 2 1865.

In 1861, and until 1866, the CKPR was financially independent of its existing western neighbour, the CWR - and, in a sense, this independence continued until the railway Grouping of 1923. However, the linking at Cockermouth of the existing CWR and the projected CKPR was an essential feature of the Keswick Company's scheme, as only by this means could its powerful friends to the east be enabled to operate important end-to-end through traffics. The completion of arrangements with the London & North Western Railway and the Stockton & Darlington Railway (soon to become part of the North Eastern Railway) was a priority for the Keswick Board. This would associate it with two railways which served a major part of British industry and which, through the ensuing 60 years, clearly appreciated the extent of their mutual interests. Negotiations during February-September 1862 produced agreements with the LNWR, as also with the SDR, confirmed and signed in each case. The CKPR Act of June 29 1863 followed, each of the other Companies being allowed to subscribe £25,000 to the CKPR. The LNWR was to operate all passenger and goods trains on the CKPR line and was to receive 33 1/3% (increased in 1889 to 35%) of the relevant receipts. The NER was to operate mineral trains and receive 35% of receipts from minerals. The Keswick Company was thereby relieved of the need to provide rolling stock or guards for commercial traffic. Locomotive power and engine crews, as discussed in detail later, were likewise to be the responsibility of the larger Companies.

A potential community of interest between the giant LNWR, with headquarters at Euston, and the small Companies of West Cumberland (CWR and WJR) was apparent. During 1864 and 1865, both the LNWR and the CKPR, acting independently, were in touch with the CWR

concerning prospects for traffic working, or merger. Also, the CKPR secured some agreement with the LNWR to respect Keswick's relations with the WJR.

However, hurt feelings followed when it emerged in December 1865 that Mr Fitzsimons, of the LNWR's Lancaster & Carlisle Division, and Mr Stephenson, Traffic Manager of the SDR, had recently agreed, without reference to Keswick:
1) That the LNWR would convey coal arriving at Penrith from the north for stations on the Keswick line by its goods trains; and:
2) That the SDR would carry pig iron from Workington for stations on the SDR system by its mineral trains.

The latter point is significant, as it indicates that a west-to-east traffic in pig iron from blast furnaces in West Cumberland was available by the close of 1865.

Nevertheless, the considerable discussions between the LNWR and the CKPR, regarding traffic handling and terms, were amicably concluded and, in May 1866, the 'LNWR, Whitehaven Junction and Cockermouth & Workington Amalgamation Bills' were passed unopposed by the Bill Committee of the House of Commons, and became law as an Act that summer. An interesting provision was that the short line to the Lonsdale Dock at Workington was deemed a continuous line of railway for traffic purposes from the WJR and from the CWR (the access being at Derwent Junction) and the LNWR was authorised to ship through mineral traffic and pig iron either at Lonsdale Dock or Merchants Quay, Workington. Lonsdale Dock was a new development of 1865, but the Merchants Quay branch and shipment facilities had existed for at least 10 years.

The coastal route between Maryport, Derwent Junction, Workington and Whitehaven Bransty, and the line from Cockermouth Goods and Cockermouth Junction to Derwent Junction, thus came to constitute the West Cumberland Lines of the LNWR. There was a degree of local autonomy, but the lines were subservient to the Lancaster & Carlisle Division's Superintendent, based at Lancaster.

Another development peaceably concluded was the extension of the Whitehaven Cleator & Egremont Railway northward of Rowrah to join the Cockermouth-Workington line at Marron Junctions, forming a triangular layout with the CWR route and believed to be opened in January 1866 (for minerals) and April 1866 (for passengers). It was doubled in 1873. In October of 1866, the SDR/NER–promoted double track link from Eamont Junction, on the LNWR's Anglo-Scottish main line, to Redhills Junction, on the CKPR just westward of Penrith, was opened. Thus, by the end of 1866, there existed a route for coke traffic from County Durham to Marron Junction and thence to Cleator Moor iron works, also to Workington and those ironworks at Workington and further south, as well as Workington quaysides. These routes were likewise available to any balancing traffic, such as the products of West Cumberland's furnaces, ironstone mines or other industries.

Euston was alive to these matters and some ten years later produced the first LNWR (WCE) Leasing Bill; this became the Act of June 26 1877, giving the LNWR control of the WCER. The CKPR became concerned early in 1878, when a Bill was prepared to authorise leasing of the WCER to the LNWR *and the Furness Railway*; the Keswick Board sought protection against traffic from West Cumberland being diverted from the CKPR to the Furness Railway route. Joint control of the WCER by the LNWR and the FR was in fact authorised by Act of June 17 1878 and the line was thereafter generally known in Cumberland as the 'the Joint Line'.

The CKPR did not oppose the entirely new railway, to be built from Cleator Moor northward to the town centre of Workington on an inland route broadly parallel with the LNWR's coastal route (to its west) and 'the Joint Line' (to its east) - and competitive with both of these. This was the Cleator & Workington Junction Railway, authorised by Act of June 1876 and opened from Cleator Moor, via Distington, to Workington Central station on October 1 1879. This link

became highly significant to the CKPR when its Workington Bridge branch opened on March 16 1885. This branch provided a direct curve of only 30 chains length but including a major bridge over the Derwent river and permitting through running from the CKPR by the CWR line, Workington Bridge Junction and Cloffocks Junction to the CWJR main line, (serving potentially Distington and Cleator Moor ironworks) and also the CWJR's new branches from Harrington Junction to Moss Bay, Harrington Harbour and Derwent. Note the existence of coastal ironworks at these three sites!

Thus the CKPR-CWR (LNWR) lines became fully established and developed progressively between 1866 and 1885 as a through route of great industrial significance.

BUILDING THE COCKERMOUTH & WORKINGTON RAILWAY

The decision to build this railway was taken at a meeting of interested gentlemen, held in the *Green Dragon Inn*, Workington, on July 26 1844. A committee was appointed and George Stephenson, whose preliminary advice and estimates had influenced the decision, was to be asked to complete a full survey. The proposed title was 'The Workington and Cockermouth Railway Company' but by October this was amended to the Cockermouth & Workington Railway. Capital of £70,000 was to be raised, amended to £75,000 in December. A survey was to be carried out by John Dixon, nominally under the direction of George Stephenson; the resulting estimate of £72,000 was close to that of the master himself. John Dixon (1796-1865) of Darlington, was a respected figure, with experience on construction of the Stockton & Darlington Railway and the Liverpool & Manchester Railway and with recent responsibilities in North East England. Parliamentary plans were deposited in December 1844 and the Act of July 23 1845 resulted. On

Above: No. 48362 leaves Penrith with a Workington-bound train on August 12 1950. The locomotive is an '18in goods' of a class familiarly known as 'Cauliflowers', this nickname deriving from the appearance of the LNWR arms sometimes carried in pre-Grouping days. The Eden Valley track is seen to the right of the train, the Down and Up roads of the West Coast Main Line to right again and the goods yard beyond those. *Neville Fields*.

June 28 1845, John Dixon was formally appointed Engineer for the duration of construction and J.C. Fearon was the Assistant Engineer, the latter being resident during the execution of the works.

In July and November 1846, George Stephenson was again consulted, when problems arose over acquisition of essential lands at Workington Cloffocks and Merchants' Quay, which belonged to the Earl of Lonsdale, of Whitehaven Castle, the most influential landowner in the territories to be traversed by the CWR. It was November 1845 when the tender of Jacob & William Ritson was accepted, as contractors. They were also building the Whitehaven Junction Railway, which was reported well advanced in January 1846, and they started on the CWR works in mid-February 1846, when an adequate part of the requisite lands had been secured.

The route of nearly nine miles crossed a major river, the Derwent (six times) and subsidiary channels and tributaries were also crossed. Leaving aside the Derwent viaduct at Workington, a responsibility of the WJR (although to be crossed by CWR trains) the CWR had itself to commission 11 bridges of nominal lengths between 50ft and 300 ft; they are discussed in *Chapter 5*. Notwithstanding, the single track route was constructed in only 15 months and opened on April 28 1847, immediately after inspection by Captain Simmons for the Railway Commissioners.

As early as August 15 1845, at the first general meeting of the CWR, (soon after its Act had been obtained) there was a hint of possible connection by rail between the Kendal & Windermere Railway (at Windermere) and the CWR (at Cockermouth). This C&W Extension Railway was independent of the CWR, which in January 1846 decided that the Extension Railway's section between Cockermouth and Keswick (for which an Act was passed in the ensuing summer) would cost more than £180,000 and would not pay 4%, so they decided against the monetary commitment. The Extension Railway's powers were never exercised.

BUILDING THE COCKERMOUTH KESWICK & PENRITH RAILWAY

There had been earlier surveys, but pressure for a through cross-country route by way of Keswick developed when a protege of the Stockton & Darlington Railway secured its Act in 1857 for a railway across the Pennines, via Stainmore. Serious surveys via Keswick followed and that carried out by Thomas Bouch in 1859 produced an estimate not exceeding £200,000; the CKPR's Act of 1861 was based on its findings. Thomas Bouch (1822-1880) was the younger brother of William Bouch, the latter being noted for both mechanical and civil railway engineering and for water engineering, and in general based at Darlington.

Below: The 'Cauliflower' 0-6-0s were staple motive power on the Keswick road for many years. Here, No. 58396 (with Belpaire firebox) pilots another of the same type (but with a round topped firebox) away from Blencow with a Penrith-Workington train in August 1949. The stock is a mixture of LMS and LNWR designs. *P.B. Whitehouse.*

Left: A static memorial - one of the two boundary stones still to be seen today in Station Road, Keswick, recalling the Cockermouth Keswick & Penrith Railway Company, which in 1923 became part of the London Midland & Scottish Railway Company. *Harold D. Bowtell.*

Below: From Workington to Cockermouth the railway was virtually level, but thereafter the general trend was uphill, with increasingly severe gradients as the summit was approached at Troutbeck, 889ft above sea level. *Author's Collection.*

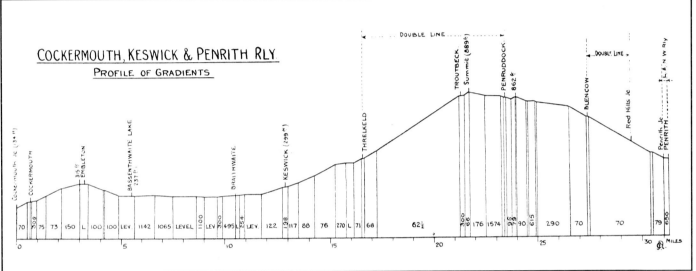

Thomas established himself in Edinburgh and he was - among many interests - Engineer during construction of the Stainmore line. He was appointed Engineer for construction of the CKPR and in May 1862 the main contracts were let to George Boulton & Son (later - & Sons).

As on the CWR, bridgeworks dominated the engineering of the CKPR. They are of special interest in view of Thomas Bouch's notable viaducts on the Stainmore route and his ultimate - and fatal - concern with the bridging of the Tay and the design of a proposed railway bridge (not built in the form he proposed) for the Firth of Forth. See *Chapter 5* for development of this subject.

During 1862-64, work seems to have proceeded without significant hitches or hold-ups, under the direction of John Wood, Resident Engineer under Bouch, who was fully occupied elsewhere. Wood reported periodically to the Company's Board and works committee, which made its first trip by rail from Cockermouth to Keswick on May 4 1864. They commented that the pitching (protective stonework) on the shore of Bassenthwaite Lake was of inferior material and workmanship, and must be renewed. On June 1 1864, they travelled on an engine (would it be the property of the SDR?) from Penrith station to Keswick station. On July 13 1864, they traversed the full length of the line, from Cockermouth to Penrith. Again, on September 30 1864, they inspected the whole line, stating that the only obstacle to opening was 'the condition of the

viaducts at Thornthwaite', delayed by non-delivery of timber. The subject of their concern would have been the screw-pile structures over low-lying lands on the Keswick side of Braithwaite station.

It is interesting that in March 1864 the CWR agreed to lend a locomotive to the Keswick Company's contractors for two hours per day, for about a week, at £1 per day. Considerably later, on November 29 1864, a CWR engine was on loan to the Keswick Company but the CWR enginemen were being kept for excessive hours, and it was decided to withdraw the engine. Earlier, following the CKPR works committee's journey of May 4, arrangements were made for the SDR to hire to the CKPR and send to Mr Boulton a locomotive and 30 wagons - for use in ballasting. The loan dated from May 25 1864 and was charged to the CKPR at £3 per day (for the engine) plus £1 monthly (for each wagon).

Boultons probably had at least one locomotive of their own engaged from early days on the CKPR construction works: *Grant*, an 0-4-0ST, with 9in x14in cylinders (clearly a small locomotive) built by Manning Wardle, of Leeds, Works No. 62 of 1862. It was despatched on November 21 1862 to 'George Boulton & Son, Penrith'.

Again, on February 19 1864, Isaac Watt Boulton, the locomotive dealer of Ashton-under-Lyne, sold to 'G. Boulton & Sons, contractors, Penrith' a four-coupled tank locomotive with outside cylinders (14in x 20in) and 4ft 9in diameter

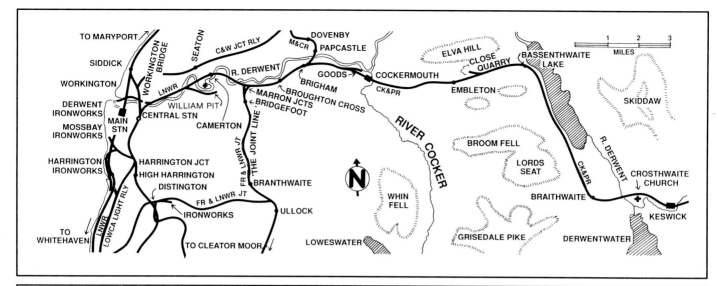

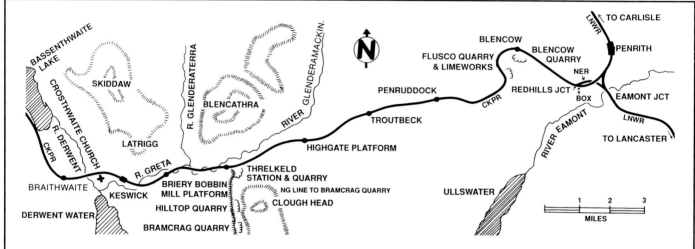

wheels (evidently much more powerful than *Grant*). Alfred Rosling Bennett, in his 'Chronicles of Boulton's Siding' reports this sale and states that the locomotive had been purchased not long before from the LNWR. Another reference in the same work *may* identify this locomotive with a type of outside-framed 0-4-2, having *inside* cylinders (14in x 20in) and 4ft 6in diameter wheels, built originally by Sharp Roberts & Company, of Manchester, as tender engines. There is also reason to believe that Boultons (of Penrith) secured the ownership, or use on hire, of a locomotive (from Gilkes Wilson & Company, locomotive builders, of Middlesbrough) during the course of the CKPR works.

Board of Trade inspections were made on October 24 and 25 1864 by Capt F.H. Rich, RE. Opening of the line to minerals was effective from November 4 1864, but the Captain declined to authorise passenger traffic on account of 11 listed shortcomings - notably the still incomplete pitching of the railway bank alongside Bassenthwaite Lake and the state of various abutments and parapet walls, also the lack of firm bearings for the wooden cross beams of some viaducts. Interestingly, the west distant signal for Blencow, and its siting, was criticised, although Blencow was not a crossing place, nor understood to play a part in signalling in those early days. Thomas Bouch personally joined the works committee on a line inspection of December 15 and all were satisfied; so was Captain Rich on

December 22 and the confirmatory letter from the Board of Trade was dated December 24, probably delivered at Keswick on Christmas Day.

Opening to passengers followed on January 2 1865, seemingly without significant ceremony. The event was something of an anti-climax as opening should - by contract and anticipation - have been on July 1 1864, and for long it was confidently expected that it would be achieved by the end of August 1864, with two days of special trains and a cold collation for guests. John Wood, as Thomas Bouch's Resident Engineer, earned the respect of the Company, which granted him a gratuity for 'extra services rendered during the construction of the line.' On January 5 1865, he was appointed Company Engineer, the appointment to be effective on ending of his commitment to Mr. Bouch.

While the Railway Company went on to a passably successful career, its Board and its contractor enjoyed strained relations for many years. A dispute was proceeding in 1867-69, with a figure of £2,500 mentioned as likely to meet the contractor's claim. Ten years on, after awards by an arbitrator and then the Court of Appeal, the dispute continued during 1876-79 - nearly reaching the House of Lords - with the final cost to the Company, in 1879, approaching £5,000, presumably accompanied by handsome legal costs. As in many works of civil engineering, expenditure on additional requirements was central to the dispute.

Chapter 2

A LEISURELY JOURNEY
The route described: Workington-Penrith

This chapter takes a leisurely journey over the 40 miles of largely country railway from Workington to Penrith, via Cockermouth and Keswick, covering a timescale of 125 years, from 1847 to 1972.

Introduction to the route

This itinerary takes in the tiny Cockermouth & Workington Railway of 1847-66, with its subsequent career as part of a through route (1866-1966) leading to Cockermouth-Keswick (1865-1966) and Keswick-Penrith (1865-1972). For much of the time embraced, the first six miles (to Brigham) provided recurring glimpses of industry - it is smiling countryside today - while from just beyond bustling Cockermouth, the scene is spectacular with fells, lake and mountains. Later sections of the book discuss permanent way, doubling of portions of the line, the many exciting bridges, its signalling and also the unique acetylene lighting - thus amplifying the descriptions in this itinerary. In summary, the stations and major junctions of the full route were:

MILES	STATION OR JUNCTION
0	WORKINGTON (MAIN)
1/4	Derwent Junction
1 1/4	Workington Bridge Junction and station
3 1/4	Camerton
4 1/2	Marron Junction
5 3/4	Broughton Cross
6 1/2	Brigham
8 1/4	Cockermouth Junction
9	COCKERMOUTH
11 3/4	Embleton
14 1/4	Bassenthwaite Lake
19 1/4	Braithwaite
21 1/2	KESWICK
25	Threlkeld
27 3/4	Highgate Platform
29 3/4	Troutbeck
32	Penruddock
36	Blencow
38	Redhills Junction
39 3/4	PENRITH

This is the LMS version of September 1929 and is taken as broadly representing maximum development. The Up direction was from Workington to Penrith (namely, heading for Euston) and Down from Penrith to Workington. The terms Up and Down will be used without inverted commas, as in normal British and derived railway practice the world over. Our journey is in the Up direction, from west to east.

WORKINGTON-COCKERMOUTH & KESWICK

Workington Main Station

When, in 1866, the LNWR took over the Whitehaven Junction Railway's coastal route between Whitehaven, Workington and Maryport - as well as our Cockermouth & Workington Railway - the passenger station at Workington was an uninspired structure. It comprised two through passenger running lines, two platforms and poor buildings, but

also a pair of goods lines to the west. Southward, blast furnaces only existed at Harrington and Cleator Moor. In Workington district, north of the Derwent, blast furnaces were found at Oldside Works and the newly-established and progressive West Cumberland Works. There were no great flows of mineral traffic or products of the iron industry passing through the station. Soon, in 1872-73, the new works with blast furnaces at Whitehaven and also on Workington's southerly shore changed all this and the railway's services were in constant demand by industry and its people.

Admittedly, the Cleator Moor-Marron route began to offer a little relief, but only when the opening (from 1879) of the highly competitive Cleator & Workington Junction Railway brought into sharp focus the congestion on the coastal route, did the LNWR take modernisation in hand.

A new layout at Workington Main was opened in November 1886, giving four roads through the station, with lengthy passenger platforms on the outer roads and further independent lines passing by on the west side; there was also a bay platform at the south end on the eastern side. The brick buildings of this new station for long looked dirty, drab and undistinguished, but cleaning and detailed improvements have revealed hitherto unsuspected colour and decoration, especially in the east front. This faces the small forecourt and access to the long Station Road.

Workington Main-Derwent Junction

Northwards, under the South Quay road bridge, the six tracks dating from the 1880s converged to form a double track across the Harbour Bridge, with the old harbour to westward, and the low-lying 'Cloffocks' are crossed. For many years, the branch trailed in (left) from the Merchants Quay, so favoured in the 1850s for loading of coals from the familiar chaldron wagons to seagoing vessels; after Lonsdale Dock was constructed, in 1865, the installations of the Quay declined in use.

The Derwent Viaduct follows closely. The cramped Lowther Iron Works, in production 1873-1911, but never a steel-producing works, was to the left. Now came the eastward divergence of the double track route for Cockermouth, which we follow (albeit closed and abandoned in 1966), under the control of Derwent Junction signalbox. This box also controlled the intriguing single track lead of 1864, trailing off the Cockermouth line, crossing the coast route on the level and reaching Lonsdale Dock, which was remodelled and extended as the Prince of Wales Dock circa 1927. This trailing lead closed nominally wef February 21 1953. Oldside Iron Works (1841-1930, never steel-producing) was over to seaward of the coast line and West Cumberland Works (1862-1900, with steel production between 1870 and circa 1900) was on the landward side, having a trail-in at its south end into the Up Cockermouth line. The maps reproduced in these pages show the main features of these once-complex track layouts.

Right, upper:
Workington station in
the early 1880s, looking
north. The layout shown
is much as taken over
from the Whitehaven
Junction Railway in 1866
by the LNWR. The stan-
dard LNWR signal box in
the middle distance was
an addition. *Richard L.
Pattinson/Cumbrian
Railways Association.*

Right, lower: A similar
view at Workington in
April 1985, showing
essentially the layout
developed in the mid-
1880s and the buildings
of that period.
Harold D. Bowtell.

Heading east on the Cockermouth & Workington line

The double track CWJR dated from 1879-80 and crossed the CWR line by a bridge; immediately southward the CWJR and the 'navvies bridge' footway also crossed the broad Derwent. Final closure of this section of the CWJR, between Harrington Junction, Workington Central and Calva Junction (this being north of the Cockermouth line) was recorded by British Railways as effective from Sunday September 26 1965. The Cockermouth line passed under the A596 and reached Workington Bridge.

Workington Bridge Station and Junction

Following pressure from residents of the higher, easterly part of the town, the station in basic form was first provided in 1847. Although the buildings were always modest, they enjoyed some rebuilding in 1867 and 1877. The stationmaster occupied a house near the CWJR bridge. The station site was very cramped. Closure to passengers and goods was wef January 1 1951. The Railway Company had a riverside pumphouse adjoining the station, with a lineside pipe to the large tank in Workington Main Yard; it supplied two loco-motive water tanks and the needs of the locomotive shed.

Workington Bridge Junction signalbox (right) controlled the CWJ double track link of March 16 1885 from Cloffocks Junction, with its own bridge over the Derwent and trail-in (right) to the Cockermouth route. Very limited sidings existed for exchange of the vital coke traffic from County Durham to ironworks served by the CWJR, and the return-ing 'empties.' The traffic declined after about 25 years, rapidly after the first world war, and disappeared circa 1926. The line fell into disuse and its formal closure is obscure, but was probably in 1930. It was removed by 1933.

Derwent Tin Plate Works, Barepot (Beerpot) village and level crossing

This site was 'tucked in' under the wooded bluff to the north of the Cockermouth line and a single track branch diverged leftwards from the CWR, actually trailing off the

Down road across the Up line. It was one of the earliest sites exploited industrially in West Cumberland, and its lease from Sir James Lowther dated from 1762, with a blast furnace soon erected by Spedding Hicks & Co. A feeder canal from the Derwent, upstream, a mill reservoir and a tailrace to the river indicate water power and their alignments necessitated three bridges to carry the CWR (1847) these still being traceable today. Adam Heslop is understood to have designed a steam engine for the iron works in the 1790s. In 1819 the works came under common ownership with the Lowca Iron Works (which was at Parton). The proprietors, by then titled Tulk & Ley, are known for their building of main line locomotives from 1840 onwards and, as Fletcher Jennings & Company, of industrial locomotives from 1858. The locomotives were built at Lowca Works.

From 1852, the Derwent Works belonged to Henderson & Davis/William Henderson, who manufactured iron bars in a puddling furnace near Workington harbour. The bars were conveyed to Barepot (Derwent), perhaps two miles, where the rolling of tinplate commenced. It was during this period that the branch railway was laid. In February 1855, these proprietors advertised these assets: a blast furnace, rolling mills, both water and steam power and a railway branch to the works. By August 1856, Samuel Wagstaffe Smith/S.W. Smith & Company (alt: Derwent Tin Plate Company) was paying interest to the CWR on the costs of making the siding. In that year, the Railway was conveying coke and limestone from Workington to the site and pig iron outwards (at April 1856). Later in the year, the railway traffic comprised pig iron from Workington and export of tin in boxes from 'Beer Pot' to Merchants Quay. The CWR's contemporary title for the traffic sidings was 'Seaton Iron Works'. Smiths were soon (by January 1857), delaying the Railway Company's wagons and using them (contrary to injunctions) on the incline to their furnaces to deliver charges of ore. By December, the Railway held five of the firm's own wagons as surety for unpaid debts. Three of Smiths' employees were prosecuted for walking on the CWR main line, and fined. Soon after this incident, of 1857, it was recorded that "another piece of wood has been found laid across the lines near Beerpot!"

Mr Spence was seemingly proprietor from 1858 to 1861, but with very intermittent operation of the blast furnace and

Above: The scene at Derwent Junction, looking south. In the left background is the Derwent viaduct, with a footway beside it and the Merchants Quay branch slighting beyond the viaduct (right). The main line to Workington station disappears into the mist. The Cockermouth (and Keswick and Penrith) route is just visible curving off sharply left (eastward). To the left of this field of view, the Keswick road was joined by the direct link from Lonsdale Dock and Lowther Iron Works, which crosses the main running lines close to the old Junction signalbox. *Richard L. Pattinson Collection/CRA.*

despatch of tinplate to Workington. Surprisingly, 200 workers were said to be employed in 1860 but failure was reported in June 1861. After a brief period of production by Samuel Sandys Briggs, of Workington, sale of the works was achieved in 1869 to William Ivander Griffiths, lately of Treforest, who came with a background in tinplate and a group of skilled men. A siding agreement of January 12 1874 and opening for traffic on June 11 1875 involved Messrs Griffiths and Walters and the LNWR. There were good years, then intermittent bad trade, takeover of the works in 1885 by West Cumberland Hematite Iron & Steel Company Ltd - and then closure in 1890, owing to their

problems. LNWR records implied little rail traffic after 1881. Dismantlement, mainly in the 1890s but completed about 1909, has today left one building, used as a store for milk bottles, various ruined walls and water channels and a handsome new house of 1984-85 in the walled grounds of the one-time manager's 'Derwent House'. The imposing old entrance has gateposts, 'with knobs on'. The village includes a terrace of former tinplate workers' houses and Workington's music festival traces its origins in the Eisteddfod brought by the Welshmen to the district

The LNWR titled its signal box 'Derwent Tin Plate Works Sidings' but they and others down the years have referred to

Right: Workington Bridge, the first station on the CWR line from Workington, seen in LMS days. Workington Bridge signal box (closed around 1950) is just glimpsed above the LNWR timber station buildings. The station itself closed from January 1 1951. *Richard L.Pattinson/CRA*

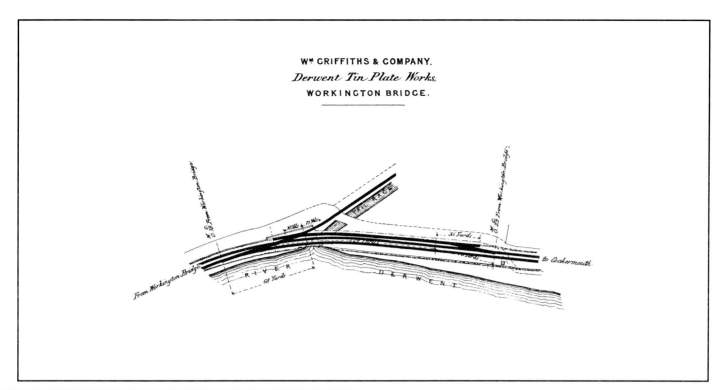

Wᴹ GRIFFITHS & COMPANY.
Derwent Tin Plate Works,
WORKINGTON BRIDGE.

Above: The branch into Derwent Tin Plate Works, Barepot, east of Workington Bridge: this is the 1874 plan but the layout was virtually the same in the 1915 version, which includes a signalbox in place of the tiny cabin (bottom right).

Left: Seaton Mill level crossing and crossing house (still occupied today) are pictured, eastbound, with the lever frame at the foot of the right hand signal. The bridges crossed in close succession beyond were: Nos. 37 (Mill Race), 36 (Byefalls), 35 (Culvert), 34 (Salmon Hall No. 2) and 33 (Salmon Hall No. 1). Overline bridge No. 31, at William Pit Sidings, can be discerned in the distance. *Richard L. Pattinson/ CRA.*

the works variously as Beer Pot, Beerpot, Barepotts and Barepot. The isolated LNWR house adjoins the site of 'Derwent Tin Plate Works Level Crossing'. A lane from Barepot village to the river side and Seaton Cornmill crossed the 'main line' here, right back to 1847, when it was known as Beer Pot Gate. The actual Works Sidings signal-box was a blockpost until at least 1910 but by 1916 only had signals and indicators for protection of the crossing, the siding connections being removed in 1916 and the box and signals (probably) in 1917. In latter days of the railway, during the 1960s, Mrs Briggs, at the house, was crossing keeper, while her husband, Henry held a railway post in Workington.

Seaton Mill and its many water channels

Leaving Barepot, eastward, the mill race was on the left of the line, and was shortly crossed, with the broad and swift-flowing Derwent close at hand on the right. The water-driven Seaton Corn Mill eventually became an

adjunct of the adjoining farm - all forming an attractive group of buildings between the railway and the river. Immediately eastward again, was Seaton Mill Level Crossing, styled Seaton Gate in 1847. Its stone-built house, on the Up side, is not of obvious LNWR origin and is still a residence. No less than four bridges followed, in close succession. They were: No. 37 over the mill race, No. 36 over the subsidiary channel, Nos. 34 and 33 (Salmon Hall No. 2 and No. 1) over the main channels of the Derwent. Salmon Hall and the associated buildings form another pleasant group, in open lands to the left of the railway route.

William Pit Sidings

Within the wide arm of the Derwent, between Salmon Hall No. 1 and Stainburn bridges, a considerable layout developed on the Down (right) side, with a signalbox on the Up side and a private single track mineral railway climbing from the sidings steeply south eastward to William Pit Colliery, more than a mile distant, near Great Clifton village. This colliery superseded the various coal pits of the Fletcher family, which had provided the CWR of 1847-66 with its main reason for construction and its principal traffic. Already in 1865, I. & W. Fletcher & Company were sinking their new William Pit colliery at Clifton and suggested to the CWR that they would need to connect by private tramway

Above: A westbound passenger train, hauled by a 'Cauliflower' 0-6-0, is seen crossing the Salmon Hall bridges over the River Derwent. This is believed to be the No.1 bridge, which had three spans aggregating 125ft in length. *Richard L. Pattinson/CRA.*

to the railway, primarily for shipments via Workington Harbour. They saw alternatives of connecting at Lowther Pit Siding, at Camerton station, or between Stainburn and Salmon Hall bridges. In September-October 1865 the CWR agreed in principle to install two pairs of points and crossings to connect with the sidings to be laid by Fletchers and to put a small arch in the wall of the overbridge connecting portions of the Stainburn Estate. The overline occupation bridge in later times had a 29ft span over the Colliery Company's sidings and 17ft over the LNWR. William Pit of Clifton Collieries was leased from 1873 by the West Cumberland Hematite Iron & Steel Company Ltd, of Workington, but taken over by Allerdale Coal Company on its formation in 1887 and worked by that company and the

National Coal Board in succession. The junction signalbox in its final form dated back to circa 1881 and the Colliery locomotives are traceable back to 1890; there were three for most of the 20th century, until closure in 1959, and dismantling by Cohens in 1961. The signalbox remained open as a blockpost until January 1965. In 1983-84, the lands at 'William Pit Sidings' (site of) have been in part reclaimed for farming and the overbridge abutments became a heap of stones, but the general alignment may be seen, by prior per

Below: William Pit Sidings (1874 plan) depicted during the period after the West Cumberland Company had taken over from the Fletcher family company.

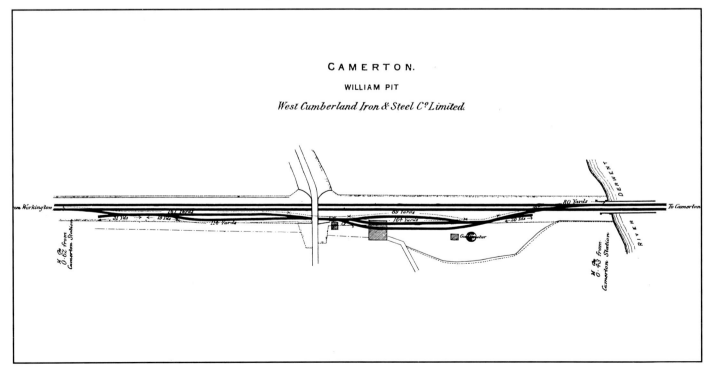

CAMERTON.

WILLIAM PIT

West Cumberland Iron & Steel Co Limited.

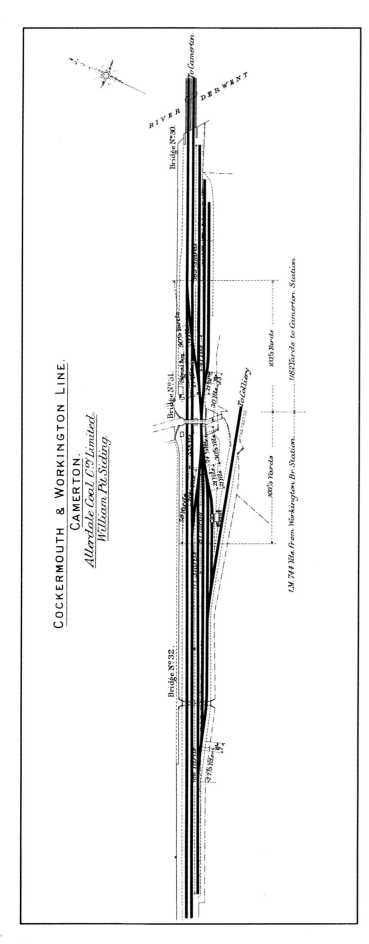

COCKERMOUTH & WORKINGTON LINE.
CAMERTON.
Allerdale Coal C.º Limited.
William Pit Siding.

Above: An eastward view at William Pit Sidings showing traffic in the exchange sidings between the CWR running lines and the steep private line to the colliery on the hill. *Richard L. Pattinson/ CRA.*

Left: The 1916 version of William Pit Sidings shows their development and the private branch railway heading off to the Allerdale Company's colliery on the hill south eastward.

mission of Mr. Gordon Ferries of Stainburn Hall Farm. The steep route by which the privately-owned colliery locomotives laboured with their 'empties' can still be followed today.

Onward to Camerton station

Eastward of Stainburn Bridge, the railway soon reached the attractive overline bridge which still carries the lane to the isolated Church of St Peter and its graveyard. A byway formerly crossed the line on the level, before Camerton station, where the two station houses (dating probably from 1882) on the Down platform have been combined by building on the yard which separated them and also extended, as a present-day residence. The station was an original CWR facility. It acquired a timber booking office and waiting room circa 1879, before the houses were added. It closed to passengers and freight wef March 3 1952, about a year after the demise of Workington Bridge station. This was the period (circa 1946-1956) when the LMS and BR (LMR) eliminated little-used stations one-by-one, but without accompanying the closures with any constructive overall plan for compensatory acceleration and improvement of services between busier centres.

A devious lane came down from Camerton village, located on higher ground to the north, and a mile-long and even more hilly footpath connected with Great Clifton village on the ridge southward, crossing the Derwent river by the footbridge, which was Railway-owned, now rebuilt by the County Council.

Camerton Colliery and Brickworks

Between the station and Camerton Bridge over the River Derwent, the colliery site was on the Up side of the line. The CWR opened on April 27 1847 and on Wednesday June 2 1847, the first train of coals was run over the new line. It was despatched from the Greengill Colliery, Camerton, of William Thornburn, who resided at Papcastle, for shipment at Workington. The Railway's locomotive *Cocker* hauled 21 loaded wagons. Ten years later, Mr Thornburn was still

Above: William Pit Sidings signalbox (c1881-1965) is framed by the overline accommodation bridge, as a westbound goods passes. The 'Cauliflower' is carrying a 12D shedplate (Workington, post 1935). A Kilmarnock-built (Andrew Barclay) saddletank locomotive owned by the Allerdale Coal Company is working beneath the right hand span. *Richard L. Pattinson/ CRA*

Right: East of Camerton station, the lead into the Camerton colliery and brickworks is seen, probably during the 1930s. *Richard L. Pattinson/CRA*

consigning coals from here for shipment, but in small quantities. William Thornburn Junior was a member of the CWR board from 1856 to 1863. In 1859, bricks were forthcoming from Camerton (Mr Cook), for conveyance to both Cockermouth and Workington. The coal came out of drift mines or 'levels' in the hillside behind the colliery buildings and by the later 19th century, from Wood Drift just to the

north, tubways being employed from the drifts to the colliery screens from as early as 1864. Camerton Colliery & Brickworks Company were the proprietors by the 1870s.

Later came Camerton Brick & Coal Company (J. Mulcaster), subsequently amended to the Camerton Colliery Company. By April 1917, it was Camerton Coal, Fireclay & Ganister Company (Messers Mutch), for whom the LNWR

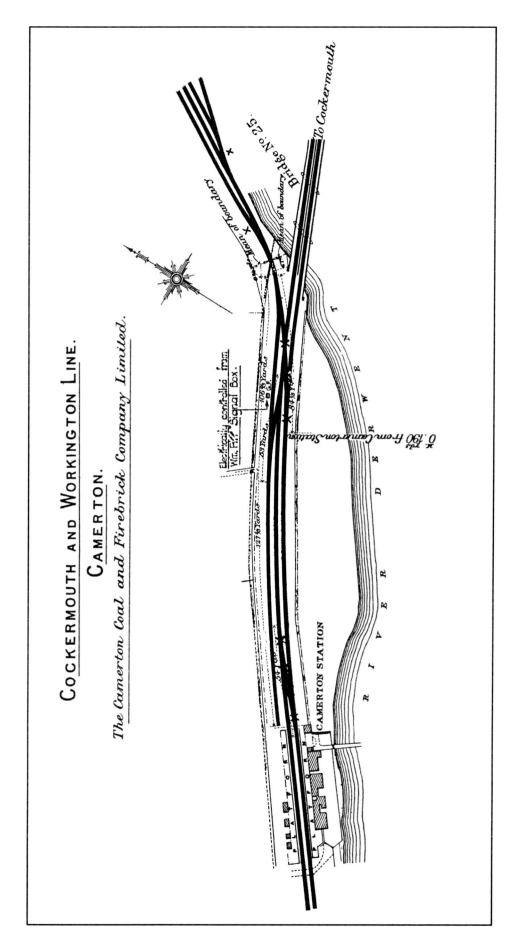

COCKERMOUTH AND WORKINGTON LINE.

CAMERTON.

The Camerton Coal and Firebrick Company Limited.

Bridge No 25.

To Cockermouth

Rear of boundary

Rear of boundary

CAMERTON STATION

Electrically controlled from Wm. Pit Signal Box.

106⅘ Yards

84½ Yards

25⅓ Yards

0.190 From Camerton Station

127⅘ Yards

30½ Yards

T Y N E W E D R I V E R

RIVER DERWENT

put the sidings in order. Then, from May 1919, the Camerton Coal & Firebrick Co Ltd were in possession. The next owners, from 1935, were Camerton Firebrick & Coal Co Ltd (controlled by J. & J. Dyson Ltd, fire-clay manufacturers, of Hunnington, Sheffield) with a siding agreement which was adjusted on February 26 1938. Wilkinsons' Wagon Works used part of the site and produced rail movements. T. McKay & Sons (Fireclay & Concrete Products Ltd) of St Bees, took over the works and sidings in January 1939, with a siding agreement of March 15 1940. However, the Admiralty had established a depot at Broughton Moor, absorbing the Allerdale Coal Company's Buckhill Colliery, closed in 1939, and part of the former CWJR 'Northern Extension line' (which had extended in its time between Calva Junction-Seaton-Buckhill Colliery-Great Broughton-Linefoot). This development led to the Admiralty establishing a depot for ammunition in Camerton clay mine. At their instance, the Camerton sidings (CWR line) were extended; the work was carried out between October 1941 and February 1942 and December 1942 and May 1943, with a fresh siding agreement negotiated between February and September 1947. In (or by) 1950, Sebrix Ltd, of Newcastle upon Tyne, took over the sidings from the Admiralty, the agreement with BR being dated September 30 1953, with amendments in 1957. They provided high quality firebricks, but the brickworks premises were demolished in 1956-57.

Wilkinsons may well have reappeared in the post-war years, breaking up wagons here. The signal box, for many years open 'as required', was replaced by a ground frame in 1935.

The site of the railway lead-in to Camerton's colliery and brickworks activities is still clear to see and in 1984 one building still stood, although landscaping was in hand. The lead was reached by setting back off the Up line and drawing forward to the branch or, earlier again, by setting back across the road from the down main line. Just west of this point, there is a hint of a probable one-time tramway, maybe from early drift mines, running southward to the river and crossing in its course the alignment used by the railway.

Ribton Hall Sidings

Beyond Camerton Bridge over the Derwent and the ensuing Ribton Bridge of six spans, there were short-lived sidings on the Up side of the running lines. Under the title 'Ribton Hall Sidings', an agreement of October 1 1873 between I. & W. Fletcher (also Edward Waugh) and the LNWR, two connections were put in, 13 chains apart. These were completed and opened to traffic in April 1874, the West Cumberland Hematite Iron & Steel Company having meanwhile taken over; an agreement with the LNWR dated September 27 1876 ratified the change. The property reverted to Messrs Fletcher and Waugh in March 1887 but the sidings were closed by then, or soon after, and were lifted in November 1888. It is particularly interesting that, in the period 1874-1878, the Iron Company ran its engine between Lowther Pit (mentioned later) and Ribton Sidings, thus traversing the LNWR double track over Ribton High Bridge in their trips to and fro. Until 1878, a signalman was maintained at Ribton, in charge of the points. A gradually descending footpath from the vicinity of Buckhill Colliery (northward of the CWR Line) to the route may have followed the course of a tramroad to the river - possibly of earlier date than the 1873 project. The third crossing of the Derwent between Camerton and Marron was by Ribton High Bridge. This brought the line to sites of earlier industry, also to the railway junctions at Marron.

Early coal pits: Lowther, Harrygill, Linefitts and others

The Fletcher family were leading promoters of the CWR - they provided its successive chairmen and its staple

Right: Ribton Hall Sidings (located between two bridges over the Derwent) only existed from 1874 to 1888. The plan is of 1874. By the time of the Ordnance Survey in 1898, the private branch line (arrowed) was a footpath.

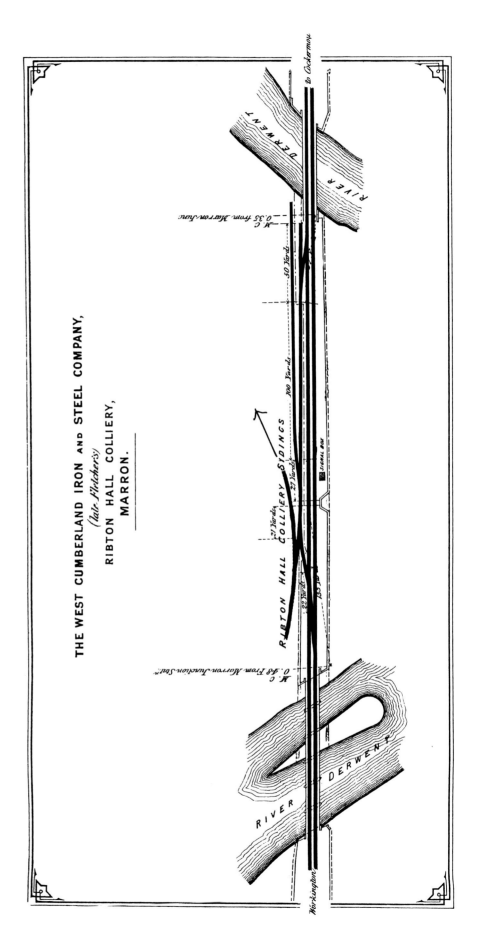

THE WEST CUMBERLAND IRON AND STEEL COMPANY,
(late Fletcher's)
RIBTON HALL COLLIERY,
MARRON.

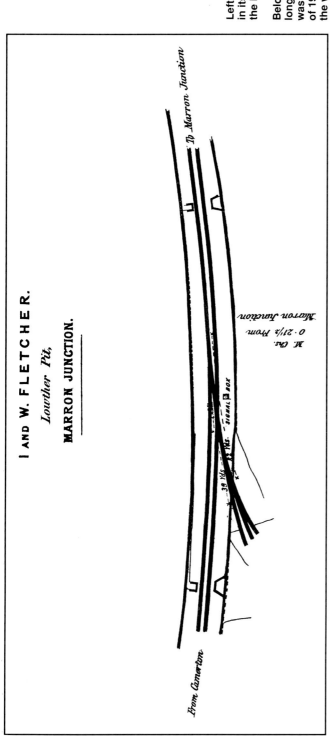

I AND W. FLETCHER.

Lowther Pit,

MARRON JUNCTION.

To Marron Junction

Marron Junction.

M. Chs.
0. 21½ from
Marron Junction.

39 Yds. 13 Yds. SIGNAL BOX

From Camerton.

Left: The lead-in from Lowther Pit, in its early form, as recorded on the LNWR's plan of 1874.

Below: By 1916, Lowther Pit had long closed and its brickworks was moribund. The large signalbox of 1902-60 is seen in the angle of the west junction, at Marron.

COCKERMOUTH AND WORKINGTON LINE.
MARRON JUNCTION.

Allerdale Coal C⁰.
Lowther Pit Siding.

To Broughton

To Bridgefoot

S.B.

1ᴹ 629ʸᵈˢ to Broughton Cross Station

1ᴹ 421ʸᵈˢ to Camerton Station

4.MP

From Camerton

Right: Reverting to 1874, both passenger platforms are shown at Marron. The branch line to Linefitts Colliery is also shown, being private property from its bridge (inclusive) and crossing on the level the south east curve of the triangular layout at Marron Junctions.

traffic in coals to Workington. The Railway Company had to steer a careful course between extracting maximum revenue from Isaac & William Fletcher & Company and yet also obliging them in every way. It was a difficult balance to achieve, for lesser coalowner clients, represented by Directors and shareholders, were ever-ready to criticise if more favourable terms were accorded to the Fletchers.

The Fletchers developed Clifton Old Pit (as it became known) from 1827 and Crossbarrow (alt: Crossbarron) followed - both in the relatively elevated country traversed by the Workington-Cockermouth Road. Lowther Colliery (from 1852) was in the meadow southeast of the CWR's Ribton High Bridge and was skirted by the railway. Westray Pit was up the hill behind, towards the main road and Crossbarrow. Harry Gill Pit was close to the railway, between Lowther Colliery and Marron Junctions. By 1856, Lowther and Harry Gill had sidings on the CWR, indeed, even in 1847 a switchman was required for 'Fletcher's Siding'. Clifton and Crossbarrow were sending coals by 'the Marron branch', which would be this 'Siding', but the Fletchers proposed building a tramway to link them with Lowther Pit Sidings or Harrygill Siding. On October 20 1856, they pressed their demand for seven years of preferential terms by writing to the CWR Board, emphasising that a private tramway from the pits to Workington harbour would be more direct and economical to operate than the existing arrangement. Lord Lonsdale was said to own virtually all the necessary land and it was claimed that he had given his consent. The Railway's Board speedily accorded them a meeting and agreed special terms.

Strenuous objections from shareholders followed but, broadly, the terms were amicably agreed by the general meeting of January 31 1857. The complete tramway to the CWR does not seem to have been built, but a link was constructed from Westray Pit, with a concluding steep descent to Lowther Colliery. A decade or so later the old pits in the hinterland were replaced by the Fletchers' new William Pit, of which the later ownership has been discussed. This brought early beehive ovens to Lowther Colliery, used to provide coke for the lessees' blast furnaces at Workington - more traffic for the CWR's successors. The Allerdale Coal Company took over at Lowther in 1887, from West Cumberland Hematite Iron & Steel Company, along with the modern William Pit;

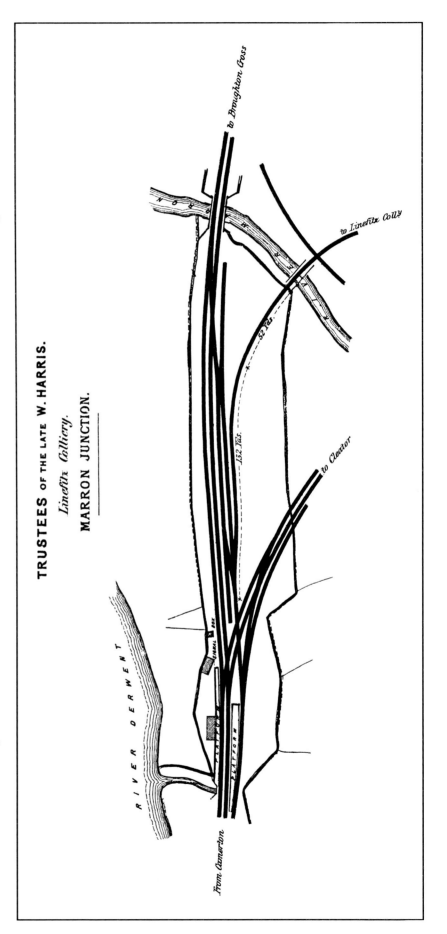

there was a Fletcher interest in Allerdale, but in later years Directors from South Yorkshire were prominent. Lowther Colliery was closed, and by January 1893 only brickworks traffic remained. Lowther Colliery Siding, with its link to the Joint Line under control of Marron Junction signalbox, survived, almost moribund (the subject of a limited rental in the period 1915-21) but was disused as a stub of line in 1923. Its site and that of the tramway from Westray are still clear on the ground.

Linefitts Colliery was the only mine in the vicinity not owned by the Fletchers and was in the Harris family, a recurring name on the CWR Board. Its access, in 1864, was by a short south east curve off the CWR's Marron loop line; the east curve from the Joint line to the CWR was built across it 'on the level', in 1866. Joseph Harris, of Greysouthen, constructed the private branch from the pit to its timber bridge over the Marron (inclusive) in 1847 and the CWR connected it to their original Siding, namely the Railway's 'Marron Branch.'

The Greysouthen (pronounced 'Greysoon') Colliery of Joseph Harris & Company was in the country south eastward of Marron Junctions and was never fully rail-connected - but by 1857 it was consigning shipment coals in small quantities, via the CWR, to Workington and in 1859 Captain John Harris (died 1863) of this Company, who was also a Director of the CWR, was preparing to send coals from Marron Sidings to Maryport. The Harris Company is on record in 1865 as planning to employ its own private-owner wagons over the CWR. By February 1870, the wooden bridge had become unsafe for the passage of Railway Company engines, so men from the pits pushed the wagons across by hand, but by this date the pit was virtually worked out. The bridge and the private line beyond (east) were removed before 1887, when the siding rent ceased to be paid.

Marron Junctions

The railway layout here was essentially triangular, with West and East Junctions on the CWR line and a South Junction on the route to Cleator Moor - this was the WCER, which became FR & LNWR 'Joint Line.' Favoured opening dates at Marron are January 15 1866 (minerals) and April 2 1866 (passengers), seemingly on both east and west curves.

The first ordnance survey, of 1864, shows a complete layout, with the CWR main line then single, with a passenger platform on its north side, just on the Workington side of the West Junction. There was double track on the west curve and single on the east curve, a single track from the South Junction to Bridgefoot and double track at Bridgefoot station. A loop line for mineral traffic paralleled the CWR from near the Lowther Colliery connection, past the Harrygill connection and as far east as the Linefitts Colliery branch. The route of that early branch, described above, is even today identifiable at the site of its timber bridge over the Marron river and its crossing of the east curve a little to the north of, and behind, Marron Junction locomotive shed. A single pointsman had charge of Lowther Pit Siding, Harrygill Siding and Marron Siding in the CWR's early days. The junctions of 1866 called for pointsmen in their respective cabins and from about 1871 LNWR signal boxes were in use at the three corners of the triangle. By this time the CWR route (LNWR) was double track and a southerly island platform figured by 1874, possibly installed when the line was doubled. The passenger station, such as it was, had been constructed at the joint expense of the CWR and WCER in its initial form; this was intended solely for changing trains. It officially closed to passengers wef July 1 1897. Direct working of the odd cattle or passenger train between the Joint Line and Cockermouth ceased with the taking out of the East Junction in (it is believed) 1902. A new signalbox was built at that time near West Junction. Much later, November 7 1960, it in turn was replaced by a ground frame of two levers. The short portion of the Joint Line between Bridgefoot and Marron Junction (meaning the new west junction) was still double in 1924, although converted later to single track. From Rowrah to Marron Junction, normal traffic ceased in November 1953, with an official closure date of wef May 3 1954. The 'West Cumberland Rail Tour' a special passenger train for the Stephenson Locomotive Society and the Manchester Locomotive Society, was privileged to run through, northbound, on September 5 1954. After years of disuse, the final abandonment between Rowrah and Marron Junction, was wef November 7 1960, followed eventually by lifting.

The Marron river was crossed just west of the one-time Marron East Junction; the bridge survives and the layouts here are interesting to reconstruct on the ground today.

Left: The western approach to Marron Junction. The independent line from Lowther Colliery site is in the foreground, right of the double running lines - and note the ground signals mounted on the cutting sides. The main line signal is 'off' for the Cockermouth route; the right-hand signal arm controls the divergence (right of the box) to the 'Joint Line' for Rowrah and Cleator Moor.
Richard L. Pattinson/CRA.

Right: Melgramfitz Colliery screens and loading siding were in the next section east of Marron. This shows the layout in 1874.

Melgramfitz Pit.

A siding connection was made in the latter half of 1860, about half-way between Marron East Junction (to be) and Broughton Cross station, in order to serve this new colliery, then being sunk by the Fletcher family. Two tracks passed through the screens and connected at west and east ends to the running line. Coals were first despatched in November 1863 and production continued through the 1870s, the West Cumberland Hematite Iron & Steel Company being proprietors from 1873. The colliery became exhausted in 1880 and the rail connections were taken out in July-October 1883. The site is lost today in the A66 road of the 1970s.

Broughton Cross station

This was an original station on the CWR, with a bend in the Derwent sweeping close by to its north. On the single line, in 1864, it had one siding but the ensuing double track layout provided no sidings or goods facilities. The substantial stone buildings were on the Down platform, adjoining the (old) main road and village, in which some houses were built by the Fletchers for workers at Melgramfitz Colliery of 1860. The station was never a blockpost and it closed wef March 2 1942, a wartime economy. The buildings survive today as a house, whilst the A66 road occupies, broadly, the railway alignment.

The village of Greysouthen is about one mile south of Broughton Cross station. *Tarn Bank* is to the east of the road to the village. It figured in the 1850s as residence of both Isaac and William Fletcher, the coalowners; also of John Wilson Fletcher, chairman for most of the years 1845-1857 of the CWR. Isaac Fletcher, of *Tarn Bank*, was son of J.W.Fletcher, and became Chairman of the CKPR from 1867; he was also MP for Cockermouth from 1868 to 1879.

Hotchberry Limestone Quarry - and its intended siding.

The Hotchberry limestone quarry was located to the east side of the Brigham-Eaglesfield road, about 1 1/4 miles from Broughton Cross Station and about one mile south of the village of Brigham. Jno. Todhunter, the proprietor at that time, signed a siding agreement with the LNWR on June 8 1883. The 'Hotchberry Limestone Siding' was to be at Broughton Cross, presumably on the Down side of the double track, and Mr Todhunter planned to build a tramway from the siding to his quarries. In the event, neither tramway nor siding were built and the scheme was abandoned at June 19 1885. The quarry was the only one in the vicinity to remain in operation in 1923 and the output went by road to the railway at Brigham, like that of Ellerbeck limestone quarry - which employed two generations of steam lorries for haulage. The Hotchberry quarry used its own horses and carts for the trip to Brigham Limestone Siding, so it is recalled.

Brigham Limestone Sidings

From west of Broughton Cross station to Brigham station, and beyond, the route of the line today is occupied by the A66 road. Approaching Brigham station from the west,

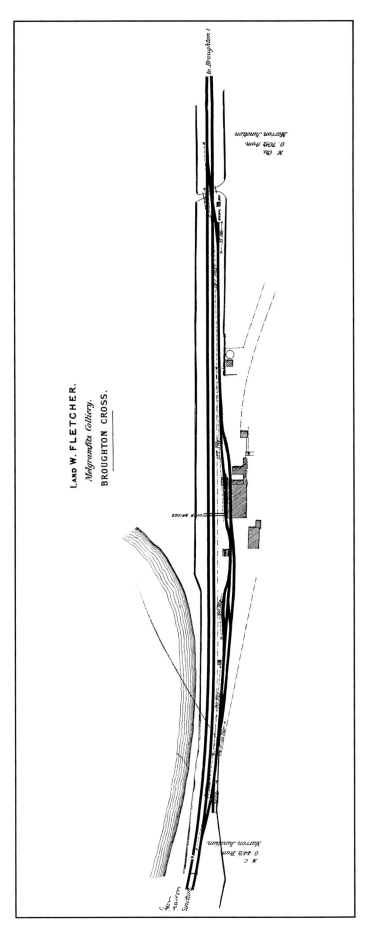

LAND W. FLETCHER.

Melgramfitz Colliery.

BROUGHTON CROSS.

Above: Broughton Cross station had neither sidings nor signalling, but the Up distant signal for Brigham is prominent in this eastward view. *Richard L. Pattinson/CRA*

sidings were laid on the Down side at MP2 (from Cockermouth old station) to handle output from Brigham limestone quarry and kilns. Captain Harris, a member of the CWR board, was principal of the limeworks, from which consignments were being made to Whitehaven in 1856, using by arrangement wagons belonging to the Whitehaven Junction Railway. Traffic expanded and in 1860 agreement

was given for the Captain to construct a standard gauge tramroad from the firm's kilns to the sidings. The resulting branch and layout was well depicted in the ordnance survey of 1863-64, also being shown by the LNWR on its diagrams of 1874 and 1915, by which latter date the owners were the Allerdale Coal Company. The tramroad passed diagonally under the old main road near the Limekiln Inn. Workings and layout expanded but were abandoned by the early 1920s, leaving an impressive hole at the quarry site. The West Cumberland Hematite Iron & Steel Co Ltd, which produced pig iron from 1862 and steel from 1872, devel-

Above: Brigham station, looking east over the level crossing, showing the sturdy stone buildings of 1863 adjacent to the Down platform and the LMS (Midland derived) design signal box of 1933. The loading dock for limestone is located in the foreground - the quarry branch once climbed away to the right - and 'Old Vicarage' farm (see text, page 29) is apparent, the church being out of sight, right. The scene is from April 1968, two years after total closure of the Keswick-Workington section. *Harold D. Bowtell.*

oped its own limestone quarry at Brigham by 1872. This had an internal narrow gauge line and a short standard gauge branch to the same sidings. Its lines were clearly delineated in 1898, but they disappeared early in the 20th century; indeed, the LNWR recorded lifting its own connection to these (one-time WCHIS Co. Ltd.) private sidings in March 1910. From 1882, by activating a section of the Brigham Station Agreement of January 1 1878, Maryport & Carlisle Railway locomotives started working to and from the limestone sidings, sharing traffic with the LNWR.

Above: This delightful scene depicts the Up platform at Brigham, in pre-Grouping days. The train has come via Bullgill, maybe from Carlisle. The engine has run round and is seen signalled to emerge onto the LNWR and head for Cockermouth. The attractive LNWR bracket signal provides for running from Workington to the MCR (left) or Cockermouth (ahead). The locomotive may be MCR No. R1 (No. 19 until 1884), a 6ft-wheeled 2-4-0 built in 1867 at Maryport. *J.D. Hinde Collection.*

Facing page: LNWR plans of May 1874 (above) and 1915 showing the developing private siding arrangements at Brigham station. *Author's Collection.*

Brigham station

The level crossing and road to Brigham village curtailed the limestone sidings at their east end. In 1847, the crossing was known as Brigham Gate. The station was immediately to its east, with the original single platform on the south side of the line and good stone buildings erected in 1863. Doubling of the track by the LNWR during 1868 and the opening in the previous year (wef June 1 1867) of the MCR line from Bullgill (and thus from Carlisle, by way of its main line) prompted the construction of an Up platform, and a back platform face (for MCR use) to this Up platform. A turntable at the extremity of this MCR road (in early days) and an independent run-round loop facilitated reversal of the Carlisle-Brigham-Cockermouth trains. The MCR, from

the outset, exercised running powers to Cockermouth. Their running powers to Marron do not seem to have been used on any regular basis. The LNWR shuttled over the MCR's massive Derwent bridge to reach Broughton Craggs Quarry, at Papcastle. Papcastle Limestone Siding derived from an LNWR agreement of December 14 1889 (with the Allerdale Coal Company) A further agreement, of July 15 1910 (with Walker Brothers) provided for extension into their freestone quarry at Papcastle.

Signal boxes at Brigham receive later mention. From April 29 1935, the MCR line was closed by the LMS, although some 20 years later the station signs on the MCR route still declared 'Bullgill, change for Cockermouth.' From May 16 1960, the Brigham to Cockermouth Junction

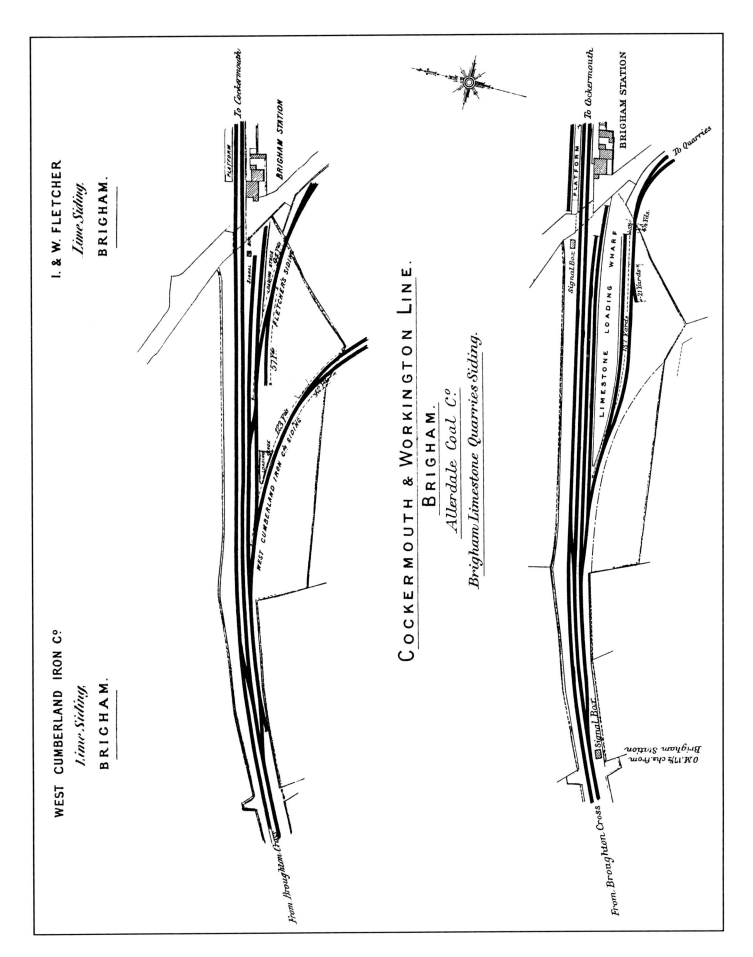

WEST CUMBERLAND IRON C°.

Lime Siding,

BRIGHAM.

I. & W. FLETCHER

Lime Siding,

BRIGHAM.

COCKERMOUTH & WORKINGTON LINE.

BRIGHAM.

Allerdale Coal C°.

Brigham Limestone Quarries Siding.

To Cockermouth

BRIGHAM STATION

Platform

Signal Box

Loading Stage

Fletchers Siding

West Cumberland Iron Co Siding

Loading Stage

From Broughton Cross

To Cockermouth

BRIGHAM STATION

Platform

To Quarries

Signal Box

LIMESTONE LOADING WHARF

Signal Box

O.M. 17½ chs. from Brigham Station.

From Broughton Cross

Right: The steam lorry *Vino*, outside its shed in Higher Brigham. Harry Wire and Tommy Dunn are in attendance, circa 1910. The lorry carried coal from Brigham station yard to Ellerbeck limestone quarry, and stone from the quarry to the loading dock. *J.D. Hinde Collection.*

section reverted to single track, with the Down road being in general the one abandoned. Total closure of Brigham passenger station, with the Derwent Junction-Cockermouth route, was wef April 18 1966. The goods yard, connected to the MCR branch until its demise, was closed wef June 1 1964. Away back in 1856, establishment of coal cells at Brigham, on the SDR/NER model for bottom-door wagons was agreed following a request by the Fletchers, as coal owners. In 1858, the depot was a traffic siding where coal and coke could be handled. Through into BR days, several merchants received and distributed coal from here.

Brigham church and vicarage

St Bridget's Church is sited beside the road from Broughton High Bridge (over the Derwent) to Brigham village. The Rector, 1833-75, was the Reverend John Worsdworth MA, eldest son of poet William Wordsworth. About the time of his appointment, John and his father chose a delectable site for his vicarage, with an extensive garden northward of the house and ending only on the river bank. Trouble followed, therefore, when the CWR's 'plans and sections', accompanying its Bill in 1844, showed a railway route running roughly midway between the vicarage and the river, bisecting the garden. When the Act of July 21 1845 received the Royal Assent, it included a 29th clause, providing for the construction of a new vicarage at the Company's cost. In December 1845, the Reverend Mr Wordsworth and architect Charles Eaglesfield were consulted, a site selected south eastward of the church and the Railway placed the building contract. This allowed £590 for taking down and rebuilding the vicarage, but in fact a new building was put up and handed over in June 1847. It is interesting to note that the Wordsworths invested in the CWR, with £500 of mortgage bonds allocated to William in

December 1846 and £200 to John in the next month; interest was payable at 4 1/2% per annum. The location is nowadays less delectable, as the railway has been exchanged for the road, with its heavy lorries going by at 60 mph, accompanied by countless commercial representatives passing at 70-80mph in their companies cars.

Right: An eastward vista from Cockermouth Junction: the original route of 1847 (double line) leads to the (lower) goods station, taking in the CWR's cramped passenger and goods site. The CKPR route, (opened 1864-65) climbs steeply on its right hand curve, heading for the (upper) passenger station. The extremity of 'the Stockton siding' is on the right; it was used for holding westbound coke trains from SDR territory before 'tripping' of the traffic to West Cumberland's ironworks. *Richard L. Pattinson/ CRA.*

RAILS THROUGH LAKELAND

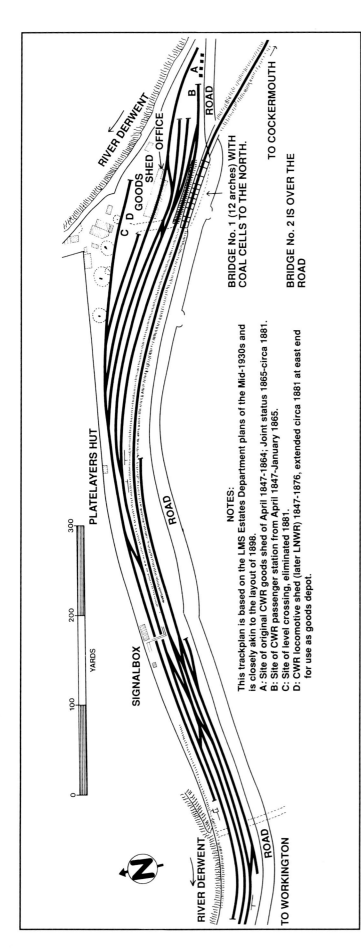

Left: Cockermouth Goods station layout.

The 'Old Vicarage', on rising ground south of the LNWR/MCR junction, ante-dated the vicarage house of circa 1833 and was already Vicarage Farm in 1847. It remains occupied in 1985, still as a farm.

Cockermouth, 1847-1864 - and a second station, 1865.

The Cockermouth & Workington Railway opened its terminal station on April 27 1847, initially as a temporary structure. Its approach by rail was restricted by an awkward bend in the river on the northern side of the site and the main road and the Senhouse family estate in the south. The road was slightly diverted to accommodate the railway but a cramped site resulted, well short of the built-up area of the town. Accommodation at the east end of the site included a goods warehouse, with two tracks and wagon turntables, whilst coal merchants' cells were provided by the main road. A small covered passenger station was squeezed between shed and cells and a locomotive turntable was located at the north west extremity of the site. Adjoining was a locomotive shed with two tracks and ancillary buildings and two more roads to its north. Here were based the CWR's locomotives – three initially and five eventually, along with the Company's workshops.

The Cockermouth Keswick & Penrith Railway, constructed 1862-64, made a physical junction with the CWR significantly west of the terminal station, in order to ease the curve and rising gradient on their chosen route. One notes that the CWR line approached Cockermouth as single track until early in 1868, when it was doubled, but the CKPR route climbed away from the junction on single track - never doubled - and skirted the southern border of the town, past the gasworks, to reach Cockermouth (upper) station. This was designed from the start for through running of passenger trains between Workington, Keswick and Penrith. Commercial mineral traffic started nominally on November 4 1864, passenger traffic on January 2 1865.

The Cockermouth stations, 1865-1876.

Representatives of the CWR and CKPR had met at Workington on January 28 1864, with W.N. Hodgson, a Director of the LNWR and also by then of the CKPR, present. It was decided that passenger traffic would be concentrated on the new (upper) station at Cockermouth, where the MCR services would also be handled. CWR and CKPR mineral and merchandise traffic would use the CWR (lower) site. The coal depot here was to remain unchanged: with some extension, it lasted until 1964, and is in use today, although not now rail served. The CWR passenger station became a 'temporary' goods station for both Companies, their existing goods building being taken down.

The LNWR took over the Whitehaven Junction Railway and the CWR in mid-1866. On August 1 1866, Richard Moon, Chairman of the LNWR, travelled via Penrith and the CKPR line, then in its second year of passenger operation (but not, be it noted, ownership) by the LNWR. He was bound for Whitehaven, doubtless to view critically his new domains, their facilities and staffs. With Mr Moon present, a meeting was held in the Boardroom at Cockermouth upper station. The management of this station was to be shared by

NOTES:

This trackplan is based on the LMS Estates Department plans of the Mid-1930s and is closely akin to the layout of 1898.

A: Site of original CWR goods shed of April 1847-1864; Joint status 1865-circa 1881.

B: Site of CWR passenger station from April 1847-January 1865.

C: Site of level crossing, eliminated 1881.

D: CWR locomotive shed (later LNWR) 1847-1876, extended circa 1881 for use as goods depot.

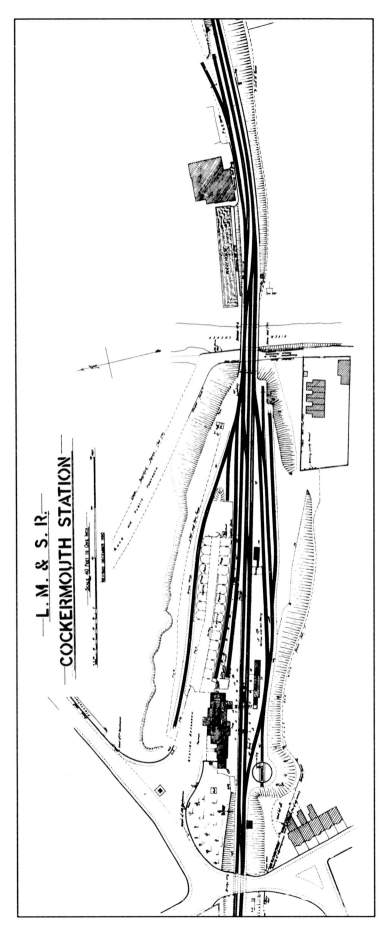

L.M. & S.R.

COCKERMOUTH STATION

Scale 40 Feet to One Inch

Henry Cattle, Secretary and Manager of the CKPR, and John Mayson (who restyled himself John Myson about this time). Mr Mayson had been the last Secretary and General Manager of the CWR and became District Manager of the LNWR's West Cumberland lines and secretary of the Cockermouth joint station committee - until his resignation from the service, around August 1869. No LNWR director was appointed to the joint station committee at this time, in 1866, but by 1881 the LNWR was represented by Richard Moon and William Cawkwell, respectively Chairman and General Manager, with Miles McInnes (LNWR director, of Carlisle) replacing Richard Moon in 1883. The CKPR also included a Director among its two members.

From November 1 1867, the MCR was given the full use of the new joint station at Cockermouth, including 'for sidings and carriage sheds'; they were to work traffic from and to their system. In the same year, it was decided to construct a cattle loading dock adjoining the upper passenger station, to supersede the cramped arrangements at the lower site. This early provision for expansion was justified in after years. Less foresight was shown concerning the goods station, still in the cramped, former passenger building at the lower site. In January 1876, the dilapidated condition of the office was blamed by Mr Bewsher, the goods agent, for the poor health of the clerks and himself, and for the accounts falling into arrears. He was cautioned and assistance was proposed, but by February 9 1876 he had absconded, leaving a deficiency in his accounts. He was dismissed *in absentia* and Mr Patrickson, Chief Goods Clerk at Penrith, was appointed in his stead, with a salary of £100 pa.

Locomotive sheds at Cockermouth - and the North Eastern Railway

The LNWR provided motive power for the CKPR passenger and goods trains from the opening of that line in 1865, and from 1867 it was doing the same job for its own newly-acquired CWR and Workington Junction lines. A minute of January 1864 (meeting at Cockermouth) had recorded that sufficient accommodation would be provided for engines working the traffic of the Keswick Company, either "in connection with the present engine shed or at such other site as may hereafter be agreed upon..." The "present shed" was at Cockermouth. It was soon supplemented by a shed at Penrith and, from 1876, by a large locomotive shed at Workington.

The NER locomotives which came through from Kirkby Stephen with mineral traffic for West Cumberland did not proceed beyond the lower yard at Cockermouth. They were serviced by their crews and, after turning, worked back east. Thus, they did not initially require a locomotive shed at Cockermouth. However, there was an early undertaking, or at least implication, that the former CWR shed would be available to the NER. It was some 10 years later, in December 1875, when J.E. McNay, Secretary of the NER's Darlington Section (doubtless based on the old SDR) approached Peter Thompson, by then Secretary and General Manager of the CKPR, with a proposition. The NER planned to work its traffic between Kirkby Stephen and Clifton under block signalling regulations

Above, left: This was the CWR's locomotive shed (of two roads) of circa 1847, seen from the west in September 1966. It was extended by 25ft in 1858 (represented by the fourth and fifth arches in the side wall) and, after probably a 10-years span housing LNWR locomotives, it was further extended east to form a new goods shed.

Above, right: One track ran through the goods shed to this eastern (town) end, where an office wing was provided, also stone-built. Observe the continued use of the coal cells ('vaults') in the foreground, in August 1983, 17 years after the railway through Cockermouth closed. *Both: Harold D. Bowtell.*

and when this took effect they would need to station two locomotives at Cockermouth *(sic)*. Mc McNay presumed - maybe tongue-in-cheek - that there would be no difficulty, as the CKPR "already have the accommodation for two of

our engines." After inconclusive exchanges, the issue lay dormant. Then, in 1880-81, there was a renewed flurry of activity. Henry Tennant, General Manager of the NER, wrote from York in October 1880 asking the CKPR to provide accommodation at Cockermouth for three NER engines engaged in the coke traffic to Workington. He believed: ".... there was an arrangement of this character some time ago."

Previously, the only real obstacle to the CKPR making the old engine shed available had been the tendency of the LNWR to make use of "the old workshops and tools." Now, there were other problems. Mr Thompson enlisted the help of George Findlay, at Euston, who was soon to be General Manager of the LNWR. In the meantime, F.W. Webb, the

Above: Cockermouth town gasworks had long existed, but only secured its railway siding in 1928. The single track on the left climbed from the Junction (for which the Down distant is in sight) to the passenger station. Working traffic at this siding called for extreme care by operating staff, in view of its direct divergence from a steep single running line with a junction at its foot. *Richard L. Pattinson/CRA.*

LNWR Locomotive Superintendent, indicated from his Crewe headquarters that he could provide accommodation for two or three NER locomotives at his Workington shed on terms to be agreed, as a temporary measure. However, Mr. Tennant made it clear that what he wanted was stabling at Cockermouth - he did not want the extra mileage involved in running to and from Workington. The CKPR therefore asked the Cockermouth joint committee to erect an engine shed for the use of the NER, but its members decided against "the site in the field adjoining the high level station" (there had been a plan dated November 1878 for such a shed, for NER use) and preferred (May 1881) to use ground recently acquired for extension of the goods station. This itself was not easy, as Mr. Senhouse, influential landowner of *The Fitz*, overlooked the area from his residence and had made it clear that he would not have a locomotive shed on land which he had sold. Mr Wood's plan, as CKPR Engineer, seems to have placed the depot further west and more remote from *The Fitz*. However, at that time (July 1881) the NER decided to postpone the project. No new locomotive shed was ever built at Cockermouth.

The Cockermouth goods shed

Cockermouth has always been a place of varied activities, with an emphasis towards the agricultural community. Thus, the Railways could not postpone indefinitely the provision of an adequate goods warehouse, needed for the transfer of merchandise between railway vehicles and road carts, also for storage, accompanied by offices. A high-powered meeting was held on November 1 1878, in the Chairman's room at Euston. LNWR Engineer S.B. Worthington presented his plan, estimated to cost £6,900 including about two and a half acres of additional lands. There could be a saving of about £1,000 if the old engine shed were converted into a goods shed.

This modified scheme was agreed, together with extensions of cattle facilities at the upper station yard, where this traffic would be concentrated, while timber would be transferred to the lower station; these rationalisations were effected in course of a few years.

The land required was purchased by the LNWR from Richard Senhouse and his wife under conveyance of November 24 1880, for £1,725. For an agricultural site, this sum represented a substantial part of the project's costs. J.B. Worthington made a new road between the railway yard and the river to give Fitz flax mill an access, eliminating the lane behind the old engine shed and the lane's level crossing over the main lines (Fitz Road Gate, in 1847). This permitted development of the sawmill and timber siding in the north west and the bringing of a track into the old engine shed from its western end. The stone-built shed was roughly doubled in length, with the extension at the east (or town) end with a single through track, plus internal platform, and a neat office block attached at the east end. The job was done by Mr Boulton, the CKPR's original contractor, for £749 (agreed March 1881). It is interesting today to view this building, well-kept in its present use, with five infilled arches in the south side wall distinguishing the old CWR engine shed. These may have contained windows in 1847.

Cockermouth yard

The long siding, trailing for westbound trains and maybe dating from 1873-75, would be 'the Stockton siding' for holding of block loads of coke from the NER, pending breaking up and 'tripping' to Workington Bridge (or beyond) by the LNWR. There were likewise a couple of sidings trailing off the yard line, suitable for holding Up traffic. The yard itself and its buildings changed little after the alterations in hand circa 1881. Timber and Armstrongs' woodyard remained. West Cumberland Farmers handled traffic at the warehouse. Fertilisers became another staple traffic in later days. Decline was rapid under the Beeching policy of 1963; the yard closed wef June 1 1964 and the whole route through Cockermouth wef April 18 1966. But the site remains active, served of course by road.

Cockermouth Gas Works

To avoid carting fuel from the lower yard, the Gas Committee of the Urban District Council proposed a railway siding in 1905-06 but the single track and steep gradient past the works were probable reasons for the CKPR's objections. The connection was not made until LMS days, evidently early in 1928, with the trail-off for Up (ascending) trains and three diverging (east facing) internal sidings. The sidings were disused by July 17 1960 and the siding agreement ended on December 31 1962. The ground frame and trailing lead were removed under authority of January 1963 and the sidings were lifted by August 1964. A proposal (plan) dated March 1 1915 would have given access more safely, by extending the short siding which trailed off the Up platform line at Cockermouth passenger station. This siding would have paralleled the running line, on its northerly side.

Cockermouth Joint station (The upper station of 1865-1966)

Development of the site was mainly carried out between the opening to passengers in 1865 and 1881-82. The plans and photographs presented give a good idea of this spacious station as it appeared from the 1880s onwards, but with progressive constriction of facilities from the 1930s. The Monday cattle market (supplemented by special sales from time to time) was a salient feature of the town which generated activity virtually all through the life of the railway. By 1882, there were two sidings and 24 cattle pens. Cattle have been recalled coming from Ireland, via Silloth and Carlisle, as well as from the mainland. Keswick did not compete.

The main buildings at the passenger station were impressive. The illustrations show them to advantage, also the attractive and practical protection provided at the front entrance and on the platform face by use of glazing. A Boardroom was included until 1869, on the ground floor, under the tall gable and with entrance by way of the stationmaster's garden from the forecourt. The refreshment room was a feature from 1868, when Fred Rapley rented a room. The Whitehaven Cocoa and Coffee House Company put up a purpose-built wooden refreshment room at the east end of the station buildings, completed and occupied from about April 1890. Prominent on many pictures, it closed down circa 1935 and was demolished. The single platform proved inadequate and potentially hazardous. An island platform, with passenger access by subway, and an independent Down platform line and loop platform line, was provided in good time for the concentration of signalling; the signalbox of 1875 remained a feature through to 1966.

Left, upper: A general view of Cockermouth station approach and buildings. This was 'the Joint Station' discussed in the text. The town's war memorial is on the right. Cockermouth's fire station now occupies this site. *Harold D. Bowtell.*

Left, lower: A detail view of the entrance porch at Cockermouth passenger station. *Roy Anderson Collection.*

By 1875, there was a back road to south of the site of the MCR's carriage shed - lasting until at least 1934 but removed by 1948. The LNWR carriage siding was elaborated into two roads accomodating a carriage shed - designed, in 1881, to take 12 carriages each of 34ft length. The shed vanished in LMS days and the surviving siding and loop road to its north were removed under a decision of 1955.

A 42ft turntable was agreed in principle in 1864 and installed by July 1867, on the Down side, at the west end, and may have been the one-time CWR table from the lower station, which it replaced. It lasted until 1954-55.

Space was always restricted at the Up (east) end, owing to narrowing for the Cocker viaduct, which carried the Up and Down running lines and a siding, on their north side. Notable, eastward, was the steam-driven Tweed Mill of the Cockermouth Tweed Company, erected 1872-74, for which a siding was approved in May 1872. After 1883, the premises became the Atlas Confectionery Works and from 1913 cyclecars were made here. In 1919-20, John Hulbert Jnr, of Manchester, demolished the main part of the tweed mill, evidently as an entrepreneurial activity. The CKPR agreed to a private siding, branching off the 'Old Tweed Mill Siding', and were promised 1,000 tons of building stone,

derived from the old mill, at 5/9d per ton, bound for Embleton, Braithwaite and Keswick. Oil depots for the Anglo American Oil Company (much later, Esso Ltd) and Shell Oil Company (Shell Petroleum) took over the use of the sidings east of the river viaduct from 1920 or soon afte and Esso survived there until the end of goods working. A ground frame controlled immediate access. The viaduct was reconstructed between October 1944 and October 1945 and is discussed in the bridge section (see *Chapter 5*).

An attractive aspect of Cockermouth station was its tidiness, and as late as 1953-54 it received BR awards. The station nameboards proudly announced:

COCKERMOUTH
FOR BUTTERMERE

Closure was from June 1 1964 (goods) and April 18 1966 (passengers).

The town war memorial was placed prominently on the station approach, the site being given by the CKPR under decision of July 1919, approved by the LNWR, but preliminaries and construction took several years. The memorial stands today, but the station has been totally erased from the landscape. A new fire station building now occupies the goods yard area; it was completed in 1984-85.

Staff at Cockermouth

The staff at Cockermouth were, from 1865 until 1922, 'joint' employees; from 1923, they were LMS staff, and BR workers from 1948. The first stationmaster was Joseph Wales, who enjoyed free occupation of the station house to 1870. He was then appointed accountant of the CKPR, in 1870, a career which ended under a cloud in 1885. Mr. Mitchell, booking clerk at Cockermouth, became Stationmaster but was given notice in 1881, after a court case. W. Cook followed, in 1881, until he was transferred in 1886 to Greenore, the LNWR terminal in Ireland. R.A. Holt, Stationmaster from 1887 to 1891, was removed from office by decision of the Company Secretary. Happily, Robert Little served here successfully from 1891 to 1921. J. W. Ewart (from Embleton, via Bassenthwaite Lake) was appointed in 1921, and then promoted to Keswick by the LMS in 1924. The last stationmaster was Thomas Hughes, in 1955-66, following a career in the West Midlands and Furness territory. The stationmaster was, in 'Joint' days, supported by separate booking, parcels and telegraph clerks, as well as a foreman porter and colleagues on the platform. Joe Carruthers was a regular signalman in the station box, from 1936 to 1966, following service in boxes mainly on the West Cumberland coast. Back in 1913, the men in this box were M. Allinson (the senior) and J.W. Stanley, with G. Sanderson (senior) and Joseph Dowthwaite in the Junction box. The senior appointments at the Cockermouth boxes then rated with Keswick A, Threlkeld and Redhills as the best-paid on the CKPR. In earlier days (1872), the sole full-time man in the Junction signalbox was on duty daily from about 5.30am until about 10.00pm, with limited relief; no wonder that the Board decided to engage a second regular signalman!

Right: The 1863 architect's elevation of Cockermouth passenger joint station, facing the platform on the Up side of the line. The stationmaster's house is at the left (west) end. On the ground floor, behind the porters' room (the window and door of which are shown here), was a Boardroom entered from the station forecourt. The Stationmaster's office was below the gable of the single storey section, the main entrance was through the double doors from the booking hall, with waiting rooms to the right. *J.M. Hammond Collection/Carlisle Record Office.*

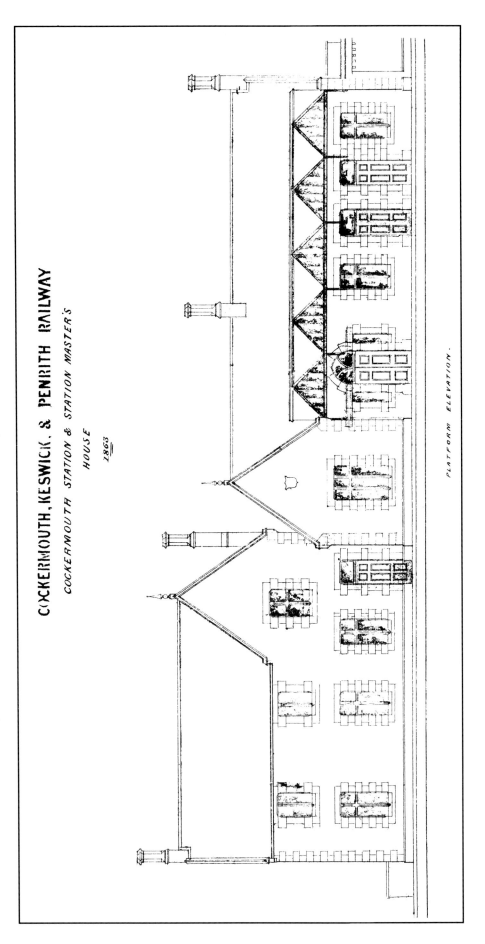

COCKERMOUTH, KESWICK, & PENRITH RAILWAY

COCKERMOUTH STATION & STATION MASTER'S HOUSE
1863

PLATFORM ELEVATION.

Right: On a summer morning around the turn of century, Cockermouth folk are smartly turned out; perhaps some are bound for a CKPR Board meeting at Keswick? The handsome refreshment room of 1890, built in timber, has added a prominent east wing to the original buildings. *Roy Anderson Collection.*

Left: Probably contemporary with the previous view is this picture, from the west end of the station. At the Down platform, the LNWR 'coal tank' 0-6-2T locomotive is highly-polished and in charge of a single coach. The shelter on this platform, and the signalbox, can be discerned, also the ever-present cattle wagons beyond the refreshment room. *A.G. Ellis Collection.*

Right: A companion view, on August 7 1950, shows LNWR 'Cauliflower' 0-6-0 No. 28589 leaving the Down platform with the 10.20am Penrith-Working-ton train. Staff have been reduced through many economies from circa 1930 onwards and the refreshment room (closed in the 1930s) has disappeared. *E.S. Russell.*

Above: A fine study of Cockermouth station from the signalbox on August 20 1964, as the Up 'Lakes Express' prepares to leave, in the charge of Ivatt Class 2 MT (Mickey Mouse) 2-6-0 No. 46432. Note the cattle pens on the right. *Derek Cross.*

Below: Here is a study of Cockermouth's waiting shelter, on the Down island platform. The station was lit by town's gas, provided by the local gasworks (see page 31). Portable steps were provided to help less-agile travellers to board trains. *Roy Anderson Collection*

Climbing from Cockermouth to Embleton, and beyond

The CWR section, terminating in the lower yard at Cockermouth, was essentially a river level line but from Cockermouth Junction the CKPR single line climbed at 1 in 70, flattening after about three-quarters of a mile for the upper station. The resumed single line eastward to Embleton involved a stiff climb at 1 in 75 and 1 in 73, with the prominent farm of Strawberry How on the right, before

Left: At the west end of the island platform, Cockermouth's small turntable is squeezed in against the embankment. NER locomotives hauling mineral trains were turned here in earlier times. *Richard L. Pattinson/ CRA.*

cuttings and an easing of the gradient to 1 in 150. After Embleton station, (2 3/4 miles from Cockermouth) the gradient fell at 1 in 100 and was then generally level by Bassenthwaite Lake station (three miles from Embleton) to Braithwaite station (a further five miles). Most of these nine easy miles of railway have been exploited by the road engineers and the new A66 absorbs the formation.

Embleton station

The station was actually in Lambfoot, but named after nearby Embleton. The single platform was north of the line, its one storey building having mullioned windows. A level crossing was at the Up (east) end, with the stationmaster's house (built by Bolton & Graham in time for the opening) on the Up side; the house survives today beyond

the crossing. There was never a running loop, nor crossing facilities for passenger trains although, from about the 1890s, tablet instruments were provided in the station office and a goods train could then be stowed in the small yard while a passenger train was handled. Signals were worked from an unprotected ground frame, adjacent to the crossing. The yard had two short sidings, one serving coal cells, but was extended in, it is thought, 1904, at the request of Mr Bewsher, the local timber merchant, for his sawmill. His succesor, T. Rutherford, closed the sawmill in 1926 and the Railway Company removed the connection in 1929. Other railway traffic in timber at Embleton declined in the late 1930s but was livened during the 1939-45 war, by the despatch of pit props from Forestry Commission plantations. In 1955, the yard was reduced to just two short sidings, one being occupied by a couple of camping

Left: Embleton station, with the stationmaster and his staff on the single platform. Also shown are the level crossing at the east end of the platform, the Stationmaster's house and the signal post with arm for each direction. Signalling instruments (illustrated on page 148) were in the station office. A66 traffic now sweeps by the site but the house survives. *A.G. Ellis Collection.*

coaches, adapted from LNWR vehicles. The acetylene gas-house was a lean-to structure at the back of the station building and supplied gas for lighting.

A promotional effort in 1906 was the offer of 'golfers' season tickets' between Cockermouth and Embleton, from April 1 to November 30, for £1 10s (2nd class) and £1 (3rd). The station closed to all traffic wef September 15 1958. Plans at that time to transfer the instruments to the east-facing porch of the house, relocate the groundframe on the lawn and convert the platform building as a camping cottage were not carried out. Token exchange was effected right to the end, in April 1966, latterly by the two ladies qualified to operate the instruments, frame and gates. They worked in contact with signalmen at Cockermouth and Bassenthwaite Lake.

Rakefoot Crossing.

Nearly a mile east of Embleton station, a by-road was crossed and a gatekeeper's cottage adjoined; the provision of a station at this point was briefly considered in 1862. There was a tragedy here at an early date (February 1867) when the gatekeeper's wife was killed by a train. This was not a blockpost, but over some years an open frame was used to work the signals, which later were operated by wires connected to the gates. In the 1930s-1940s, Tom Sanderson, porter at Bassenthwaite Lake, lived in the house and his wife was gatekeeper, succeeded from about 1946 by their daughter, Mrs Mary Davidson.

Close Granite Quarry

This quarry was just north of Rakefoot Crossing and the (old) main road. The proprietor, Mr Glossop, was carting his stone to Embleton station in 1908-09, when he first applied for a siding. The connection was actually made in 1912, at a point about half-a-mile east of Rakefoot gates. It was controlled by 'Close Quarry Ground Frame' (dated 1912) always released by the section token and with no cabin or signals. In 1912, the quarry belonged to the Cumberland Granite Co. Ltd. (proprietor William Spencer, of Skipton, until 1919), the Company becoming Keswick Granite Co. Ltd. in 1936, also controlling Threlkeld Granite Quarries, from which men and activity were soon trans-ferred. In 1949-50, production ended at Close and activity reverted to Threlkeld. A little railway ballast was seemingly brought out of Close - for transfer to the ED siding at Keswick by an Up goods train - until effective closure of the siding in 1952. It was derelict by June 1954 and the connec-tion was lifted in 1956. Narrow gauge tubs ran from the quarry down a self-acting incline to tip into hopper, con-veyor, crusher, screens and final hoppers for loading to road or railway wagons. The rail outlet was under the old main road bridge, then by weighbridge and office, over the Dubwath beck and reaching three exchange sidings. An internal-combustion tractor, mounted on rail wheels, figured in the 1930s-1940s, propelling wagons (empties) up the grade to the crusher and loaded wagons from weigh-bridge to exchange sidings.

Bassenthwaite Lake station

About 1 1/4 miles from Close Quarry Ground Frame, an eastbound train would run over the level crossing, with attractive signal box to its left, and into the Up platform at

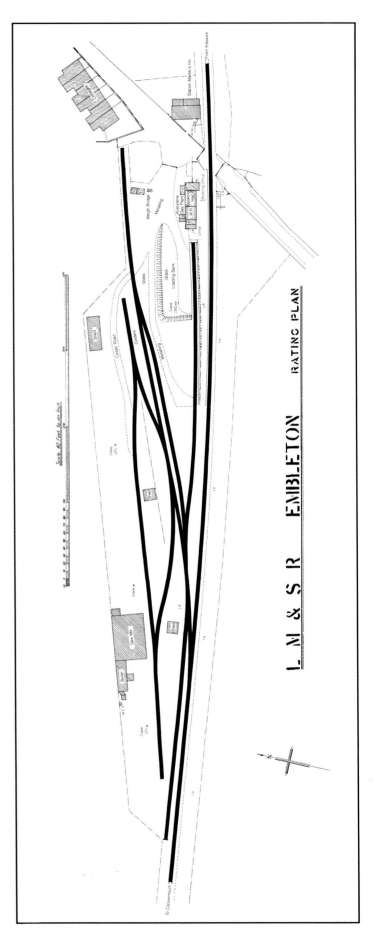

L M & S R EMBLETON RATING PLAN

Left: The Rakefoot level crossing keeper's cottage, on April 17 1985 and looking roughly westward. The single line passed to the left of the building (the gable end faced the track) and the road seen in the foreground passes over the crossing. The A66 road now occupies the former trackbed in this vicinity. *Harold D. Bowtell.*

Below: In the section from Embleton to Bassenthwaite Lake, this access ground frame (left) was released by the token for the section and the lead trailed off the single line for Up trains, to reach the group of exchange sidings and the short private branch to the processing plant of Close quarry. *Richard L. Pattinson/CRA.*

Bassenthwaite Late station - often affectionately known as 'Bass Lake' by railway folk. While the Up platform never achieved more than a timber structure (albeit featuring waiting and porters' rooms) the Down side had a pleasant single storey stone building in the general style of those at Embleton and Braithwaite, and provided booking office, general waiting room and ladies' waiting room. This building was flanked to the east by a pair of cottages erected in due course for the two signalmen and their families. To the west was a handsome house for the Stationmaster, built by Bolton & Graham contemporary with the station and notable for an attractive internal stairway.

From (seemingly) February 1910, the Stationmaster acted also as Sub-Postmaster and the Railway Company built a Post Office immediately behind the booking office; it was completed in October 1911 and the Stationmaster was charged a rent of £6 pa for its use.

The station was a crossing place from the start, in 1865, and the Up and Down platform roads were used strictly for movements in the respective directions. A signalbox was built in 1874, and electric token instruments, working at that time with Cockermouth to the west and Keswick to the east, were provided in (probably) 1889. The crossing loops were extended westward of the crossing circa 1899 and eastward later. This latter extension would lead to the installation of the 'auxiliary frame', in a rudimentary small cabin, at the east end of the layout, to work the points (facing for Down trains) at that end. This refinement was completed in December 1902. The same small box remained to control the resited points following a further eastward extension of the loops.

The 'blind' approach by road from the direction of the Pheasant Hotel, south of the level crossing, caused the CKPR board anxiety in the early days of horseless carriages, which were devoid of effective brakes! In 1908, a large 'caution' board was proposed 'to appraise approaching motors of the danger', but on July 23 1909 Mr Milne's motor car nevertheless sustained damage at the gates. Hence, a proposition before the Permanent Way Committee was the installation of a signal on the road, each side of the crossing, to warn drivers of the status of the crossing! The signal was to be 10-12ft high and designed to operate when the gate locks were bolted. In fact, a larger wheel was installed

in the box, to speed gate-opening and closing. Finally, with completion in October 1911, a new signal box was erected, closer to the road, so giving the signalman better visibility.

The goods yard was behind the Up platform and had four sidings, which were unchanged and well-used for many years by cattle, timber and varied traffic, and of course, coal. There were three coal cells on the back road and three merchants were represented; after Mealsgate station closed (wef December 1 1952) a merchant from as far distant as Ireby (six miles north eastward) was installed too. Two sidings were taken out in 1951.

To operate the small box, the porter on each turn of duty had to walk or cycle out. Often trains crossed, so the stationmaster was hard-pressed to look after both Up and Down trains, and their passengers, simultaneously. Stationmasters at this delightful site had included Samuel McKenzie (with uniform and house provided) until 1867, John Scott to 1872, William Reay until appointed to Keswick in 1876, Thomas Allison from 1879, John Blackburn in 1908-10, J.W. Ewart from 1910 to 1921 (with later promotion), and Joseph Todhunter from 1921 until his retirement in 1933. Then came Messrs Grimley and Whelan. After the transfer away (circa 1957-58) of Sam Whelan, there was an interregnum and the sub-Post Office was closed. Jim Airey, the last 'Bass Lake' Stationmaster (1959-1964) did not have that responsibility. After his time, the station was under the charge of Mr Hughes, based at Cockermouth.

DISTANT SIGNAL 640 YDS

TO COCKERMOUTH — THREE COAL CELLS — GAS SHED

GOODS SHED · SIGNALBOX · PLATFORM · STN MASTER'S HOUSE · P.O. · PLATFORM HOUSE

TO KESWICK

BASSENTHWAITE LAKE · PLATELAYERS HUT

YARDS 0 25 50

NOS. 1&2 LEVERS HERE WORK THE EXTREME EAST-FACING POINTS

Nos.	RELEASES	LOCKS	BACKLOCKS
13: UP HOME	14	6,7	9,16
14: UP DISTANT			11,12,13
15: WICKET GATES	2,3,13		15
16: GATE STOPS	2,3,13		
GATE WHEEL			(THESE BACKLOCK THE WHEEL AND ALSO LEVERS 1 &2 IN GROUND FRAME)

Nos.	RELEASES	LOCKS	BACKLOCKS
7: CROSSOVER ROAD	3	2,6,12,13	
8: UP FACING POINTS		9	
9: POINT GUARD	13	8	
10: SPARE			
11: UP ADVANCE	14	2,6,7,4	6,7

Nos.	RELEASES	LOCKS	BACKLOCKS
1: DOWN DISTANT			
2: DOWN HOME	1	7,11,13	2, 3
3: DOWN STARTING	1	7	16,4
4: LOCKS FP LEVER IN GF		11	8,7,16
5: SIDING GROUND SIGNAL			6

NOTE: LEVER No. 11 is released by lever No. 1 in ground frame.

LOCKING DERIVES FROM TWEEDY OF CARLISLE NOVEMBER 15 1902, WHEN SMALL CABIN AND FIRST EXTENSION WAS INSTALLED. SMALL CABIN OR GROUND FRAME CABIN WAS LOCATED 285 YARDS FROM SIGNALBOX.

In LMS days, Bassenthwaite Lake became, with good reason, a 'favoured resort for camping coaches and BR continued this tradition. Before 1939, the vehicles were brought in spring and taken away for overhaul and storage in the winter. In 1959-64, there were two coaches and they stood in one of the two surviving short sidings but the points for this siding were taken out so the occasional move for repair or painting necessitated the temporary slewing of the stabling road into the 'operational' siding.

The gardens, especially on the Up side, were a 'picture', beautifully set against foliage in the summer, with the lake and, beyond it, Skiddaw (3,053ft) seen ahead, eastward, through a short rock cutting. James Shrives, the Company gardener from Edwardian times until 1921, made 'Bass Lake' his speciality, and Frank Bragg, Porter here in the 1920s was also a particularly keen gardener. The Reverend Simmons, Secretary and a mainspring of the Friends of the Lake District from the beginnings (in 1934) of this notable organisation, had a special word of praise for Bassenthwaite Lake station and its people. Surely, too, the weekly residents in the camping coaches and the travellers who arrived in early evening by the 'The Lakes Express' from London, or left on the last morning of a stay nearby, would echo this pleasure and praise. Closure to goods was wef June 1 1964, while the station and both signal boxes closed with the line, wef April 18 1966. The 'new' road sweeps by the surviving station buildings.

Bassenthwaite Lake-Braithwaite

Sir Henry Vane had given land for the railway in the Bassenthwaite Lake station vicinity and he was soon provided with wicket gates and the right to cross the line to his boat landing.

Beyond the rock cutting, the line emerged onto the very brink of the lake itself, the formation supported by walls on the left and thus protected from erosion by wind and water. Only half-a-mile from the station, the railway negotiated the point at Castle How, briefly in a cutting with the original main road abobve it, on the right, supported by massive stone retaining walls and backed by a cliff face. Across the water, on the left, the supremely impressive vista of Skiddaw and its supporting heights opens out. From MP6 1/4 to MP9, the line was on a southerly course, then from MP9 to about MP10 1/2 it crossed water meadows to Braithwaite station, five miles from Bassenthwaite Lake station. On the waterside section, there was a backing (right) by precipitous Wythop woods and the heights beyond. Beck Wythop cottages, a pair built by the CKPR circa 1904 for platelayers, were above the line (right) and are now above the new road. Beyond Powter How, where the meadows were crossed by a low embankment. Thornthwaite village, on the (old) main road in the trees above was a community which mined and processed lead and zinc. Nearing MP10, the unusual farm lanes-cum-aqueduct crossed over the line.

Braithwaite station

This station (which very nearly originated as 'Thornthwaite') was on a curving stretch of the railway route, which brings it from north-to-south to its more familiar west-to-east alignment - and also detaches it from the present-day A66 road, which has usurped its magnificent lakeside course. The gently-curving platform was on

Above, left: The approach to Bassenthwaite Lake station, looking east, as seen from a Penrith-bound diesel multiple unit on July 27 1963. A green and cream liveried camping coach is glimpsed through the trees on the left. *Preston Whiteley.*

Above, right: Stationmaster Jim Airey, resplendent in his uniform, and Mrs Airey are on the Down platform at Bassenthwaite Lake. Note the acetylene gas lamp, and their house. *Jim Airey Collection.*

Right: Today, the A66 sweeps past 'Bass Lake', whose buildings survive to interest the historian and modeller. In this view, Keswick is to the left. *Harold D. Bowtell.*

Changing seasons at 'Bass Lake', as this station was affectionately known in local railway parlance. Above, left: A pleasant, sunny day on the Up platform, as three passengers and two railwaymen await the arrival of a Penrith-bound train. Note the colourful flower beds and the neatly-trimmed bushes further down the platform. Above, right: A crisp winters day at 'Bass Lake' with plenty of snow. The camping coach (an LNWR-built vehicle) is on the left, in this pretty scene. *Jim Airey Collection.*

the Down side of the single line, with a minor level crossing at the Bassenthwaite end. The single storey stone building has much in common with those at Embleton and Bassenthwaite Lake, with mullioned windows and a steep roof profile, backed in this instance by a substantial stone house, an original structure. The house was extended about 1889, by building an additional room for station purposes behind the waiting room and an additional bedroom above it. With further extensions at the other end, the premises represent a residence of fair size. The staff developed topiary on the Up side banking, opposite the platform, and a garden beside the platform. In 1954, traveller Eric Hannan remarked on the fine display of roses.

The goods yard, on the Down side behind the platform, had trailing access for Up trains. In general, there were four rather cramped sidings, the two longer (back) ones forming a loop. Minerals figured. Barely a year after opening, the CKPR agreed to build a warehouse for leasing to the Goldscope Mining Company (April 1866) and in the next year (August 1867) agreed to construct a coal depot for the use of G.I. May of the Goldscope Mines. Twenty years on (in April 1887) the Company approved extension of the shed to accommodate lead ore of the Cumberland Lead Mining Company, with a rental charged.

Thornthwaite Mines Ltd. (sometimes, by 1920, using the style 'Threlkeld Lead Mines, Thornthwaite - proprietors Marple & Gillott Ltd, Sheffield') mined lead and zinc from 1873 to 1921 and advertised their operations as 'via Braithwaite station.' Anthony Wilson was Managing Director in 1920. Former footplateman Joe Tinnion, often firing the engine of the Workington-Keswick pickup goods in 1938-39, recalls that a wagon or two of barytes would often be picked up at Braithwaite, the mineral having come by horse and cart from Newlands Fell. Timber too was evident. The LMS (and subsequently BR) installed camping coaches. Trifling layout extensions were made during the years from 1898 to 1923 and curtailments between 1948 and 1954, and after, leaving only a siding for the coaches and one (new) short internal loop. Coal sales were evidently handled here from the earliest days, as the Stationmaster was dismissed in 1868 for irregularities in the coal business.

As at Embleton, the signals were worked from an unprotected ground frame, adjacent to the crossing, and the instruments were in the station office. The electric tablet probably dated from 1893, replaced as elsewhere on the route, in LMS days, by miniature staff instruments. A goods train could be 'locked in' the yard, to allow another train to pass. A second frame appeared in time. The personnel were reduced and in the last last six years of operation (1960-66) there was just one man on each turn of duty, and as this was a blockpost, he had to be a qualified signalman. Bob Bond, relieving at that time in boxes west of Keswick, remarks that the acceptance and offering-on of a train had to be conducted in the office on the platform, after which one crossed to the far side of the line to 'set up the road' before returning to receive the token for the section in rear and give the driver the token for the section in advance. The received staff would be put in the appropriate instrument, the signals restored to danger and maybe the gates opened. There would also be tickets to issue and any merchandise to handle, often crated chickens to load. The train was then despatched with all customers safe and satisfied, including any arriving visitors or walkers who required directions to the village (one half-mile south) or by Whinlatter Pass, up behind Braithwaite, to the Lorton Fells and Loweswater. In quieter moments the signalman refilled the trays of the lighting plant and kept everything tidy. Closure to goods was wef June 1 1964 and to passengers wef April 18 1966, when the railway west of Keswick closed.

Above: The rock cutting at the Up end of Bassenthwaite Lake station, looking back westward to the station. Following extension of the loop at this eastern end. 'Bass Lake' provided a crossing facility with ample capacity for lengthy trains. *Richard L. Pattinson/ CRA.*

Braithwaite-Keswick

It was 2 1/4 miles from Braithwaite to Keswick, by rail. The first mile and a half or so traversed low embankments and a multitude of bridges. In this area, Bassenthwaite Lake and Derwentwater threaten to combine from time to time, and this created perpetual and considerable problems for the railway company.

Between bridges Nos. 45 (Pow Beck) and 47 (River Derwent), the CKPR built Howe Cottages, a pair erected in 1888, on the Down side, where a lane crosses by bridge to reach nearby How Farm. The building tender was for £283 13s 0d. The nearest community is in Portinscale. Jack Stamper, ganger in charge of 'the Braithwaite length', lived in one of these cottages during the years before 1940. The houses remain, very pleasant, and one has been extended. Bridge No. 47 was the only bowstring girder structure on the CKPR line west of Keswick. Just beyond the last of the bridges over water, near MP12, St Kentigern's church and vicarage are quietly situated to the south of the railway route. This is Crosthwaite Church, which has long played a significant part in the life of Keswick and gained special

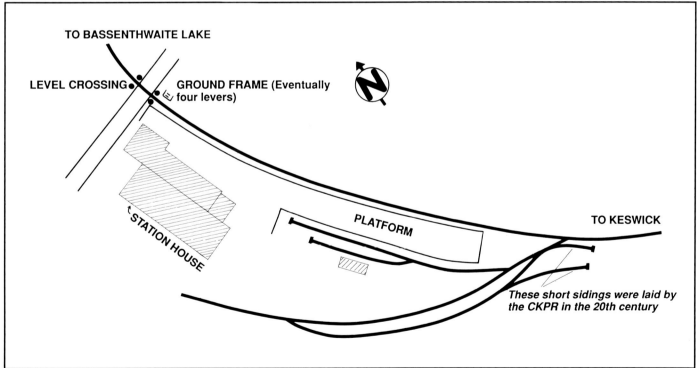

TO BASSENTHWAITE LAKE

LEVEL CROSSING

GROUND FRAME (Eventually four levers)

STATION HOUSE

PLATFORM

TO KESWICK

These short sidings were laid by the CKPR in the 20th century

fame when Canon Rawnsley was the incumbent. The memory of Bishop Eric Treacy is also honoured. In this vicinity, the A66 crosses and recrosses the line of this route today. The railway crossed the A591 (to Carlisle) by an underline bridge and swung briefly south over a lane which developed residentially and so, by an embankment above Fitz meadows (public park), reached Keswick station.

Top: On Bassenthwaite Lake shore, 'Cauliflower' No. 58396 is in charge of the 11.50am Workington-Penrith train of August 5 1950. This location is south of MP7 (from Cockermouth Junction) and north of the Beck Wythop overline accommodation bridge and cottages. *E.S. Russell.*

Above: Braithwaite station plan.

Above: 'Cauliflower' 0-6-0 No. 58389 makes haste with the 11.50am ex-Workington duty of August 7 1950. The train is leaving the southern shore of Bassenthwaite Lake, with O.S. Nock riding on the footplate. Thornthwaite is in the woodlands to the left. *E.S. Russell.*

Above: On July 27 1963, looking eastward, the 2.55pm Penrith-Workington DMU is entering Braithwaite station, which boasts its camping coach (right) while, on both sides of the line, the station gardens are a picture - sadly, to be tended for only two more summers at this stage. This was surely the English country railway at its best. *Preston Whiteley.*

RAILS THROUGH LAKELAND

Left, upper: The substantial house at Braithwaite was built directly behind the station buildings. The CKPR starting signal is shown as a train still painted in LNWR 'plum and spilt milk' livery leaves westward. A uniformed member of staff is dividing his attention between despatch of train (with token) and receiving the lady passenger. He will also have to restore the signals and operate the level crossing gates. *Richard L. Pattinson/CRA.*

Left, lower: Happily, the station house and platform buildings at Braithwaite escaped destruction by the road builders and have been well looked after. Here is a study of detail in the platform buildings, in January 1983. *Harold D. Bowtell.*

Below: A tranquil general view, looking west at Braithwaite on July 27 1963, just three years before closure of the route betwen Keswick and Workington. A quite delightful sight.
Preston Whiteley.

Above: The CKPR identified its bridges by attaching oval cast iron plates of this design. *Author's Collection.*

Right: A 'Cauliflower' approaches bridge No. 52 (note the CKPR bridgeplate) over the lane near Crosthwaite churchyard. Today, the stone abutments carry a footbridge for ramblers.
Richard L. Pattinson/CRA

KESWICK AS A RAILWAY HEADQUARTERS
Aspects and atmosphere

Workington hid the sea away behind several steelworks. Cockermouth's setting has always been rural rather than rugged. Penrith, too, is a pleasant town, below Beacon Hill, but most of its vistas are distant. Keswick, however, is superbly dominated by lake and mountains; climb gently for a mere 250ft and the scene is breathtaking. This has never been a major county or administrative centre but it has developed steadily with tourism, during 150 years and more. The town was pleasantly enlivened by appreciative visitors arriving on its railway, without becoming congested or overwhelmed. Only in the era of the popular motor car and the intrusive motor lorry has it suffered. Since 1972, it has lived without its railway and has instead embraced one of the most hazardous roads in Britain, prominent on the foothills a little to the north of the former station.

Keswick's station was attractive to the eye. It was the headquarters of the CKPR Board of Directors from the 1860s and its discreet development continued under the LMS until 1939. It was quietly businesslike with out-of-season traffic and alive with anticipatory and active bustle several times a day in the holiday season. Its staff established and maintained this air of a headquarters and assumed automatic superiority. They would have it that 'The Lakes Express', bound for London started here - and not from Windermere or Workington, as might be supposed by the uninitiated! In CKPR days, the stationmaster donned a top hat and complementary attire to receive Directors and distinguished visitors; some say he wore it whenever on duty.

The passenger station - a closer study

The lands required at Keswick were purchased from General le Fleming, and the contract to build the station was placed in 1863, with Boulton & Sons, the contractors for the Railway. It was based on a plan presented by Thomas Bouch, the engineer. The alignment was west-to-east, one third of a mile north of the town centre and with little beyond and above it except the 1203ft summit of Latrigg a

mile away, with the greater heights of Blencathra and Skiddaw up behind that. The route was always single line in each direction, but with Up and Down running lines for the length of the platforms, and for a roughly similar distance at the western end, from which direction there was access to the goods yard. The Up passenger platform originally carried only a waiting shelter and (at its east end) a water tank for the use of locomotives. On the Down side, a workmanlike stone building of two storeys was built, using local materials. It was well gabled, ostensibly much the sort of building which a comfortably-off local Director might have built for his own occupation. As it weathered, against a background of growing trees, and the horse-drawn equipages drew up before its entrance, the analogy would be the more apparent. A glazed 'portico' was added to Bouch's design before construction started. This was a happy touch, affording protection and softening the lines of the building. This building survives today, and may still be studied.

Upstairs, the Boardroom was in the west wing, whilst the Secretary's office was under the west gable of the centre block. The Traffic Manager's office was under the next gable and the Accountant resided in the east wing.

The ticket office and usual waiting rooms and other premises occupied the lower floor, opening onto the platform; these were rearranged in the 1890s. The Keswick Hotel (of which more later, see pages 61-62) was built for the Railway Company in the 1860s, when it was considered to be an essential part of the project; it faces onto the forecourt from the eastern side. Happily, it continues to offer hospitality to visitors.

A surprising aspect was the short life of Keswick station's refreshment room. It opened in 1865 (or very soon after) and was let from the outset to the Hotel Company. Around 1871-72, other parties volunteered to operate the room at

Facing page: An impressive view of Keswick, from the slopes of Latrigg, around 1890. The station and hotel are prominent in the foreground, with building work for the island platform in progress. Once again, the splendid surroundings are clearly apparent. *Valentine.*

higher rentals than the £45-£50 per year being paid. Then, on August 8 1872, the CKPR Board unanimously agreed that it was desirable to withdraw the refreshment facilities. The Hotel Company acquiesced and it was duly closed by April 10 1873. One is left assuming, perhaps, that a rowdy and possibly drunken element had caused problems, on days when excursion trains predominated. After closure, a first class gentlemen's waiting room and an additional lavatory were constructed in the space relinquished (1873) - which itself had been curtailed in 1871 by creating a second class ladies' waiting room and modifying the lavatories.

Below: A plan of Keswick, based on the LMS drawing of the 1930s. Observe the alternative sites being considered for the turntable.

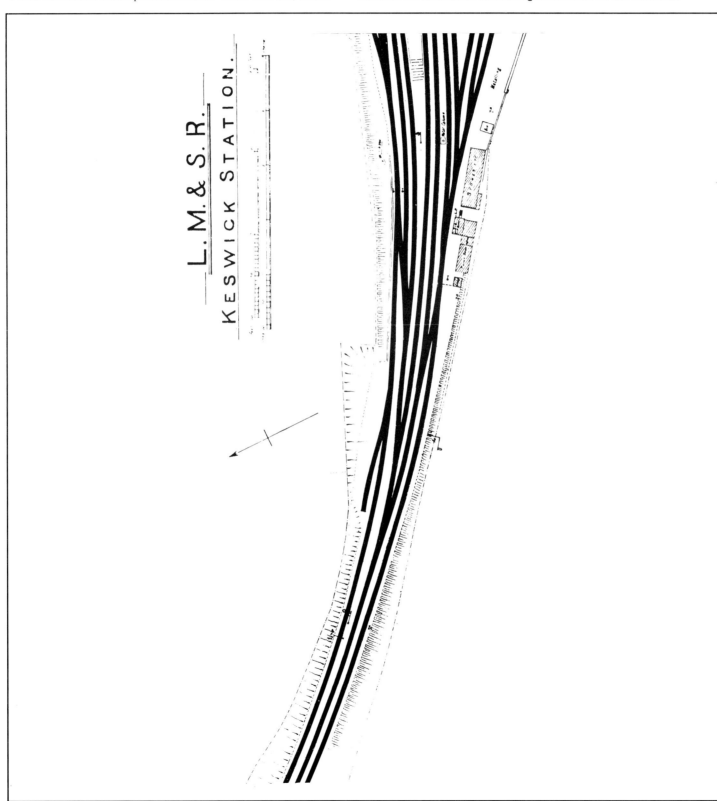

L. M. & S. R.

KESWICK STATION.

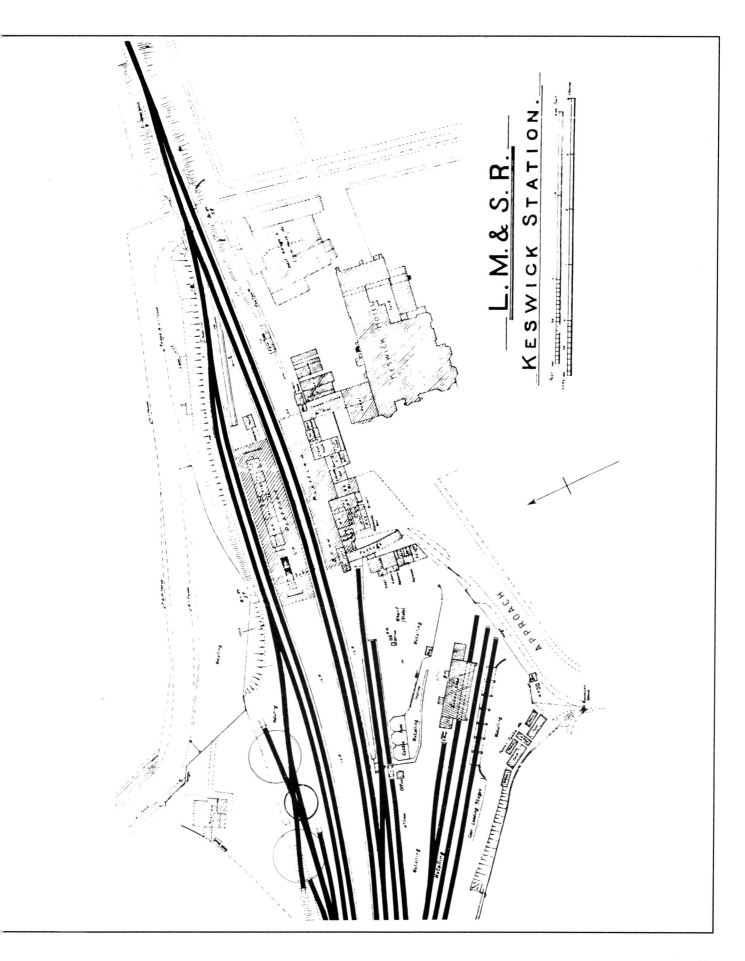

L. M. & S. R.

KESWICK STATION.

Bookstalls

The CKPR board, which always cast a jealous eye towards Windermere, wished to have a bookstall, selling all newspapers, either at their published prices or at least on the same terms as at Windermere. That was in their first year of traffic, in 1865. It is not clear whether any arrangements were made at this time, but in 1869 the matter was taken in hand by Charles Mason, Assistant General Manager of the LNWR. He agreed terms with W.H. Smith & Son for the opening of bookstalls on the stations at: Keswick (CKPR), Cockermouth (CKPR/Joint Committee), Workington (by this time, LNWR) and Whitehaven (also LNWR). The arrangements took effect in 1870 or early 1871. The LNWR and W. H. Smith renewed the agreement for this group of bookstalls from time to time, but Smiths declined to continue the arrangements for Keswick and Cockermouth stations after December 31 1905. It was not until February 1909 that the CKPR formally concluded an

Top: The exterior of Keswick station in later CKPR years; the Company's war memorial plaque is mounted above the post box, under the porch. The old Company's Boardroom was formerly upstairs, in the left gabled wing; its chimney stack is prominent. *Roy Anderson Collection.*

Above, left: The original porch canopy at Keswick station was similar to that at Cockermouth. It sheltered many comings and goings and was focal to local life. Here is quite an occasion in the days of the early horseless carriage. At the time, the various hotels' omnibuses would all be horse-drawn. *Author's Collection.*

Above, right: The LMS substituted a smaller, neat canopy with delicate tracery, although the evidence of the former gabled porch remained on the stonework. *Roy Anderson Collection.*

alternative agreement with Wyman & Sons for the operation of a bookstall (with advertising privileges) at Keswick station, and with Kershaw Ltd for Cockermouth station. By 1914, Wyman ran both bookstalls but Kershaw were permitted to advertise. In January 1921, Wyman may well have

Above: Within Keswick station, in June 1919, the atmosphere of the era is captured by Ken Nunn's shot of No. 1675 *Vimiera*, a 6ft 6in 'Jumbo' 2-4-0, in charge of the 11.20am Up passenger from Cockermouth, comprising six-wheeled stock. Through carriages are standing in the short Up bay (right). Note the ring (uncommon - maybe unique - on the CKPR) on the diverging signal arm and the brake van of a Down goods train. In the yard beyond are cattle wagons, pitprops and other timber. *LCGB/Ken Nunn Collection.*

Left: A pleasant portrait of Keswick's distinctive water tower, at the eastern end of the island platform, and the attractive buildings. *Peter W. Robinson.*

The prominent water tank

The water tank for locomotives, at the east end of the Up platform, dated from 1864, but was reconstructed and enlarged under a contract of July 1880 with Cowans Sheldon & Company, of Carlisle. This tank was a very prominent feature through to closure of the station in March 1972, with Cowans, Sheldon's number 44 and date 1880 carried upon it.

Expansion and improvements in the 1890s

Whereas most daily trains ran through to and from Workington, the excursions normally terminated at Keswick towards noon and had to start homeward at early evening. The engines and carriages had meanwhile to be accommodated. Increasingly, too, through carriages were kept overnight at Keswick and attached to popular trains in the morning. Thus, resources became overstrained.

A loop line had been laid behind the Up platform by 1889, when lengthening of that loop at the west end (and laying in of a second loop, behind it) were proposed. For these developments, a strip of land was purchased from Mr le Fleming, owner of the adjoining field. Between 1890 and 1893, development was carried out progressively, bringing the passenger station and its layout to essentially the form known during the ensuing 70 years, with Board of Trade

taken over the Cockermouth bookstall entirely but at that time the right to operate at Keswick station had recently been granted to A. Chaplin, stationer, of 19 Station Street and (in line with current LNWR practice) advertising rights at the station were secured by Frank Mason & Company, of Maxwell House, Arundel Street, Strand, London.

Around 1931, Wyman again took over the bookstall (also the kiosk on the island platform) at Keswick (from Chaplins) but closed down the bookstall during the 1950s. Wymans closed Cockermouth's station bookstall round about 1961.

Keswick's well-known subway

It was decided in 1873 to build the subway, which became a familiar feature of Keswick station, linking the platforms and providing also direct access to and from the forecourt, by way of a passage with glazed roof.

inspection of the virtually completed works taking place on November 2 1894. The Up platform was moved back somewhat and reconstructed as a lengthy island, broad in its central portion. This permitted slewing of the main Up and Down running lines and widening the Down platform by about 7ft 6in, in front of the station buildings, accomplished 1894-95. Behind the island, another platform track took the form of a long loop, parallelled by a second long loop, suitable either for running engines round their stock, or stabling a train. A short bay road was provided at the Up end of the island and a bay in the western end of the main Down platform. Handsome glazed roofing was installed over a substantial part of both platforms, also a range of attractive timber buildings on the island, which featured free-standing glazing. A locomotive turntable was installed near the boundary of the site, as extended a little northward, behind the station. It was probably at this period when the Down platform was lengthened at its east end by a narrow extension, in timber. This proved a source of trouble in the prevailing climate, being found decayed and unsafe in 1919, and likewise in 1946.

Electric light

Opportunely, within a few years of completion of these improvements, which aided railway operating and the comfort of travellers, there came the offer by the Windermere & District Electricity Supply Company to install electric lighting. This company undertook to provide a regular supply of electric current and their tender of £303 was accepted in November 1899, for a comprehensive installation. In view of the early date, and this being the only station on the CKPR route (except Penrith, and that in relatively recent times) ever to benefit from electric light, the initial list of lamps is quoted, slightly summarised:

Upper Floor: Board room: Four drop lamps, each of 8cp (candle power); Secretary's office: Two drop lamps of 8cp and one lamp of 25cp; Clerks' office: Five drop lamps of 16cp; Accountant's office: Four drop lamps of 16cp.
Ground Floor of the main buildings: Station entrance: One lamp of 50cp and two outside lamps of 16cp each; Booking office (Down): 4 lamps of 16cp each; Stationmaster's room: One lamp of 16cp.
Island Platform (There were also lamps in waiting and other rooms, and in the subway):
Booking Office (Up Platform): Three lamps of 16cp, one being outside; Stationmaster's office (Up): Two lamps of 16cp.(Also lamps in other rooms on this island platform).
Signal box 'B' (on Down platform): Two lamps of 16cp.
Signal box 'A' (westward): Two lamps of 16cp.

Above: An Ivatt '2MT' 2-6-0 (or 'Mickey Mouse') of 12D (Workington) shed calls at Keswick on August 20 1964 with the Down 'Lakes Express'. The glazed screen design of the island platform buildings is shown to good effect. *Derek Cross.*

Left: No. 46432 leaves Keswick with 'The Lakes Express' in July 1964, pictured from the western end of the station and included to show the bay platform layout and loading gauge.

Workshop and offices: Eight lamps of 16cp.
Goods warehouse: Two lamps of 16cp.
Goods office: Two lamps of 16cp.
Goods yard: Two arc lamp.s

Any reader who can recall the dim glow from a carbon filament electric bulb of 25 candle power, deriving power typically at 110 volts dc from public generation, would not have been overwhelmed by the brilliance of Keswick station and yard as the new century approached! Before completion of Keswick station and hotel, in the 1860s, the CKPR had planned to take gas from the Keswick Gas Company. One is left doubting whether this supply materialised for the station and goods yard, as the prospect of electricity was seized upon without hesitation.

Hydraulic power and problems
In 1900, a hydraulic lift was installed between the Up (island) platform and the subway and another in the Keswick Hotel. The water came from the lands of Mr Spedding - who was Chairman of the Railway Company's Board - but his farm needs were paramount. By February 1902, there was concern at the inadequacy of the supply in times of drought. An engine and hydraulic pump were installed, the cost being shared by two-thirds by the Hotel Company and one-third by the CKPR. In the 1930s, when Roy Hughes was the LMS engineer responsible for the CKPR section, he encountered problems with this supply. The farmer modernised his operations by installing a milk cooler - which promptly took all the water – necessitating a long period of diplomacy and pipe-cleaning to secure the needs of hotel and railway.

Telephones
Another refinement was the telephone, provided by the National Telephone Company, whose business passed to the Post Office in 1912. The first instrument was placed in the Company's office (upstairs), along with one in the Stationmaster's office (downstairs), in 1910. Next year, extensions were made to the goods and parcels departments - following upon representations by tradespeople.

Later changes
A shed for bicycles and luggage was placed at the west end of the Down platform in 1913, whilst in 1914 some modification of Down side waiting rooms seems to have followed. Eventually, a plain glazed roof was substituted for the decorative portico, but the LMS superimposed quite an attractive and airy structure bearing the name 'Keswick.' Following some previous use of light coloured paintwork, the station was finished in green and cream, around 1960.

Keswick Goods Station
Unlike its passenger counterpart, the Goods Station at Keswick was positively and honourably parochial. The east-bound ironstone (or empties) and coke (westbound) all passed it by, the trains pausing only long enough for their engines to take water or enlist assistance in the rear. The yard was at first tucked neatly into a near triangular site. On its south side was a coal road, traversing seven coal cells. There was one track between the coal road and the one which passed through the stone-built goods shed, and a short siding which terminated just short of this building. Finally, there were two fairly long sidings close to the Down running line and one of these came alongside a loading bank, or platform, with a five-tons capacity crane handy. The yard tracks converged into the Down running line (without a headshunt) just before it joined the Up line - and there was also a siding on the north of the site. All major changes in the yard were made before the end of the 19th century. A short stage (platform) was built beside the approach line to the coal cells, to ease discharge of side-door wagons. The neat and matching goods office was added circa 1877 to the west end of the shed and the short track was cut back to accommodate it. The loading bank acquired three cattle pens and the track next to the running road became effectively a bay platform line. Significant, however, was a widening of the formation, westward, circa 1880, and the creation of a useful headshunt. This permitted the shunting of all roads in the yard without fouling the running line. A weighbridge for railway wagons eventually appeared on the line beside the loading bank and this probably derived from the demands away back in 1880 of the traffic from the Buttermere Green Slate Company. Just inside the road entrance was a weighbridge for carts and lorries; beside it, a charming weighhouse, in vertical tim-

Right: A view into Keswick goods yard from Station Road. The timber-built weighbridge cabin was of a pagoda-like design, with the stone-built goods shed beyond. Today, a leisure centre occupies the yard site.

Below: The track entering the western end of Keswick goods shed is obscured, but Percy Sanderson's one-time office is shown. The coal cells are beneath the right hand siding, which is designed for the discharge of NER bottom-door wagons.
Both: Roy Anderson Collection.

bering with slated roof and tall, decorative finial, presented the air of a small pagoda. A relatively late development was the provision of a small oil store, near the southern boundary of the goods yard, left of the road entrance. The Anglo American Oil Company (much later becoming Esso) and the British Petroleum Co. Ltd. (BP) were both permitted to establish their first oil stores at Keswick station yard in 1912.

Signal cabins and workshops

A Saxby & Farmer brick signal box, with slated roof, hipped at the ends, was built in 1874, on the Down side near the yard outlet. This brought together the operation of most of the running line points and signals, also giving the signalman an oversight of shunting movements. A quaint little signal cabin was provided on the Down platform,

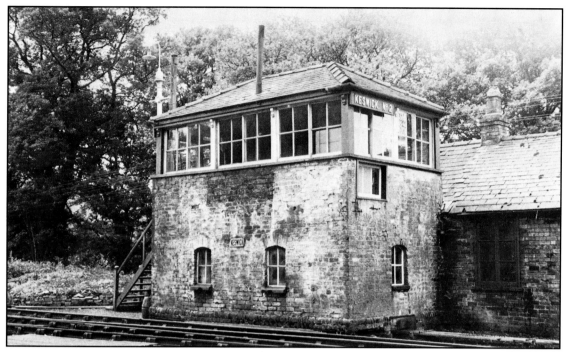

Left: Keswick No. 2 signalbox, a Saxby & Farmer structure built in 1874. The single-storey brick building to the rear was the CKPR's joiners' and plumbers' workshop.
Roy Anderson Collection.

Below, left: William Greenhow, the CKPR Keswick carter, is in town, in April 1917, with his horse and heavy duty Company cart, collecting waste paper for sale in aid of the local military hospital, established in Lord Rochdale's home *Lingholm*. This collection was the initiative of Mrs George Hogarth and the family shop appears. *Fitz Museum Collection.*

towards its east end, in (probably) 1889; it was superseded by a new box in 1932. The 1874 box became 'Keswick A', whilst the 1889 box became 'Keswick B', although in LMS days the styling was No. 2 and No. 1 (respectively). The woodwork of both boxes was painted green and cream by the 1960s.

Workshops and stores (single storey brick buildings) were clustered close behind the 'A' box, originally accommodating the CKPR's joiners, plumbers and blacksmith, who shoed the Company's horses, amongst other work. The stables were to the right, when entering the yard gates, and eventually a garage was added to the block.

Traffic in Keswick yard

Coal was always the major inward traffic. Prior to 1923, that for CKPR stations was primarily a NER responsibility and, accordingly, bottom-door wagons were used. The staff liked them, for side-door wagons – sometimes received from pits via Brayton (MCR), Whitehaven or

Workington way, occasionally too from Durham or Yorkshire pits - called for much shovelling. The town gas works was a regular customer, with one cell reserved; it sent its own lorries, which backed in for loading. Other cells were rented by merchants, who bagged their coal as required and undertook their own cartage to customers.

A staple outward traffic by rail was slate from the Buttermere Green Slate Company's Honister quarries, certainly back to the early 1880s and probably before that. This Company not surprisingly undertook its own cartage of the prized slate, using two-wheeled carts for many years, each pulled by a single horse, over the hilly route to Keswick. Before the 1914-1918 war, a steam lorry was sharing the job. By the 1930s, a Sentinel steam lorry was employed by the quarries on the run to Keswick station. There had been talk of a link by steam light railway - and quite some railway it would have been - and this is touched upon later.

Timber merchants, with their own sawmills in Keswick, delivered planks and the like by road to the station yard, for despatch by rail. Pit props were sent mainly to West Cumberland. There was also wood bound for the short run by rail to the Briery Bobbin Mill's siding. Keswick was proud of its two pencil manufacturing mills, amalgamated in 1912 and reduced to one from about 1939. The railway carters collected their consignments. There are still pencils made in Keswick today, by the Cumberland Pencil Company.

West Cumberland Farmers' Trading Society maintained a depot at Keswick, receiving supplies by rail. In autumn, the Railway sought orders from the farmers round about - to load sheep for despatch to winter pastures, often via Gretna, and to bring them back in the spring.

Traffic for NER destinations was consigned to Penrith or Carlisle for transhipment, or for onward transit if in full wagon loads.

There was a siding at the west end of Keswick, on the north (Up) side, lengthened westward sometime during the first 20 years of this century. In LMS days, it was favoured for the stabling of Engineers Department wagons of railway ballast, from Close Quarries at Embleton.

Right & below: Traffic destined for Keswick in the late 19th century was indeed varied. On notification cards despatched to William Reay (CKPR stationmaster from 1876 until his death in 1908) is recorded a range of merchandise from fenders to straw and sugar. This example was posted from T.R. Metcalfe, of Tangier Street Whitehaven, on March 21 1889 and carried a halfpenny stamp. The message reads: "Please deliver 3 bags sugar ex Liverpool consigned to my order to W. Thomas Barnes, Grocer, Keswick." *Courtesy J.M. Hammond Collection.*

Familiar carts and carters, at Keswick

In October 1866, well over a year after opening, the CKPR decided: "to purchase a lurry, horse, etc, in order to execute the Company's cartage work at Keswick," and in May 1867 the purchase of a second horse was authorised. Joseph Tinnion was the carter, but he was promoted to Foreman Porter at Keswick in 1867. Mr Fearon, a platelayer, took the carter's job from August of that year. Isaac Atkinson succeeded as 'cartman' at Keswick, his pay being increased in May 1873 from 19/- to 20/- (£1) per week. In November 1877, the lurry (a spelling maintained by some Railway Companies until the 1920s!) was worn out and replaced. There was only one horse in these times and nine years on it was reported 'too old' and another was purchased. Similarly, in April 1907, a horse was superannuated and replaced.

Two horse-drawn carts were maintained by the summer of 1913, when an increase in wage levels led to carter W. Greenhow receiving a pay rise from 23/- to 24/- weekly. His colleague Fleming Barnes was advanced from 22/- to 23/- for a week's work. Mr Greenhow drove the four-wheeled cart used for the heavier deliveries whilst Mr Barnes was in charge of the parcels cart, said also to have four wheels but of lighter build, with a detachable cover. The two carts comprised the fleet in the CKPR's later years, from 1920 to 1922, when Jack Tyson was one of the carters. It is believed that the carts remained in use for some years after this; the carters worked from 7.30am until 4.00 or 5.00pm.

Rather surprisingly, during the war, in September 1915, the Company considered introducing motor traction for the delivery of goods at Keswick but this was not pursued and new stables were built instead. In July 1919, a scale of charges was compiled for delivery of parcels beyond a one

mile radius from Keswick station. In general, delivery was not charged to Chestnut Hill or The Forge, towards Penrith, nor to Portinscale, about a couple of level miles in the opposite direction. Eventually, a motor vehicle replaced the parcels cart and its horse and the new vehicle undertook longer journeys, for a fee. A garage was built onto the southern end of the stable block, as indicated by a drawing of 1946. Finally, there were two motor vehicles and their drivers. In 1953, reconstruction of the stable, to accommodate two motors, was proposed.

The locomotive turntable at Keswick

At the planning stage, in November 1863, a turntable and a shed for one engine were proposed, also a shed for six (small) passenger carriages. The LNWR, which undertook to provide locomotives, carriages and train crews, did not require the CKPR to provide engine or carriage sheds at Keswick and none were ever built there. The turntable was implicitly of early date. On Tuesday June 2 1914, quite likely the day after Whit Monday holiday and with excursion traffic still at a peak, a girder of the table was broken while turning a NER locomotive. The Cowans Sheldon company, of Carlisle, was invited to tender for the repair.

As the LMS programme for strengthening of bridges progressed through the 1920s and 1930s, the time for running of more powerful locomotives through from the main line, to Keswick, approached and the inadequacy of the turntable had to be faced. The relevant drawing came from the Chief Engineer, then based at St Pancras, under date July 12 1938, and showed replacement of a 40ft diameter turntable by one of 60ft. It was vacuum operated and sited just west of the old table, its well extending into the field between the former northern boundary of the railway territory and the detached house provided for the Stationmaster. Connection was to the 'Jubilee Road,' namely the back loop line, beyond the platform loop and, like the old table, it could be reached from either west or east. It is generally recalled in railway circles as being completed around the end of 1939, or early in 1940. The LMS drawing of the works is dated 1940,showing the new connections. However, contemporary reports are clear that the new turntable was first used commercially on Saturday June 24 1939 and that Stanier 'Black 5' 4-6-0 locomotives worked the summer Sunday expresses from Glasgow and Newcastle upon Tyne to and from Keswick on the immediately ensuing Sundays, and were turned. There was little demand for turning class 5, 5X and 6 4-6-0 engines during the war years from autumn 1939, nor indeed during the following years, so this handsome table saw comparatively little use and (although retained in a review of 1963) was taken out of use before April 1966, when the last trains ran west of Keswick on the route. At the time of writing, the turntable well can still be viewed as a monument to 'what might have been.'

The approach and environment at Keswick station

The CK&P Railway Company ordered its contractors to construct an approach road to its station at Keswick; the road was straight, broad for its day and impressive, with a bridge over the Greta river and a concluding sweep past the goods yard gates to reach the spacious forecourt shared by both station and hotel. Its conception was worthy of a headquarters. The bridge was of 60ft span over the river, in cast and wrought iron, with a secondary 20ft stone arch (sidespan), the whole structure being widened in the 1890s or soon afterwards. In 1890-93, a diverging road was made, passing behind the hotel, at a lower level, to afford access to the coachhouses and stables and continuing through the

underline bridge east of the station to reach the Stationmaster's dignified house. This was built to the designs of architect Mr Ross, of Carlisle, the builder being R. Harrison, under contract of March 1865; a bathroom was added in 1912 and the house still stands today. Across the road was the estate of John James Spedding, of Greta Bank, a CKPR Director from 1861 to 1909, and Major Spedding in succession.

The residents of Chestnut Hill, on Keswick's higher eastern outskirts, soon called for a short cut to the station and in 1873 the Railway was prepared to contribute to the cost, but it was not until 1898 that a committee (helped by £20 from the CKPR) had a footbridge of suspension-type built over the Greta. This provided a pleasant footway from the Penrith road, near Millfield House, to the CKPR's back road round the hotel. Also in 1898, it was decided to make an inclined path from this back road to the Down platform. The site of the bridge and the course of theinclined path are both visible but regrettably neither bridge (abandoned since the railway closed) or path exist today.

Station Road and the road round the hotel were subjects of periodical debate. In 1876, the Railway decided not to dedicate these roads to the public and in the 1880s a chain and temporary gate was placed across Station Road, suitably manned, on one day each year. Presumably, only bona fide travellers were permitted through, on sufferance! On January 1 1904, platelayers Joseph Little and Thomas Gibson held a chain across the road, between two stone boundary posts, from 8.00am to 5.00pm and this procedure was applied on Monday January 2 1905 and subsequently. Its revival coincided with a period of irritation with Keswick Urban District Council, who were pressed by the Company during 1900 to take over the roads – and especially the Greta bridge – in accordance with the Railway's interpretation of an early agreement. The Council declined. In fact, the bridge remained as Railway property until its sale (with the station) to the Lake District Special

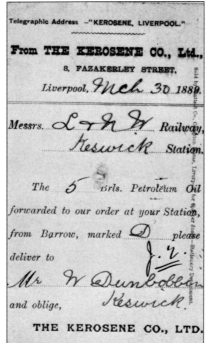

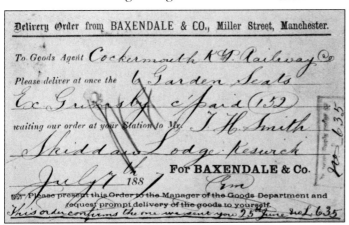

Above: A further selection of consignment instructions for Statiomaster Reay includes (top) five barrels of 'petroleum oil' for Mr W. Dunbobbin, of Keswick, from The Kerosene Company, Fazakerley Street, Liverpool. Above, left: This delivery order, from Baxendale and Company, Miller Street, Manchester, requested the delivery of six garden seats to Mr J.H. Smith of Skiddaw Lodge, Keswick. Above, right: This delivery note recorded the delivery to Keswick of one barrel of tar for the company's own use. All: J.M. Hammond Collection.

Planning Board, some years after the railway's closure. In addition to being primarily a route to station and hotel, the Station Road in time also gave access to benefactions received by the town of Keswick. Higher Fitz Park, with its gates dated 1882, was developed to the east of the road on land bought from Keswick Hotel Company and the Fitz Trust also laid out Lower Fitz Park (on land acquired from the le Fleming family) on the road's west side. This too was opened in the early 1880s and boasts gates (erected circa 1898) 'in memory of J.S. Crossthwaite' (a prominent early Fitz Trustee). The Keswick (Fitz) museum, nearing the station on the west side, is of 1897 and its northern wing, of 1905, is the art gallery 'in memory of T. & H. Hewetson, 1897'. The museum and gallery are happily cared for and quietly improved as the years go by. Henry Hewetson (1821-95) never forgot his boyhood in Keswick and Hewetson funds endowed several of these projects.

Above: The CKPR ambulance challenge shield. The inscription on the lower part of the shield reads: "Presented by the Directors for annual competition by employees. Henry Howard Esq, Chairman, 1914." It was competed for originally within the territory of the CKPR, but it still figures today as an award of standing in a much wider territory of British Railways. *Harold D. Bowtell.*

In the first year of passenger traffic (1865) Edmund Grayson wished to place a drinking fountain on the road, near the station. The fountain, designed for people and dogs, is still there today, in the right-hand wall of Station Road, on entering from the town. It can be seen before the bridge, and is inscribed:
'IN MEMORY OF FRANCES ROLLESDON 1865
Whosoever drinketh of the water that I shall give him shall never thirst.
John IV 14.'
Close at hand is a memorial stone placed 1923 by Mr & Mrs J.B. Wivell, of the Keswick Hotel, in memory of their son George Banks Wivell and daughter Mary Wivell. There is also a commemorative stone of November 1939 in appreciation of Doctor R.K.B. Crawfurd, JP.

Hotel omnibuses

The residential hotels of Keswick gained most of their business from visitors, arriving by train at the station. The 'Keswick' soon had direct access but all the others were at a considerable distance. Thus, in general, each commissioned a smartly turned-out horsed omnibus to meet arriving trains, convey anticipated guests and encourage support. Around

Above: This view takes us back to Keswick circa 1868. The Greta river bridge and Station Road have been newly constructed, as has all else here seen. Note the coal cells in the left distance, and the goods shed behind them, with wagons and derrick crane. The tall signal, the main station building (already with its porch) and the Keswick Hotel are all as yet unfinished, with no conservatory or covered way yet evident. *Fitz Museum Collection.*

Above: This was the sight which greeted many travellers arriving at Keswick by train. As they stepped out from beneath the glazed porch there was a row of smartly turned-out horse-drawn buses owned by the local hotels. *Joe W. Brownrigg.*

Above: Here, in Keswick's Fitz Museum, on February 22 1983, are the handsome spade and barrow used in 'turning the first sod' for the CKPR, on 21 May 1862. *Harold D. Bowtell.*

1903, the Railway Company sought to ease the resultant congestion by delineating individual stands - one might say, 'parking' or 'waiting' places, in return for a fee. By January 14 1904, all were allocated for the year and contention resulted, and recurred over the years. One notes, for example, that in October 1911, Mr Messenger was permitted to place a char-a-banc on his last omnibus stand, adjoining the covered way. It could have been a horse or motor vehicle. It would in either case be an open coach, with forward-facing leather bench-type seats, rising in tiers towards the back, as in a theatre, so that every passenger might have an uninterrupted view of the scenery. The vehicle would be used for a 'round tour'. Omnibuses for a short station-to-hotel run usually conveyed their passengers inside, with their backs to the side windows and a centre aisle, while the roof carried trunks and other luggage, flanked by railings and upper side boards which proclaimed the name of the hotel. Towards the end of the CKPR's independence, the omnibus stands at Keswick station were let for the year 1921 as follows:

1. Pape's Coaches Ltd	*Royal Oak & Queen's*	£47	0	0
2. J.H. Fletcher	Lodging Houses	£17	0	0
3. J. Boadle	*King's Arms*	£ 4	0	0
4. Pape's Coaches Ltd.	*George Hotel*	£ 2	0	0
5. Pape's Coaches Ltd.	*Blencathra and Park*	£ 1	0	0
6. H.T. Pape	*Lodore Hotel*	£ 1	0	0
7.				
8. T.C. Stanley	*Derwentwater Hotel*	£ 1	0	0
9. J. Wilson	*Lake Hotel*	£ 1	0	0
10. J. Young	Cab	£ 2	0	0
11. Pape's Coaches Ltd.	Skiddaw and County	£ 3	0	0
12. W.D. Wivell	Cab or Taxi	£ 5	0	0
	Total	£84	0	0

Representation of hotels

Railways were traditionally jealous of their right to restrict access to platforms but the CKPR used to allow a select few representatives of hotels on the platform to meet passengers. For example, in 1912, the annual fee was £12.10.0 and only four subscribers were accepted: Mr Messenger (*Keswick Hotel*), Mr J.S. Harker (*Lodore Hotel*), Mr D.N. Pape (*Royal Oak Hotel*) and Mr T.C. Stanley (*Derwentwater Hotel*). By the 1930s, only *The Keswick Hotel* was allowed to place a uniformed representative on the platform.

Royal Visitors.

The German Kaiser Wilhelm called at *The Keswick Hotel* for tea in August 1895 and there exists a classic picture which includes his carriage outside the hotel entrance.

On October 17 1956, the Queen (who also visited the Keswick Hotel) was photographed on the station platform, under the canopy. This would be the occasion which caused concern in railway circles; the party had travelled by car from West Cumberland and was about 20 minutes late at Keswick, with consequent delay to the Royal train, which started from there. Another Royal train, of limited load, came from Penrith on July 22 1966.

A worthy shield - and final parade

Ambulance work, on a voluntary and spare-time basis, has always been supported enthusiastically by railwaymen, with accommodation and encouragement offered by the Railways. The CKPR's ambulance teams competed for a shield. It is good to know that the competitions continue today, the 'Keswick' shield being on display from year to year at places as far apart as Carlisle and Morecambe, the competing teams being drawn from a wide area.

An occasion to be remembered was on Sunday May 22 1966. A parade of the St John Ambulance Brigade for annual inspection took place in Keswick and an impromptu bandstand was created when the band proceeded via the station subway and played on the island platform, with the appreciative audience standing on the main down platform. That was during the short period while Keswick was a terminal station but before it was reduced to a single operational platform. The weather is better not recalled!

Barrow and spade

The inscription engraved on the handsome spade, accompanied by a wheelbarrow of carved magnificence (illustrated above) reads: "PRESENTED TO T.A. HOSKINS ESQ, JP, ON THE OCCASION OF HIS CUTTING THE FIRST SOD OF THE COCKERMOUTH KESWICK & PENRITH RAILWAY MAY 21st 1862."

Thomas Alison Hoskins, of High Hall, near Cockermouth, was first chairman of the CKPR board, holding the office from August 10 1861 until his resignation on November 2

1867. His term embraced the period of practical decisions, the construction of the line and its opening to trafic in November 1864, fully effective in January 1865. The memorial wheelbarrow and spade were duly held by T.A. Hoskins. About 40 years after the opening, his son, Colonel R. Hoskins, of Fairfield, Pencraig, Ross-on-Wye, wrote on January 30 1905 to Sir Henry Vane to offer these mementos. They were received by the Railway's Board by February 25 1905 and it is understood that they were displayed in or near the Boardroom. On March 10 1923, when the LMS Railway was already in being and the CKPR board was winding up its affairs, they determined to offer the barrow and spade to the Fitz Park Museum. The Museum trustees and curator still prize these items, which are beautifully kept and worthily displayed.

In Proud and Honoured Memory

COCKERMOUTH KESWICK & PENRITH RAILWAY COMPANY
IN PROUD & HONOURED MEMORY OF THE EMPLOYEES
OF THIS COMPANY WHO GAVE THEIR LIVES FOR KING &
COUNTRY IN THE GREAT WAR
1914-1918

Wm. NOTMAN	Sergeant	Border Regiment
J. YOUDALE	Corporal	Border Regiment
J. GIBSON	Private	Border Regiment
J.W. HEBSON	Private	Border Regiment
W.P. HETHERINGTON	Private	Border Regiment
M.S. MITCHINSON	Private	Border Regiment
R. WATSON	Private	King's L'pool Regiment

This is the inscription on the copper plaque which was produced at the wish of the CKPR Board. The tracing of the design was approved on September 20 1919 and the tablet was engraved in the Keswick School of Industrial Arts, which incidentally owed its foundation to Canon and Mrs Rawnsley. It was affixed to the front wall of Keswick Station, beside the entrance and above the post box (which is still in situ and in use at the time of going to press). It faced the southerly sun and gained weather protection from the entrance canopy.

The tablet was unveiled formally on May 1 1920 by Major Hamlet Riley DL, JP, LLB (Cantab) (1851-1922), who was then Chairman of the Railway Company. He died in office on October 14 1922 after 31 years on the Board and he was the last formal Chairman of the CKPR.

Somewhat before the closure of Keswick station, on March 6 1972, the plaque was removed and, thoughtzfully, installed on the town's war memorial, in the gardens beside the entrance to Station Road. Unfortunately, the only available side of the memorial faced away from most beholders, and towards the sunless north. The result has been a sad deterioration by weathering and oxidisation and it is certain-

Right, upper: The grand portal of the Keswick Hotel, where HM Queen Elizabeth II has visited and, once, Kaiser Wilhelm called for tea. The hotel entrance is illustrated on August 31 1982.

Right, lower: Staying with the Keswick Hotel, here is the covered way which once linked station and hotel and was probably designed as a gravelled path to steps leading to an external side door, but elaborations soon followed. Here, from 1940 to 1945, Roedean schoolgirls and their mistresses held umbrellas to protect them against the rain coming in through leaky roof-lights. Also viewed on August 31 1982. *Both: Harold D. Bowtell.*

RAILS THROUGH LAKELAND

Left: This delightful stained glass screen is well kept today by Trust House Forte. The double doors are between ante-room and lobby, leading from the Keswick Hotel and its conservatory to the station platform. The artists depicted in stained glass are: Sir Peter Lely, Raphael Sanzio, Paul Veronese and Sir Godfrey Kneller. The picture was taken on March 12 1985.
Harold D. Bowtell.

ly not a worthy object as seen today. It could doubtless be far better prized and displayed in the great hall of the National Railway Museum at York but, for me, the ideal location is available in Keswick, close to its railway home of some 50 years. This is the Fitz Museum, where it could, after cleaning with the care accorded to works of art, be worthily displayed in a dry atmosphere along with the memorial barrow and spade and other mementoes of the CKPR.

Closure at Keswick

Goods traffic at Keswick ceased wef June 1 1964. The route westward to Cockermouth and Derwent Junction (Workington) closed to all remaining traffic wef April 18 1966. From December 4 1967, operation east to Penrith No. 1 signalbox was on a 'one engine' basis (which can mean equally one railcar set), the signalboxes at Keswick and intermediately closing. The station was unstaffed wef July 1 1968 and final closure took effect from March 6 1972.

The Keswick Hotel

Before the CKPR was open, its Board decided it was imperative to have a 'Station Hotel' at Keswick and arranged visits to hotels at Grasmere, Windermere and Ullswater, on the Lakes tourist 'round.' Mr Ross, the Company's architect, produced drawings, which were approved. Three and a half acres of land were purchased from General le Fleming and in December 1863 the building tender of £8,800, by David Hall, of Carlisle, was accepted. Work proceeded apace and by 1865 an impressive pile resulted. In March of that year the name *The Keswick Hotel* was adopted, furnishing was put in hand and laying out of the grounds was entrusted to Mr Kemp, of Birkenhead. The covered way between station and hotel, such a distinctive feature down the years, was to be constructed. On July 1 1865, the opening of the railway was celebrated (retrospectively) together with that of the hotel (a little prematurely). The hotel was probably not complete until 1866-67; indeed the gilded date above the main entrance records 1869.

The Railway Company would have liked to hand over the hotel and its operation to professional hoteliers. Between March and May 1865, the Cumberland Lake District Hotel Company came on the scene, with ambitious plans for the purchase and running of the hotel, and establishment also of a hotel at Bassenthwaite Lake. However, they soon withdrew from the latter project and the Railway lost confidence and created a 'Keswick Hotel Company' as a subsidiary or associate of the CKPR, from 1866, with a common chairman, Isaac Fletcher, from that year. There was a formal contract, under which the Hotel Company was required to purchase the establishment at Keswick. It is noted that, in 1869, they were paying interest charges to the CKPR, evidently on the capital cost of building, furnishing and laying out the grounds. The hotel was under lease in those early years but a conveyance was prepared in 1871.

The story of the hotel soon became linked with the Wivell family. Joseph Banks Wivell, once in the pencil trade, married Mary Wilson, daughter of William Wilson. Born on January 19 1836 at Armboth (by Thirlmere) William Wilson had been a farmer but from 1875 was Manager or Proprietor of *The Royal Oak Hotel*, Keswick, and in 1883 took over at *The Keswick Hotel*, apparently as lessee from the Keswick Hotel Company. This led to J. Banks Wivell and Mrs Mary Wivell (nee Wilson) becoming involved with the Keswick Hotel, where in due time they became managers. After 1918, their elder son, Alex Wivell, undertook training in catering and hotel matters in Switzerland. In 1931 he became joint proprietor with his father of *The Armathwaite Hall Hotel*, Bassenthwaite Lake. The younger son, W. Dennis Wivell also came out of the services. Having qualifications as an electrical engineer, he became established, by May 1919, as W.D. Wivell of Wivell's Coaches and Motors Ltd, of the Keswick Hotel Garage. This, in due course, brought W.D. Wivell into the Keswick Hotel proper. His father had already, back in 1912, figured as 'J.B. Wivell, proprietor' on the hotel notepaper, but this may have been a loose presentation of lessee, for in 1913 J.W. Pattinson, a CKPR director, was on the Hotel Company Board and Peter Thompson, Secretary and General Manager of the Railway, was also interested. True proprietorship probably came later, but still in CKPR days, and the new partnership developed as J. & M. Wivell & Son (namely J. Banks Wivell and Mary, and WDW). This was a private family Company but one of the Pattinsons (JWP, presumably) was a Director, while Chairman into these days was Robert Jackson Holdsworth, of Bolton and Thornthwaite, who was on the CKPR Board (1913-1923). W.D. Wivell and Mrs Wivell succeeded as proprietors and managers.

With the departure of Roedean school (who took their own bedding and equipment with them) at the end of 1945 the Wivells elected to sell their interest to Thomas Cooper Pattinson, of Windermere, who later vested all the shares in the Keswick Hotel Co Ltd, a Pattinson family Company. Mr Shoesmith was appointed Manager and modernisation extended over several years, resulting in 58 bedrooms with private bathrooms, and other similar facilities. The Hotel Company was sold to J. Lyons & Company on March 29 1972 - almost concurrent with the closure of the railway at Keswick - and they operated it as a 'Falcon Inn'. They resold it, in January 1978, to Trust House Forte (UK) Ltd, the present owners and operators.

The Keswick Hotel retains the external appearance which pleased the CKPR Board of Directors both in the architects' drawings and following completion, in the 1860s, and it retains an air of 'solid comfort' in keeping with its surroundings. To the student of railway history in general, and Keswick's railway history in particular, the hotel's former conservatory, with its ante-room, beautiful stained glass screens (see previous page) and entrance lobby from the one-time main station platform, is rewarding to view today.

EAST OF KESWICK, TO PENRITH

Above: Climbing again, our old friend No. 58396 is seen with the 11.50am Up service from Workington on August 5 1950. The train is heading up the bank eastward out of Keswick. *E. S. Russell.*

A CKPR spectacular: by Briery Bobbin Mill and Greta Gorge

Milepost 13 (from Cockermouth Junction) was at Keswick station, MP14 at Briery platform and MP16 1/2 on the approach to Threlkeld station. One may compare this section of the CKPR route with the Highland line in Killiecrankie pass, between Perth and Inverness. But the Greta gorge section of the CKPR and its emergence, with suddenly wider views, at its eastern end had their own distinctive character. Trains travelled too quickly for the appreciation of two short tunnels and fully a dozen bridges - including eight spectacular bowstring girder underline bridges by which the single track railway crossed and recrossed the rocky river valley. A platelayer's eye view, or that of the walker today, is however rewarding. The various structures receive more detailed attention in the sections about the bridgeworks on the line (see *Chapter 5*). At

two points, the new portions of the A66 road have broken in on the scene since 1972. On Keswick's outskirts, Brigham Forge, in the valley below (north) of the railway route, is eclipsed by the lofty skew road bridge. 'Big Tunnel' is beneath that bridge, and infilled, along with part of its approach cutting; the walker has to clamber up and over the road, or find access at Briery and walk back. There is also infilling east of bowstring bridge No. 75 (Crozier Holme) where at MP16 the new road recrosses the route.

Briery Bobbin Mill and Platform

Eastward of 'Big Tunnel', the railway barely squeezed along a rocky shelf between the river, with massive retain-

Above: Proceeding east, after leaving Big Tunnel, a 'Tweedy' ground frame was unlocked by the key token to give access to the sidings at Briery Bobbin Mill. Stone-arched bridge No. 63 carries the lane to the mill site and the platform is a little beyond. The ground frame at Fluscow was of essentially the same design.

Left: Briery Bobbin Mill platform, for workpeople, looking west. It was in daily use, except on Sundays, until 1958, when the mill closed. Its date of origin is obscure, but is probably soon after 1922, and its face was rebuilt, using precast concrete units, during the 1930s.
Both: Richard L. Pattinson/CRA

ing wall (below, left) and the protective wall (above, right). Just beyond this point, a loop in the river provided the site for the bobbin mill and its cottages. In the 1820s, waistcoats and similar woollens were manufactured here. Bobbin-making came in the 1830s, owners being in general the Coward family, but Coward, Philipson & Co Ltd from 1922 (although, strangely, a reference in 1867 is to Charles Christopherson). Import of timber was required, notably local hardwoods (sycamore, ash, beech and birch) but later teak from Burma and lancewood and boxwood from the Caribbean. Bobbins were despatched for the textile industries. As early as 1867, the CKPR agreed in principle to provide a siding but it was not until 1891 that a detailed

layout and terms were agreed with Mr William Philipson and a siding for 20 wagons, with access (controlled by ground frame) facing Up trains, and a smaller internal loop siding, were put in hand. Another internal siding diverged to run into the buildings. The bobbin trade was slack in 1902 and the charge for use of the siding was reduced from 1/- to 6d per ton. In 1906 and 1911, further short extensions were made. In those days, bobbins were despatched by rail, bound for destinations which included St Petersburg in Russia. The mill closed in November 1958, at which time the siding layout was still in place, although used only for inwards coal in the preceding few years. A major sale at the premises took place on June 3 1959 and the private siding

Right: The scene in the Greta gorge as a 'Cauliflower' approaches with a Down passenger train; it would seem to have crossed bridge No. 73 (Rowsome) and just crossed No. 72, an under-line arch over Naddle Beck. *Richard L. Pattinson/CRA.*

agreement with the railway was formally terminated on October 17 1959.

At a date which seems to have been soon after 1922, a wooden platform was constructed at Briery for use by workpeople arriving from Keswick (and also from Cockermouth) in the mornings and leaving at teatime, or lunchtime on Saturdays. This platform was placed on the Up side, with a wicket gate leading directly down into the mill yard. The condition of the wooden-faced platform deteriorated by the early 1930s. The LMS was 'watching the pennies' at this time of depression and slackness in industry but the District Engineer had surplus pre-cast concrete units in stock, so it was rebuilt with these substantial facing units, and exists today. The daily calls for workmen, made by one train each way, are understood to have ceased wef Monday November 17 1958, a week after cessation of production at the mill.

The site of the bobbin mill and some of its industrial buildings have been adapted and reconstructed tastefully to provide holiday accommodation; the workers' cottages, close by the river bank, have become an attractive part of the scheme.

Above: This view is from the elevated signalbox at Threlkeld, at 12.28pm on September 6 1948. No. 28492 is arriving with the 10.23am Whitehaven-Penrith passenger train. The fireman is preparing to surrender the token for the section from Keswick. *Harold D. Bowtell.*

Threlkeld: approach and location

The railway from Keswick crossed the Glenderamackin, tributary of the Greta, and reached the station site on the lower southern slopes of the broad valley, which it was about to follow eastward. The station site was remote from the old Threlkeld village, seen 3/4 mile distant, on the northern slopes of the valley, with the bulk of Blencathra (Saddleback) rising dramatically to its 2,847 ft summit, about one and a half miles behind the village. The station was accessible to the by-road which heads south to St John's-in-the-Vale and Thirlmere. It also, opportunely, proved to be well-sited to serve major developments in quarrying and 'Threlkeld quarry village', which derived from these, in the later 19th century years.

Threlkeld passenger station and its sidings

Threlkeld station was originally on the single line, in the section from Keswick to Troutbeck (8 1/4 miles) and it was neither a crossing place nor a blockpost. A house for the Stationmaster was put in hand in 1865, on the Up side bank above the station, designed by architect Mr Ross and built by J.R. Harrison. A pair of railwaymen's cottages was built, under plans of 1887, on the far side of the house and likewise facing west, at right angles to the line. By 1911, the near cottage was allocated to a signalman. All the houses are occupied today. By 1888, a modest waiting room, for quarry workers, was approved for construction on the platform and in 1890 a shunting neck at the west end, on the Down side, was proposed. In July 1892, the Railway's Engineer produced a plan for conversion of Threlkeld to a crossing station, with an island platform, a layout which contemplated early doubling over the 4 3/4 steeply-graded uphill miles east to Troutbeck. There was already a ground

Above: No. 58389 is seen on the 11.50 am ex-Workington train of August 7 1950. This is the eastern end of Threlkeld station, with the signalbox glimpsed and the corner of the stationmaster's house (of 1865) above the bank on the right. *E.S. Russell.*

frame on the Up side, well to the east of the station layout. Also, some form of signalling applied in 1892, as at July 1 1892 permissive block working was being operated from Threlkeld to Troutbeck for Up (ascending) trains and wef November 9 1892 Highgate signalbox opened to break this section and absolute block working was introduced (for passengers) from Keswick (or Threlkeld) to Highgate and Troutbeck. It is not clear whether any electric tablet instrument working was introduced at Threlkeld at this time.

The engineer's plan of 1892 was soon adopted. The new platform was constructed on the Up side of the existing single running line, which thereafter became the Down line. A new Up line was laid round the other side of the platform, close-in to the foot of the embankment on the northern boundary. The island platform created was the only one on the CWR/CKPR route to take precisely this form of one Up and one Down face to a single island. The neat and workmanlike range of single storey buildings erected on the platform included separate workmen's, gentlemen's and ladies' waiting rooms, with integral lavatories for the two latter rooms, also a station office (with mullioned bay window to the platform and booking window to the booking hall). The hall was reached via a porch down at road level, a subway and ascending stairs. Architecturally, an unusual and attractive feature was the signalbox which formed part of the platform buildings at the western end; internal stairs ascended to an operating floor which was at about eaves level with the main range of buildings. The signalbox was brought into use on September 27 1893. On that day (or

RAILS THROUGH LAKELAND

very close to it) Threlkeld became a crossing place, with electric tablet operation and by October 4 1893 the Board of Trade authorised crossing of trains at Threlkeld. Doubling from Threlkeld to Troutbeck was carried out between August 1893 and August 1894; the Board of Trade's provisional approval of the works followed in August 1894, with final approval in December. Double line block working from Threlkeld to Highgate and Troutbeck was thus instituted. A small addition to the buildings shown on photographs was the coalhouse-cum-lamproom (built in 1918) on the platform against the west wall of the signal box.

From the point of view of passenger traffic, Threlkeld was a fairly typical wayside station but visitors to Blencathra

Sanatorium came here from its opening in 1904 and for many years there was a morning and evening train for quarry workers, from and to Keswick. Local goods traffic was on a small scale, with limited sidings on the south west of the site. The most southerly had the odd cattlepen on a small platform and could also handle coal, but there were never any coal cells, During the circa 1890-94, Threlkeld was a railhead for receipt of masonry, pipes and valves to be carted through the vale to Thirlmere for use in building Manchester Corporation's dam and aqueduct works. Like most CKPR stations, Threlkeld acquired acetylene gas lighting and the gas house was built on the bank, on the Up side, just east of the platform end.

The way to the quarry village and quarries was by the distinctly informal road past the porch entrance to the passenger station, thence close by the railway houses and soon turning over the spidery 'fly bridge' (No. 81). The light construction of this bridge was restrictive. In 1935, drawings were prepared for a new bridge to cross the railway (two running lines and two siding lines at that point) diagonally, NW-SE, to the east of the 'fly bridge' and emerge opposite the lane which passes the west end of Railway Terrace,

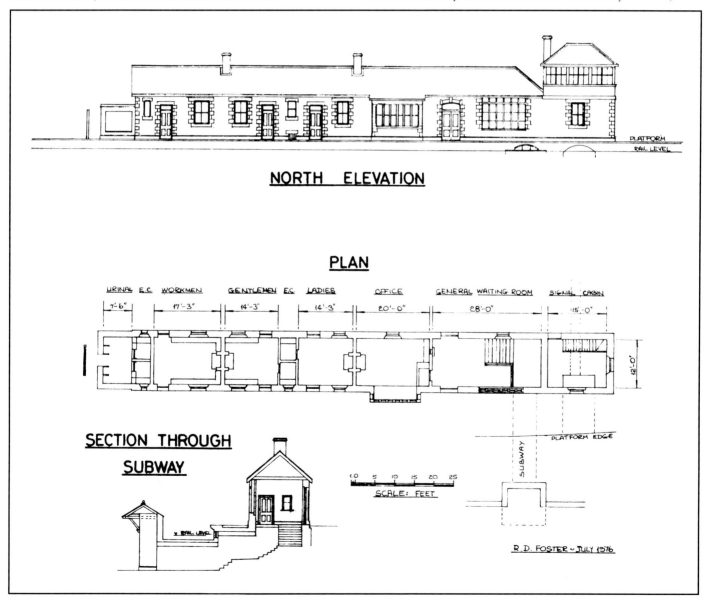

NORTH ELEVATION

PLAN

URINAL	E.C.	WORKMEN		GENTLEMEN	E.C	LADIES		OFFICE		GENERAL WAITING ROOM		SIGNAL CABIN
7'-6"		17'-3"		14'-3"		14'-3"		20'-0"		28'-0"		15'-0"

SECTION THROUGH SUBWAY

SCALE: FEET

PLATFORM EDGE

SUBWAY

R. D. FOSTER ~ JULY 1976

(now Glenderamachin Terrace). This work was not done and about 1947 a roadway was made outside the southern boundary of the railway property, so that motor vehicles need not use the light bridge. Both routes remain.

From December 4 1967, the double track sections reverted to single line working and the remaining signal boxes (including Threlkeld) closed. The station closed to goods wef June 1 1964. It was unstaffed from July 1 1968 and passenger working ceased wef March 6 1972, with closure of the line. The lever frame was taken out but the attractive signal box and other buildings have stood, vainly awaiting a saviour until 1985; demolition took place during 1985-86, the 'gas house' too being razed in spring 1986.

Threlkeld quarries and their railway traffic

Back in 1874, the CKPR erected a shed at Threlkeld, in part for the use of the Saddleback Mining Company (John Jackson of Annan), which was carting lead ore from the other side of the valley, for loading on rail; the company's

Right, upper: This is the west end of Threlkeld's island platform, with the signalbox glimpsed, shortly after reconstruction in 1892-93. Is the gentleman obscuring the locomotive bunker (second right) the personable George Schollick, the long-serving first signalman here? The locomotive over towards the loading dock is an LNWR 0-6-2 'Coal Tank.' *Richard L. Pattinson/CRA.*

Right, lower: The design of the entrance to Threlkeld station by its subway was, like the main buildings, tastefully executed. *Richard L. Pattinson/CRA.*

Below: The layout at Threlkeld, essentially as created 1893-94 and modified down the years to the 1930s. *Drawn by Richard Foster.*

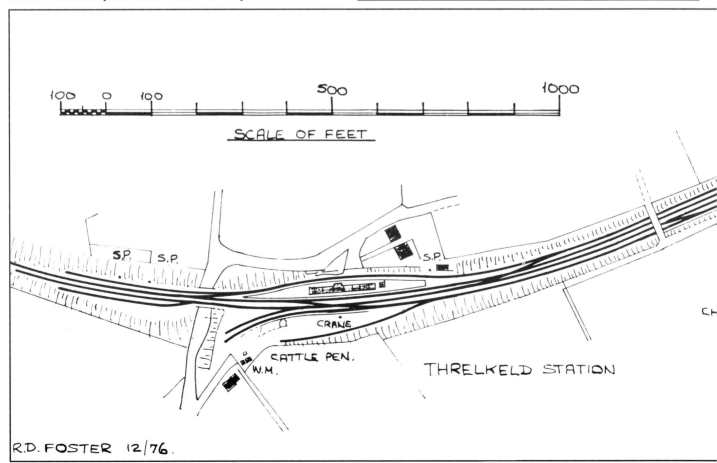

100   0   100   500   1000

SCALE OF FEET

S.P.   S.P.   S.P.

CRANE

CATTLE PEN.
W.M.

THRELKELD STATION

R.D. FOSTER 12/76.

successors brought traffic until circa the early 1920s. There had for long been a small granite quarry in the hill immediately south east of the station site, apparently a 'parish quarry' with a tradition that local people could work it at their pleasure. It was also a substantial source of stone for Boulton during construction of the CKPR, 1862-64. However, in 1877 it was taken over by Mr Bullen, of Barnard Castle, becoming known in time as Bottom Quarry, and the Railway Company undertook to lengthen the siding east of the station to accommodate, it is thought, 12 wagons. By 1883, the proprietors were the Cumberland Road Metal Company Ltd (Harkewitz & Bullen) who, while providing outward traffic, were not 'good payers.' A little later (1885-87) things were going their way and the quarry working was being expanded. In 1890-91 (by March), the huge retaining wall was built, with stone supplied free by the quarry owners, so that an extra 'back road' could be laid by the CKPR for quarry traffic - and in 1892-93, the third and final siding for this traffic was squeezed in, with lengthening eastward of these three sidings following in 1898. The Granite Company built wagon shops at the end of these sidings, circa 1901-02. Plant was then developed for making macadam as well as paving flags. This was probably the peak period for these quarries but they were still busy in

1921, when C.J. Allen reported that they provided the biggest part of the CKPR's freight. Trade declined in the 1920s, with much short-time working from 1926 (the general strike) onwards and typically three days work weekly.

The Company was reformed as the Threlkeld Granite Co. Ltd. in 1891. Mr Hermine Harkewitz was principal until his death (on October 19 1904) but the controlling Board was widened to include businessmen with CKPR (and other) interests; Thomas Glasson and, later, J.W. Pattinson were Chairmen. Following association with the Cumberland Granite Co. Ltd. of Close Quarries, Embleton, to form the Keswick Granite Co. Ltd. (incorporated September 24 1936), quarrying operations were concentrated from 1936-37 at Embleton, with a little site activity at Threlkeld itself in 1937-39, perhaps into 1940.

The Quarry Company ran a lorry morning and evening to convey its Threlkeld men to Close and home again. Emphasis was switched back from Embleton in 1948 but there was never major activity again, and one notes that the CKPR line ceased to be available after 1964. By 1973, employment was only about 50, with little actual quarrying. The last quarry working was in 1980-81, and complete closure followed in 1982.

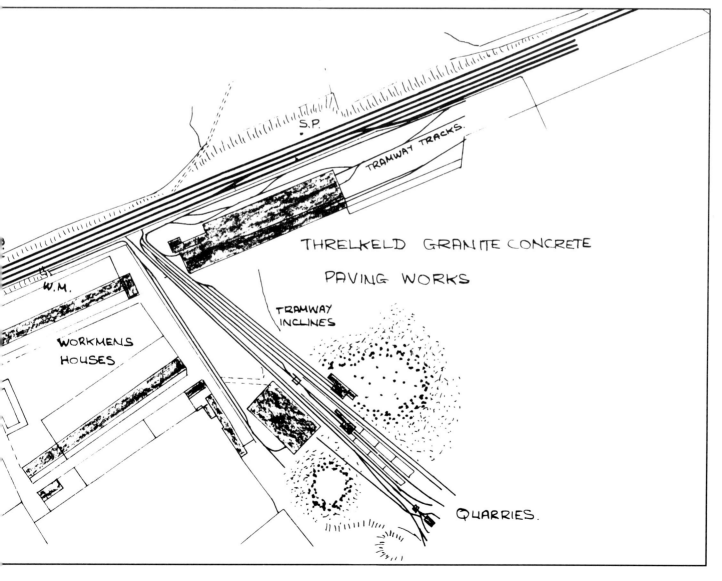

Right: A 'Cauliflower' with an Up passenger is setting off from Threlkeld for some five miles of climbing at (mostly) 1 in 62, to the next stop at Troutbeck. The Down home is a CKPR signal; the lamp top is open, the porter doubtless has his lamps out for cleaning and refilling with oil. Observe the arched lattice bridge of light construction which at the time provided the only road access to the Quarry Company's premises. An independent lead from the station layout to the quarry sidings runs parallel (left). *Richard L. Pattinson/CRA.*

Above: A view eastward of Threlkeld station, looking back hazily to the lattice bridge shown at the top of this page. The three sidings for the granite quarry traffic are on the left with their loading bank left again. The Up advance starter is another CKPR signal. *Richard L. Pattinson/CRA.*

Narrow gauge steam railway at Threlkeld Quarries

The Threlkeld Granite Co. Ltd. developed a railway system on 2ft. 4in. gauge (approx). This brought stone out of Bottom Quarry, as it was exploited, but its exciting main line diverged in a southerly direction to reach Hill Top Quarry, about one mile and above Hill Top Farm; this was the 'Spion Kop' quarry in the men's nomenclature, implying opening out about 1900. There was a locomotive water tank at the trail-in from this quarry and in due course the narrow gauge line was extended, with sinuous curves as it followed the hillside well above the vale road to Thirlmere, until it reached Bramcrag quarry; a lengthy face was developed and the main route of railway here reached about 2 1/2 miles. A little beyond the end of the line and down near the road; landmarks are The Bungalow,' built by Manchester Corporation in connection with its Thirlmere project, in the 1890s, and Bramcrag farmhouse. 'Klondyke' quarry (worked out well before the others) once had a branch line, north of 'Spion Kop'. At the Threlkeld end of the route was a locomotive shed with two roads, complete with inspection pits and adjoining site workshops; these buildings may still be seen. Close by these buildings, stone

was tipped into crushers and loaded by gravity to narrow gauge wagons, which descended self-acting rope-worked inclines (the drum side walls survive) to the tar plant and on to the buildings alongside the standard gauge sidings and adjacent loading bank, where the paving slabs were made. By 1923, the narrow gauge line continued right along the bank beside the sidings. Three locomotives are known, and all survived until around 1939, latterly in the shed:

THRELKELD: An 0-4-0ST with 8in x 12in outside cylinders, built by W.G. Bagnall, Works No. 1608 of May 1900.
EDWARD VII: An 0-4-0ST with 8in x 12in outside cylinders, built by W.G. Bagnall, Works No. 1685 of April 1902.
GEORGE V: An 0-4-0WT, with 7in x 11in outside cylinders and built by Andrew Barclay, Works No. 1734 of 1921.

All came new to the Company and the dates reconcile with the Boer War period, also with the further develop-

70   RAILS THROUGH LAKELAND

Above: During the early 20th century heyday of Threlkeld quarries, this is the vista from the top of the narrow gauge incline which conveyed trucks of crushed granite to the loading bank alongside the standard gauge sidings, shown on page 70. The CKPR line crosses just beyond the foot of the site at right angles. To the left are: the horse-keeper's house (white), the bothy or lodging house (in dark 'tin'), the reading room (white, gabled), the end gable of the terrace of 'tin' houses in Top Row, the Company office (above the tarmac plant) and the gables of the tall, permanent houses of Railway Terrace (now Glenderamachin Terrace). *John Jameson.*

ment at Bramcrag after the 1914-18 wartime slackening of quarry trade. Usually, one locomotive was 'spare' whilst two worked, their trains crossing at the intermediate loop near 'Spion Kop'. Each trip would bring down 16 or 17 thirty cwts-capacity loaded trucks; between them the two working engines made up to 10 journeys per day. Quarry workers were at one time brought down on the narrow gauge 'mail' train at the end of the working day and this naming extended to the CKPR/LMS workers' train, stabled in its short siding at Threlkeld during the day. This was the 'Boer Train,' used also by Mr Bragg, the manager, and his sons and office staff.

Threlkeld quarry village: a lively community

The commercial development of the granite quarries has been dated from 1877. with subsequent progressive expansion from 1885 to 1902, and intermittent busy periods until 1925. 'Commuters' were brought by the train from Keswick but the quarry owners encouraged immigration from other

parts of the country, including Leicestershire, known for its granite quarries. In 'Top Row' (nowadays known as 'Blencathra View') 12 'tin' houses and six narrow stone houses were built, probably all in the 1890s. In 1890, 'Bottom Row' was under construction, starting from its eastern end, with the Company office, then six particularly dignified houses. The whole terrace was seemingly not completed through to its western end until the late 1890s. Its official title was 'Railway Terrace', now 'Glenderamachin Terrace', with no view of the railway below but a fine vista of the river valley and awe-inspiring Blencathra. It was the reported overcrowding of the quarry village, in January 1887, which led the CKPR to build the two cottages near the station for its own staff. At its peak, probably in the early 20th century, the Granite Company is said to have employed around 200 men, including local residents and daily comers.

About 100 children attended the quarry village school, located on the top edge of the village. It was a delightful site and the Railway Company contributed £25 to the cost of the building, in 1897 - and this helped to stave off the appointment of a school board, which would levy a compulsory rate. Similar thoughts and altruism merged to produce a voluntary subscription of £5 per annum to the Vicar of Threlkeld in support of the Church of England school in the old village across the valley. It dates from 1849, when it replaced an earlier school, and is still active today. The quarry school prospered for many years but by 1951 was down to 11 children and it closed in July of that year. At the eastern end of the top street was a reading room and behind it the 'bothy' or lodging house (a 'tin' building), no doubt provided for new arrivals and single men. Above this again was the horse-keeper's house and, topmost, the stables; these last have become a house, as reconstructed. The Wesleyan chapel, opened October 14 1903 and converted circa 1981 to a handsome residence, accompanied by cricket and football grounds, with one-time pavilion, rounded off the facilities. Typically in the 12 months from August 1901 to July 1902, railway excursion bookings from Penrith brought the Working Men's Football Club, and its supporters, on three Saturdays. On July 19 1902 the Edenhall Cricket Club and its friends had similar facilities to Threlkeld.

Although the public buildings have all ceased to perform their intended functions, this remains a significant village,

Below: The setting, products and atmosphere of the Threlkeld Granite Co. Ltd in Mr Harkewitz's day come though on this letterhead of 1902. Note the message. *Oswald Todhunter Collection*.

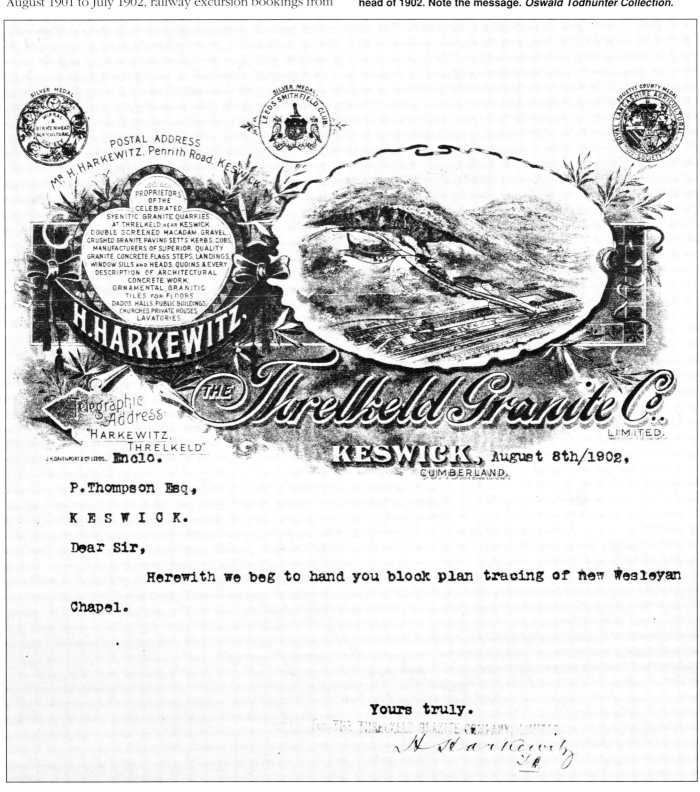

Above: Out on the narrow gauge to southward, above St John's-in-the-Vale, was Bramcrag quarry, where *George V*, an 0-4-0 well tank engine built by Andrew Barclay in 1921, is seen drawing out a load destined for Threlkeld incline top, the crusher and processing and-despatch by the CKPR line. *John Jameson.*

Left: Above the narrow gauge incline, the locomotive shed had two roads, and this survives today, although the pits are filled in. The shed housed the three small steam locomotives to work the traffic from the quarries, which were away up behind the camera and were formerly reached by the private line. Threlkeld (old) village is largely in view across the valley, on June 27 1984. *Harold D. Bowtell.*

although not all householders are all-year residents nowadays; some of the cottages are 'holiday homes.'

Threlkeld railway folk

An early stationmaster was John Smith, then soon Gresley Wolton took over in September 1866; that was still at the wayside station with no crossing facility and no industry and the pay was 18/- weekly. A uniform was also provided, together with a house and plus 2/- weekly from August 1872. The personable signalman on opening of the new box of 1893 and throughout the other major develop-

ments of that period was George Schollick. His diary, with entries through to 1927, is of much local interest. In due time, the quarry business accounted for employment of a station clerk, (Joe Ridley by the 1920s-1930s) and a yardsman; this, in 1913, was W. Notman, who joined the army and sadly was killed, as a Sergeant, in 1916. Signalmen of later days included Joseph Farrer (son of the Stationmaster) and Edwin K. Nelson, of Tebay, the latter in 1934-36 - he had previously had a year at Penruddock - and Bob Wren from circa 1961 until closure of the box on December 3 1967. He died in October 1984, a loss to many friends. The elder Joseph Farrer and then Fred Johnston were station-masters here, until Mr Johnston's death in 1936. Cecil Oldfield came from a career on the Furness Railway and FR section of the LMS, from 1912 to 1937, to be Stationmaster from circa 1937-45, and later, going on Preston way.

Above: Mosedale viaduct, the longest bridge on the CKPR. 'Cauliflower' No. 28589 is working the 2.10 pm Workington-Penrith service on August 7 1950, with its maximum permitted load of five carriages. The gradient here climbed at almost 1 in 62. The dark slopes of Blencathra are across to the right. *E.S. Russell.*

Eastward from Threlkeld: to Highgate and Troutbeck

Most of the 4 3/4 miles from Threlkeld to Troutbeck climbed at 1 in 62 and the summit of the line (889ft) was about a half-mile beyond Troutbeck station. This section receives mention under the headings, 'To school by train' (concerning the intermediate Highgate platform), 'Doubling the CKPR' and 'Bridges on the CKPR'. From MP16 1/2 at Threlkeld, the way today is clear to walk to nearing MP18 (Guardhouse underline bridge). At overline bridge No. 87 is the early pair of CKPR cottages known as Moor Cottages, later Hill Cottages, and now Hill Cottage. The house nearest the bridge was occupied by Jack Greenhow, a well-known length ganger in the early 20th century, his elder son being William Greenhow, who became Senior Carter at Keswick. Lower down, in the Wallthwaite community, there had been a public house, thought to be in demand during the railway widening of the 1890s. Up the hill above the cottages, the present handsome 'Birkett Hill' was known as 'Old Hill House' and earlier 'Old Hill Hog House' and 'Gin Hog'.

The Mosedale viaduct, between Hill Cottage and Highgate, is the longest of the route's many bridges. It is impressive as seen in evening light from the A66 road, about 3/4 mile distant, but can better be viewed by following the valley of the Mosedale beck on foot, upstream from Wallthwaite. Highgate (see 'To school by train') is reached by overline bridge No. 91, which commands a view of the site of the children's platforms of 1908-28 and the CKPR houses of 1898, with a glimpse of the little block signal box of 1892-1931 (eastwards). Gillhead viaduct is close to the A66 road, nearing Troutbeck station.

Troutbeck station

The station was immediately east of MP21 and overline bridge No. 97, which carried the road (A5091) to Matterdale and Ullswater. This bridge, like others, was remodelled for the doubling of 1893-94 - but was demolished in 1984, the road now crossing the former trackbed on the level. Passengers would come from Mungrisdale and Mosedale hamlets in the north and Matterdale to the south, along with those from scattered farmhouses and perhaps, hopefully, tourists and climbers bound for Patterdale at the head of Ullswater. In 1862, a station site near Wallthwaite was considered and 'Hutton Moor' was mentioned in this connection, so the site of Moor Cottages may have been in mind - but it was decided, in June 1862, to build the station 'at the Troutbeck road'. Thus, Troutbeck station was an original facility of 1865. It had one platform, with buildings, on the north side of the single line. A Down loop with second platform and signal box were added in 1874. The doubling eastward, to Penruddock, was carried out 1900-01. The Up platform building provided station office, general waiting room and ladies' waiting room. A house for the stationmaster was rented at the start but by 1869 a two-storey house was being built and, as can be seen, abutted directly onto the back of the one-storey platform building. The Down platform of 1874 carried a timber waiting shed, which had a long life. It became the practice from the days of Joe Cutts as stationmaster to hold Sunday afternoon services and a Sunday school in Up side premises, and later, in the room on the Down side, Furniture included a harmonium, which remained even after the station closed.

The small yard, with its trailing connection on the Up side

to eastward, was little expanded from its 1865 form. It had two short sidings close to the Up running line and was served by the loading bank, crane, cattle pens (the first of which dated from 1872) and a small goods shed. There was an original long siding with coal drops at its remote end and another long siding inserted behind it. John Stubbs was the coal merchant, then Mr Cutts (stationmaster) took over. Timber from Ullswater estates was hauled over on long horse-drawn wagons at one time. The outer siding and the coal drops were taken out in 1955, the beginnings of terminal decline. In 1966, one short siding remained. The acetylene gas house was beside the cattle pens. Troutbeck's station gardens must not be overlooked in this history; they achieved awards. Also on the Up side, near the convergence of the yard tracks, was a locomotive water tank, but in 1914 the tank was reported to be empty and the pump engine was replaced that year by a new oil engine. Locomotive water was still available in later years, with a gravity supply, with supplementary pumping from the stream when necessary. In 1955 there was a plan to convert the tank house to a tool store.

Troutbeck's autumn sheep sales were held at the mart adjoining the nearby Troutbeck Hotel, producing traffic for the railway over many years. An early industrial connection was a siding of circa 1867 to 'the tileworks adjoining the station'. This would be Mr Miller's brickyard, where, in May 1868, his men caused accidental damage to an engine and a wagon belonging to the LNWR. The brick and tile works

was on land behind the Down platform and its siding ran to stops near the Matterdale road embankment, with rail access by a trailback behind the signal box. It seems to have finished by 1914; the private siding was removed in 1915 and the Down platform was extended eastward.

The exploitation of minerals brought traffic to Troutbeck yard for despatch. Lead mined by the Greenside Mining Company (Ltd) was a long-standing, if intermittent traffic. The mines were 1 1/2 to 2 miles west of Glenridding (Ullswater), up into the mountain valley and the slopes of Helvellyn. The office was at Greenside, Glenridding and the engineer-manager resided (certainly, from 1912) at 'Greenside Lodge'. He was for long W.H. Borlase, who wrote a paper on the mines in the mid-1890s and reported frequently until at least 1928 to J.W. Pattinson, the miller, of Whitehaven. He was principal of the Mining Company and a CKPR board member, from 1903 to 1923. Mining dated from the first quarter of the 19th century and in 1867 the Company signed a 10 years agreement with the CKPR for traffic via Troutbeck station. Rates were quoted for consignment of their products to Liverpool, Skipton, Chester and Glasgow. They were then described as lead manufacturers with mine, works (namely smelting) and also 'lodging shops' at the mine for workers. There were problems circa 1867-70, as not all consignments were handled by way of the CKPR, as contracted. In October 1877, they proposed carting part of their traffic to Penrith and the agreement lapsed, but the earlier arrangements were resumed in 1879.

Above: A classic scene on the western approach to Troutbeck station, in BR days. Ivatt '2MT' 2-6-0 No. 46491 is hurrying east on Saturday July 31 1965, with a train from Keswick to Manchester and Crewe, comprised of BR and LMS rolling stock. The train is running 'wrong road' following the temporary introduction of single track working over the former Down line on this section in the spring of 1965. Once again, Blencathra ('Saddleback') dominates the horizon. *Derek Cross.*

Above: Troutbeck station, looking eastward from bridge No. 97 (Matterdale Road - A5091), seen on October 9 1966, when it was but little changed.

Right: Also in October 1966, a westward view from the east end of the station, showing that the yard had been curtailed to one siding. The signalbox, built by Saxby & Farmer in 1874, was in the first group of proper lever frames and cabins installed on the CKPR. The latter-day lever frame from Troutbeck box was removed (1984-85) by the Derwent Railway Society, for the National Railway Museum. *Both: Harold D. Bowtell.*

Hydro-electric generation powered an overhead wire electric locomotive, from circa 1892. In 1910, the mines were in a poor way, but Mr Borlase was an incurable optimist and saw prospects in the discovery, on October 24 1910, of a fresh lode of lead. In February 1911, new plant was brought over from Troutbeck station and use of a steam traction wagon was commonplace, notwithstanding the County Council having forbidden this traffic to cross Dockray Bridge on the route! On one occasion in April 1912, the 'traction' made the entire journey, Greenside Mines-Troutbeck-Whitehaven in the day and was expected to spend the next day returning. Bob Hope and Geordie Craig are remembered on the steam lorry. The mines prospered during the First World War and in December 1915 the War Office released men to work there. Smelting is understood to have ceased in 1919, with the lead subsequently sent to Troutbeck for consignment by rail to Newcastle upon Tyne for smelting. The Greenside traffic via Troutbeck station did not end until the late 1930s.

Carrock Mines, near Mungrisdale, were also using Troutbeck station in the 1930s. Their initial prospectus, of June 1904, had written up the prospects in glowing terms, under the title of The Carrock Mines Ltd., with directors

J. Wright Wilson, 'iron merchant' of Penrith, another director from Leicester and two from the City of London; the plan was to lease 5,000 acres of Carrock Fell properties, roughly five miles from the station.

An obscure reference in CKPR records was dated November 4 1885, by the Permanent Way Committee. It was proposed to remove the east end of the quarry siding further from the main line; this was quoted as "west of Troutbeck station" and the Cumberland Road Metal Company was mentioned. The implication is of a siding in section at that time.

The diary of George Schollick (of Threlkeld) recorded that on September 10 1913 a horse and cart ran away from the station at Troutbeck and headed towards Threlkeld. It ran into the waggonette from the Lake Hotel, Keswick. One horse was killed and two passengers seriously hurt. The first stationmaster at Troutbeck was William Richardson, on typical terms of 1865, at 19/- weekly, with uniform and

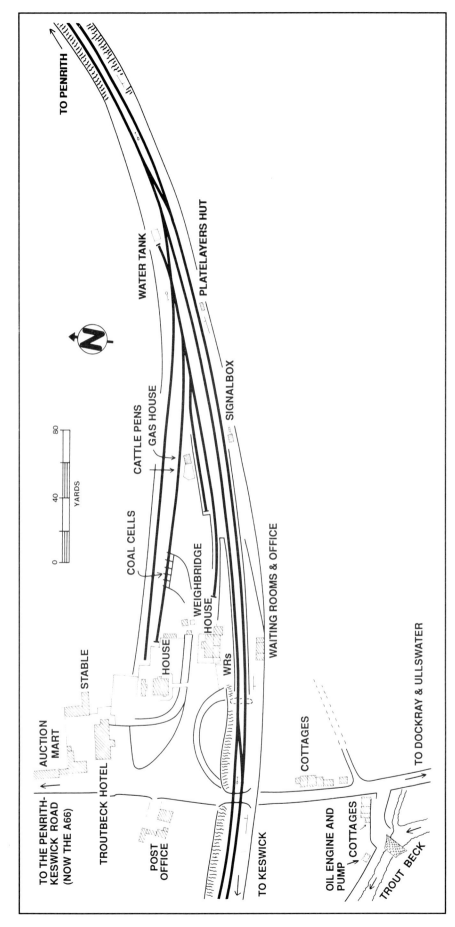

house provided. In August 1868, he was relieved on account of what was described as 'irregularities'. His successor, John Smith, was appointed in September 1868, on the same terms, rising to 21/- per week in August 1872 and 23/- in November 1874. However, in November 1874 he had 'absconded', leaving the accounts practically straight. Stationmaster Walton retired in November 1912 on account of old age after giving 'long and faithful service.' He was awarded a gratuity of £30. He was followed in November 1912 by J.M. Cutts, hitherto Foreman Porter at Keswick, and he was in charge at Troutbeck until about 1926. Thompson Simpson would be the last Stationmaster from circa1926 until 1932 after which Troutbeck was placed under the command of Threlkeld's stationmaster. Almost traditionally, there was a Watson at Troutbeck: Joseph Watson was for long the signalman, until his retirement in 1946 whilst his son, Edward Watson (still resident in the district at the time of writing) spent most of his career on the station. In 1913, Richard Hebson was the senior signalman, and had been at Troutbeck a good many years, with Joseph Watson as 'relief signalman' at that time. It is thought that the term 'relief' was used by the CKPR to indicate a porter-signalman. Nathan Routledge had shared the signalbox circa 1901-13 and tragically J. Whitham, relief signalman, had been killed by an engine, on January 12 1906. The Company's rule in 1907 was that the senior signalman at these smaller stations performed 11 hours duty daily, and for the remainder of the working day the box was operated by the porter-signalman, who *also* had hours allocated on the platform to make up a full day of 11-12 hours. In its later years, Troutbeck box was not manned constantly; a porter-signalman was in the box as required by traffic. The pair of houses opposite the station (one now the post office) was owned by the Railway. Signalman Dick Hebson and Joe Watson were long-time residents, with their families.

Goods traffic ceased at Troutbeck wef June 1 1964. The signalbox closed wef November 21 1966 (or December 5 1966). It had a closing switch so communication could be connected through from Threlkeld to Penruddock. Single line working, from Keswick to Penrith No. 1 box, applied from December 4 1967, on a 'one engine in steam' basis. The station was unstaffed from July 1 1968. Final closure (for passengers) was wef March 6 1972

Penruddock station

This was another wayside station, 2 1/4 miles eastward of Troutbeck, with a few

Right: Troutbeck's Up advance starting signal, a CKPR signal with a flat cap, is seen at the top of the bank, looking east through ' Summit bridge.' This occupation bridge was rebuilt for the track doubling with four main steel girders and concrete jack arches between them – indicative of changing civil engineering practices around the turn of the century. *Richard L. Pattinson/CRA.*

houses nearby and tiny villages at Motherby and Peruddock, each about a half-mile distant. Originally, in 1865 (or very shortly afterwards) it was a crossing place on the single line. The loop was lengthened 30 yards westwards in 1870, with a siding beyond, and in 1873 this siding was taken into the loop, in order to allow the longest mineral trains to cross. Signalling was concentrated in a box in 1874, electric tablet working (and exchange of tablets) came circa 1891 and double line block working to Troutbeck in 1901, but the line was never doubled between Penruddock and Blencow.

Unlike other stations on the CKPR, Penruddock had staggered platforms. The signalbox (as rebuilt circa 1896) prudently overlooked the midway barrow crossing between the east end of the Up platform and the west end of the Down. The neat stone building on the Up side was closely comparable with that at Troutbeck, but had a slightly hipped roof at its eastern end. Again, a small wooden building graced the Down platform. A house for the stationmaster was purchased from Mrs Sarah Bailey, widow, in good time (July 1863) for the opening in 1865. This was presumably the house on the roadside near the Up side approach,

occupied by stationmasters and provided with a path leading directly to the station approach.

The goods yard, on the Up side, effectively provided a short trailing siding behind the box, a short back siding eastward with a platform and a longer siding eastward, serving a cattle pen on the platform, a coal landing and three coal cells. A three tons capacity crane was in the original equipment. At the west end of the Down platform, a 'horse and carriage landing' (later also available for motor car vans) was installed, trailing off the down line, in 1882, accompanied by a convenient crossover. This facility met the needs of the Howards (Henry Howard was a member of the CKPR Board from 1876 to 1914) of Greystoke Castle and their guests. Before the First World War, horses were unloaded some half-dozen times each year, for hunting. In the years just before 1914 'Yeomanry' of the Northumberland Fusiliers came by way of Penruddock, with their horses, bound for summer camp held in fields beside the road between Motherby and Greystoke. Timber from Greystoke estate (for pit props) was loaded, in 1919, whilst in the war years from 1939 to 1945 this horse landing was again used for loading timber. Special cattle for export have

Right: Penruddock: 'Cauliflower' No. 28589, working the 10.20am from Penrith, is leaving the station westward, under bridge No. 103 (road A591) with Motherby and Greystoke to the left, on August 7 1950. *E.S. Russell*

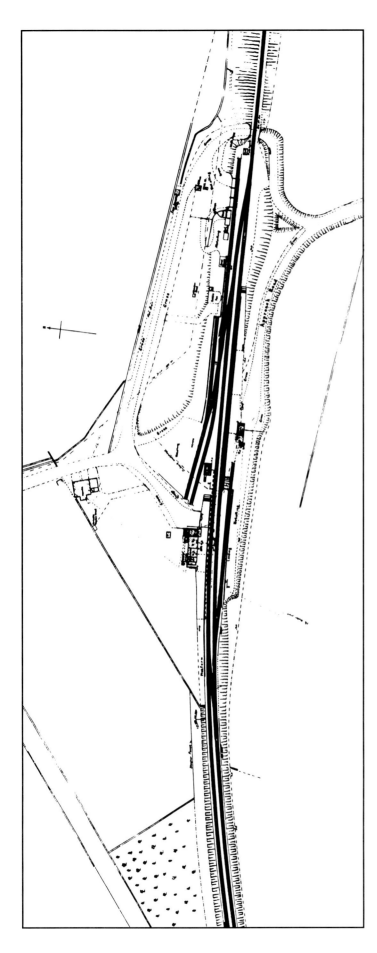

also been loaded similarly. The short Up side (east) siding was taken out in 1940 and the crossover was removed circa 1965. The station had the usual gas house and lighting.

The coal depot has been mentioned and it particularly served Greystoke and its surrounding area. Following the pattern found commonly on the NER, the Penruddock Stationmaster enjoyed coal rights, though not exclusive. The coal merchant who operated from Penruddock depot thus found himself in competition with the Stationmaster! The merchant until 1921 was Mr Thompson, who retired that autumn, in his eighties, and on October 21 1921, Mr John Mandale, of Greystoke, took over, shortly after coming out of the army. He rented two coal cells - commonly styled 'coal vaults' in CKPR parlance - for use with bottom-door wagons and for storage, but also used the 'coal landing' for the discharge of side-door wagons. In his earlier days, his coal came chiefly from Whitehaven (in bottom-door wagons) and from the Allerdale Coal Company's Buckhill Colliery (on the C &W Jn Railway's Northern Extension line). Later, coal came from Wharncliffe in Yorkshire (and Hickleton Main) and a very good quality coal from Easington in Durham - and this was ordered in side-door wagons to minimise breakage during discharge. Local delivery was achieved for many years using traditional horse-drawn four-wheeled coal carts. However, from the 1930-35 period, Mr Mandale bagged his coal and delivered it in a Ford one-ton capacity motor lorry. His railway wagons were shunted off the local goods trains into the siding behind the box and from there he pushed them to his depot in the east end of the long siding. From 29/- per ton in the early 1920s, the price of coal delivered` at Penruddock station fell during the ensuing years to 23/6 per ton. Profit to the merchant was around 1d per hundred-weight. The working day began at 7.30am. On Tuesdays, John Mandale (cheerful 90 years of age at the time of writing) would lend a hand to push loaded cattle wagons through to the siding behind the box, so that they could be picked up by the engine of the 8.15am (and thereabouts) passenger train, en route Penrith, for the weekly auction mart. Mr Keith Mandale, son of John, took over eventually and has run the coal business form Penrith, and now Blencow, station yards.

Penruddock's first stationmaster was William Reay, at 21/- weekly, with uniform and house; he was transferred in January 1872 to Bassenthwaite Lake, a promotion in status if not in pay, and later held the premier position of station-master at Keswick. John Tinnion came from being station-master, Blencow in January 1872 (a promotion) and ten-dered his resignation in October 1906, the board respond-ing with a gift of £25, in view of "very long and faithful service." John Blackburn, promoted from stationmaster, Embleton, came in October 1906, at a salary of 25/- per week, but was appointed to Bassenthwaite Lake in August 1908, when Joseph Todhunter (formerly stationmaster, Braithwaite) was appointed. He served until September 1921, when he moved to Bassenthwaite Lake. John Clapham, previously parcels clerk at Keswick, was appoint-ed in his stead, at £200 per annum, plus five per cent and he was thus John Mandale's competitor for coal sales, and stayed to be the last stationmaster at Penruddock, which

Above: An eastward view at Penruddock, showing the staggered platforms, the CKPR-designed signalbox and two CKPR signals nearest the camera. The dock for horseboxes and other like traffic is on the Down side (right) and beyond the coal cells (far left) the line crosses Penruddock viaduct. *Richard L. Pattinson/CRA.*

Above: Stanier 2-6-4T No.42594 represents the large tank locomotives permitted on the route from 1939, indeed a little earlier, as they did not require the larger turntable. This is 'The Lakes Express' to London on July 22 1960. Penruddock viaduct, which had nine arches (subsequently reduced by infilling) survives today but underline bridge No. 106, beneath the engine was demolished in 1982. *Derek Cross.*

was placed initially under Troutbeck and then, from 1932, Blencow. He lived in the house, which was afterwards occupied by other railwaymen. The first porter at Penruddock was Thomas White (appointed July 1864) at 12/- per week and, it is interesting to note, with house. Mr. T. Thompson followed him in 1873; maybe it was he who took on the coal merchant's business.

In the years before 1914, William Ridley was the senior signalman, and likewise, in 1919, his son, Syd Ridley, joined the CKPR here as junior porter. Mr J. Todhunter (then living at Motherby) was the 'relief signalman' based here - and he was 'fined' in December 1909 for "irregularity in working the train tablet." This was a serious offence, for only by rigorous operation of the tablet system could safety be maintained on a single line railway. Later, Syd Ridley (1905-1983), a stalwart character who long outlived the CKPR and even the local line itself, became signalman here, (his father having died as signalman, April 8 1927) with George Watson (Jnr) coming as his colleague, from local permanent way work, in which he had followed his father. They are not to be confused with other well-known Watsons locally, whose service was principally at Troutbeck.

Closure of the signalbox came wef the changes of December 4 1967. The station had closed to goods wef June 1 1964, became unstaffed from July 1 1968 and finally closed (with the line) wef March 6 1972.

Penruddock-Flusco-and towards Blencow

Departing eastward from Penruddock, a signal post on the Down side carried LNWR-type corrugated steel arms for the Up starting signal and the Down home signal; this arrangement lasted until the end of signalling on the line and probably dated from the remodelling of circa 1896. Separate signals had been in use a few years earlier, but the steel arms are likely to have replaced CKPR items in LMS days. The Penruddock viaduct (bridge No. 105) was reduced in 1920 from nine arches to four, by infilling but still stands today, unlike the ensuing underline bridge No. 106, demolished 1982-83. Penruddock station (MP23 1/2) to Blencow station (MP27 1/2 approximately) was always single track, mostly descending eastward, concluding on a downgrade of 1 in 70. Between MP25, at Kirkbarrow Wood, and MP27, at Bunkers Wood, nearing Blencow, the route describes a bold sweep north and then east again, in order to negotiate the contours. On the south-north portion, after bridge No. 111 (Green Lane, overline) are two limeworks sites, and a notable cutting.

Harrisons Limeworks Siding (Flusco)

Mr Joseph Harrison proposed opening-out a limestone quarry around 1907 and by 1912 his limeworks was established. However, it was not until 1916 that his Flusco siding was commissioned, south of underline bridge 113 (Flusco bridge) and precisely at MP26. The turnout faced Down trains and the groundframe was released by the Blencow-Penruddock tablet. The title became Harrison's Lime Works Ltd. The works embraced quarrying, crushing and processing, and included kilns. Traffic increased and even kept the line open for a time after closure of the Penrith-Keswick branch line on March 6 1972. 'One engine' working applied from Penrith No. 1 box to Flusco Siding until closure wef June 19 1972. The site changed hands latterly and was closed by Amalgamated Roadstone Corporation, circa 1980.

In 1923, there were a couple of internal standard gauge sidings, incorporating twin loops, on banking above the CKPR running line, and by 1954 several roads were noted; there was a cable drum for standard gauge haulage. The quarry (hidden from the CKPR line) employed a 2ft gauge internal system. In 1924, a network of hand-operated tracks are recalled on the quarry floor, with a steam-powered cable incline at one end for haulage up to the crusher. At that time, a single steam locomotive, kept clean but not in use, stood on an isolated track in the quarry bottom. It has been reputed that a steam 0-4-0T (by German builders Orenstein & Koppel) named *Fleetwood* was eventually buried at this site. A tentative identity, from recent research, is O&K No. 5131 of February 6 1912, supplied originally to Caffin & Company. The narrow gauge layout in 1954 included a steam winder by Clarke Chapman, an incline, and two four-wheeled internal combustion locomotives, by Ruston & Hornsby (of 1942 and 1944), one being in a dismantled state.

Flusco Quarry Siding

This siding connection was just north of bridge No. 113, on the Down side of the single line and with entry facing Down trains, and groundframe, released by the token. It was of earlier date than the Harrisons Limeworks Siding. It served 'Flusco Ballast Quarry' (the older spelling Fluskew being used at first). This was seemingly purchased circa 1890 by the CKPR for its own use and there was one standard gauge siding, alongside the running line. In November 1890, the CKPR proposed to purchase a stonebreaker and engine for the quarry. A tramway bogie accident on September 15 1910 implies the existence of an internal narrow gauge layout. The index entry for a CKPR plan (undated) was titled 'Flusco Engine Shed' and this may hint at a locomotive. The use of the ballast quarry declined – in 1918 the CKPR was trying to sell the engine and crusher – and it was closed about 1922. In the working timetable of October 3 1921, a call was still shown and in 1921-22 a trip was made about one day weekly to remove material, by rail.

St Andrews Cutting

North of the old ballast quarry siding, the line, on a right-hand curve, passed through a rock cutting, itself topped by Low Fluskew Woods and hemmed in at its midpoint by St Andrews overline bridge (No. 115), which featured a stone arch on rock abutments. This was a blind spot for locomotive drivers and in the exceptional snows of early 1940 it also became a snow block. The tragedy which occurred on that occasion is described later. Through the curve, and the next overline bridge, the bracketed home signals and station of Blencow came into view.

Blencow station

This station was west of underline bridge No. 117. Here, the railway crossed the by-road from the villages of Little and Great Blencow (up to two miles north) and the Clickham Inn crossroads on the former A594 (now the B5288). This road continues south through Newbiggin village (a mile south of the station) to reach the former B5288 (now merged into A66). The station was named Newbiggin when planned, but by May 1864, the alternative

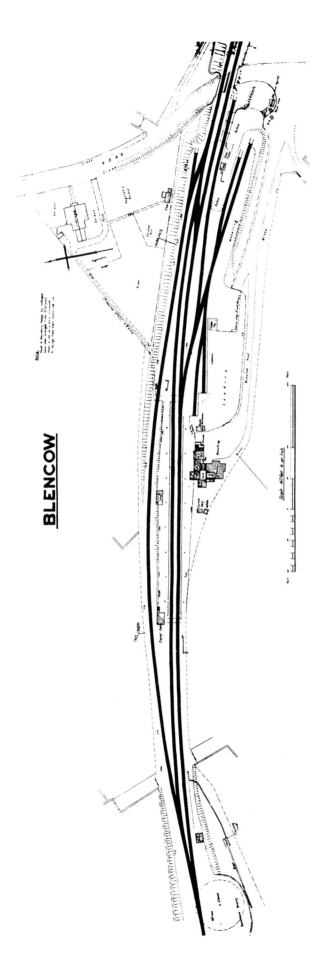

BLENCOW

names favoured were Greystoke (two miles to the west) and Dacre (three miles to the south). At the opening, in January 1865, Blencowe was adopted, but by July 1865 'Bradshaw' was listing Blencow (with no final 'e') although the archaic form was commonly used by the Railway company for a few more years. The station was on a single line, with the sole platform and buildings on the Down (southern) side. The single storey building included office and two waiting rooms but, unlike Troutbeck and Penruddock, two gables faced the platform.

The Stationmaster's house was designed by architect Mr Ross and built by J.R. Harrison, whose tender was accepted in March 1865; a substantial two-storey house resulted, behind the station premises and almost contiguous with them. Much later, the acetylene gas house (for lighting) was built, abutting on the west elevation of the platform buildings. A carbide store was a separate structure, a short distance away. There were modest sidings on the Down side and, after the dramatic runaway of December 26 1889, a shunting neck eastward was authorised.

Blencow was not provided with a crossing loop before the line eastward to Redhills Junction, two miles, was doubled; this was done between March 1900 and June 1901, the opening being on Sunday June 2 1901. Up and Down running roads were then made through the station, converging to single line to the west, and an Up platform was provided, with timber waiting shed of one room. There are indications that the additional track created through the station was the Down line, in which case the original platform face was cut back. The signalbox was built at the Down (west) end of the new platform and Blencow thus became a blockpost, with a single track (with electric token) westward and a double line block eastward. A long siding was installed at this time, entered in the facing direction by Up trains and passing behind the new Up platform to converge short of the underline roadway. This provided a useful Up goods loop, allowing a lime train from Flusco, or other goods, to be held while passenger workings were handled at the station. Coal was accommodated with three cells, on the down side siding which trailed back to near the underline bridge.

An important development of the mid-1930s was the coming of the Blencowe (note spelling) Lime Co Ltd, south of the station, established by Mr John Farrer. A peculiar lead was completed for traffic in November 1936, leaving the yard access line after its divergence from the Down running line and taking a sweeping curve which cut across the cattle siding and likewise crossed the station roadway, in order to reach the limeworks. Substantial traffic from the works was developed between 1936 and 1939, and also during the war years, notably to Lanarkshire Steel and Colville's Dalzell Steelworks at Motherwell and Clyde Iron Works, also Glengarnock Works on the GSWR line. In 1954, there was still an extensive internal 2ft gauge layout in the works area, serving crushing plant and kilns. There were many 2ft gauge wagons and two internal combustion locomotives, respectively by Hudson-Hunslet, Works No. 2194 of 1941, and Hunslet (for Ruston Hornsby), No. 3116 of 1944. There is now no on-site quarrying, although ground lime is produced from imported limestone and there is also some brickmaking.

Left: Blencow station, as recorded on an LMS plan, but drawn before the Blencowe Limeworks link of 1936 was installed; this curved off to the south.

Left: This view of the approach to Blencow station, from the east, is included to show the 'Cauliflower' turning sharply right from the Down platform road into the access line for Blencowe Limeworks, installed in 1936. Its train is seemingly standing in the Up loop (left). There is an LNWR Down starting signal (on the right) but the Up starter is of CKPR origin.
Richard L. Pattinson/CRA

Above: This August 7 1950 scene (from the east end of the Down platform) shows the Blencowe limeworks access line cutting away right, across the tracks of the small yard, round the end of the cattle dock - to cross the carriageway approach to the station and head for the works. No. 45230, a Stanier 'Black 5' 4-6-0, is climbing briskly with the Down 'Lakes Express', comprised of four corridor coaches in red and cream livery, strengthened by two non-corridors, probably from Penrith, in LMS/BR darker red. *E.S. Russell.*

An economy of 1938, believed effective from June 20, was the formal abandonment of Redhills Junction, closing of the signalbox there and conversion to single track between Blencow and the Redhills Junction site. The Up and Down platforms and platform lines, also the Up loop, were retained at Blencow, which thus became (for the first time) a crossing place on a single line, the token section eastward extending to Penrith No. 1 box.

Blencow closed to goods wef June 1 1964 and on Monday June 28 1965 the refuge siding, dock siding and other down yard facilities were taken out of use. However, from Monday December 4 1967 the Down refuge siding was restored, this probably being the trail-back down the bank created in 1938 from part of the former Down running

line, of 1901-38. Also from Monday December 4 1967, 'one engine' working was introduced between Keswick and Penrith No. 1 box, with a groundframe taking over the connection trailing from the former Down platform line to the Lime Company's siding. Stops were installed on the former Down line west of the platforms, and all passenger trains thereafter used the former Up platform; the signalbox was closed. The station was unstaffed from July 1 1968 and closed to passengers wef March 6 1972, but the line itself and the quarry connections both here and at Flusco survived until final abandonment wef June 19 1972. Blencow passenger station had earlier closed as such wef March 3 1952 but reopened from July 2 1956, to survive as seen until March 6 1972.

A pair of neat houses, gabled and with very good gardens, were built by the CKPR in 1908 near Blencow station and facing the road. A signalman occupied one and the permanent way ganger in charge from Blencow westward the other, as recalled from the 1920s-1930s. They are still smart at the time of writing.

A renowned 'character' at Blencow over many years was Stationmaster George Gaskarth, here from circa 1917 until

Above: Lime traffic is prominent in this Keswick-Carlisle goods, seen at Blencow on August 3 1963, hauled by Ivatt Class 2MT 'Mogul' No. 46455. The train is taking the Up goods loop behind the platform. *D.F. Tee.*

Right: An imposing portrait of Stationmaster George Gaskarth, in charge at Blencow c1917-1942. He would walk the platform playing his bagpipes! *Syd Ridley Collection.*

retirement circa 1942. He had also been the parcels clerk at Cockermouth in 1913. He liked to wear his Scots regalia and march up and down Blencow platform playing his bagpipes! He was an energetic figure; after Redhills box closed in 1938, he would cheerfully walk the line down to Penrith No. 1 to initiate pilot working. The romantic aura surrounding George Gaskarth diverts attention from his predecessors, who included Henry Sutcliffe (there at the start in 1865), Thomas Kidson (promoted from Blencow to stationmaster, Keswick, in April 1869), John Tinnion (moving, as noted, to Penruddock in January 1872), John Scott (here 1872-85, then resigning) and James Hutchinson (appointed 1885 and still here in 1908, when he was offered Bassenthwaite Lake, but was left undisturbed at Blencow at his own request). Jim Airey, who had been stationmaster at Bassenthwaite Lake, came to Blencow in the years 1964-66 as its last stationmaster. He and Mrs Airey had happy memories of their days at both these attractive stations. Mr Edwin Thompson and Mrs Thompson, both with earlier assignments at Embleton station and level crossing - and Edwin Thompson also as signalman at Bassenthwaite Lake - made a move to Blencow in April 1966, when the railway closed west of Keswick, and took over the station house. Mr Thompson was in the box until it closed late in 1967. He and his wife have continued to reside at Blencow and made progressive improvements, which since 1972 have included expansion over trackbed and platforms, forming a garden of CKPR memories, with a superb vista towards Carlisle and also the Northern Pennines. Back in 1913, the signalman was Fred Bewley, with Adam Watson as part-time relief. Alfred Ousby was a pre-1923 CKPR man who had been in Redhills box until circa 1935. He was pleasantly recalled as the Blencow signalman by Geoffrey Holt, who came to Penrith in 1945 as signalmen's Inspector. Teddy Foster knew Blencow box very well, from 1938. Tom Jackson, of Keswick, was a regular signalman here from about 1938 until 1967, with a background of experience as 'box lad' at Penrith No. 1 in 1929, also at Tebay, Kirkby Lonsdale, Threlkeld and Penruddock, and subsequently

having a roaming commission in the years 1967-69, between Penrith and Keswick, in the days of unmanned stations.

From Blencow to Redhills Junction

The new line of 1901 was the Down road of 1901-38. From 1938 to 1972, the original line (the Up road of 1901-38) was retained for Up and Down running. A train's length

Left: Redhills Junction was created in 1866 by the Stockton & Darlington Railway (later NER/LNER). Looking east, the LNER double track for Eamont Junction diverges left, and subsequently passed beneath the CKPR to descend to the WCML (See below). Its protecting Down home signal is of CKPR type. The old signalbox, which lasted to 1938, is of uncertain antecedents. The pair of railway houses are also seen. Ahead, the CKPR route, single track, descends to Penrith. *Richard L. Pattinson/CRA.*

Above: Looking north from Eamont Junction signalbox in 1934, the double track route to Redhills Junction diverges to the left, from the WCML. A 'Royal Scot' three-cylinder 4-6-0 is literally roaring up the bank, southbound. *Syd Ridley.*

of the former Down line was retained at Blencow in order to be available as a refuge for stabling Blencowe Limeworks traffic. The bank was on a downgrade of 1 in 70, unbroken past Redhills, to finish at 1 in 79 near Penrith No. 1 box.

Redhills Junction and the North Eastern link

Underline bridge No. 130 (Station Road) immediately preceded Redhills Junction. The signalbox was on the right, opposite the divergence (left) of the line built by the NER, which immediately became double for the remainder of its length of rather less than one mile, to its convergence with the West Coast Main Line (WCML) at Eamont Junction. This was the 'Penrith Loop' or 'Redhills Curve' and descended at 1 in 66, 1 in 50 and 1 in 131, in that sequence. At a Euston meeting in March 1864, with William Bouch representing the SDR (strictly, by then, the NER), the junctions to be formed were styled Stainton and Yanwath (eventually Redhills and Eamont) and interim arrangements were discussed for handling mineral traffic from Durham and the Eden Valley Railway (opened 1862-63 as part of the SDR) by way of Penrith until the 'Loop' was commissioned. This NER double line was constructed by 1865 but not yet connected at Redhills when, in May of that year, the CKPR insisted on seeing the NER's plans for the junction. The junction opened on September 5 1866 but some residual contention about the precise layout was apparent between October 1867 and January 1868. The NER recorded the junction signalbox as opened in 1866, at its expense. However, on April 2 1890, the CKPR agreed to erect a new cabin here, as the existing frame was 'so dilapidated.' The somewhat plain and fairly tall signalbox, with hipped roof, had the air of a Saxby & Farmer cabin of approximately 1870. Perhaps it was in essence the original cabin of the 1860s, retained in 1890 and equipped with a new frame by (probably) Tweedy of Carlisle. It lasted in operation until 1938. The 'loop' was traversed by the coke trains from 1866 until, after a period of intermittent running, a last working on February 18 1926 (C.R. Clinker's date). Excursion trains from the NER to Keswick and back used it extensively, especially between the 1890s and 1914. The LMS also used it, for circular tour trains in the 1920s, and a southbound train, remembered as being in August 1929, would probably be the last example. In 1930, the LMS Chief Signal & Telegraph engineer paid a visit and was very disturbed by the poor, indeed unsafe condition of the 'Loop'. Some immediate work was done but its use was virtually restricted to the turning of the LNER 4-4-0 locomotives of D3 (ex GNR) type during the years 1930-35 and, latterly, LMS former MR Class 2 4-4-0s - all these engines being too long for Penrith's turntable. Derailment of one or more of the LNER locomotives was reported, during these turning operations on the 'Loop.'

The line was condemned about 1936-37 and lifted in the period 1937-38. An official closing date was June 11 1938 (Saturday), thus wef June 13 1938. Eamont Junction signalbox closed wef July 11 1938 and, as already noted, Redhills box seemingly closed wef June 20 1938.

At Redhills - and its people

Following receipt by the CKPR Board of a memorial from residents of nearby Stainton, it was agreed in 1871 to provide a siding at Redhills Junction for goods and mineral traffic. Nevertheless, by May 1874, the siding and its points were to be abandoned; the Board of Trade was demanding expensive alterations, having presumably awakened to the hazards of shunting on the gradient here, with two convergences to a main line 'just down the hill!'

The two cottages adjoining the signal box were also erected under a CKPR decision of 1871 and were intended for a signalman and a platelayer. In the 1920s and 1930s, each was occupied by a signalman and his family. They were rapidly becoming derelict in early 1985.

Although Redhills was a NER junction, the CKPR employed the signalmen. In January 1872, John Scott was transferred from Redhills Junction to Blencow box. Edmund Porter succeeded him but resigned in February 1873. It is implied that he would not endure the prevailing hours of duty, for in February 1873 the Board minuted that "the signalman (clearly only one) has long hours. In future, he is to be relieved two days each week and every third Sunday by a platelayer of the Redhills length." In July 1913, there were two full-time signalmen, J.S Codling (who held this post from circa 1878 and who died on October 22 1916) and John Laycock. They each worked turns of eight hours one week and 8 1/4 hours the next week (alternating) thus suggesting that the box was open 16 1/4 hours daily. Incidentally, there had been times of pressure in the iron industry when the coke trains ran over the CKPR by night, as well as during a long day. Adam Watson and Alfred Ousby (the latter later of Blencow) were the signalmen in the 1920s and 1930s and Joseph Watson joined his father, circa 1935-38.

The NER and LNER for long employed two men (a ganger and assistant) on maintenance of their double track 'Curve', the men living just south of Redhills Junction but not in railway houses.

The concluding descent, Redhills Junction to Penrith No 1 signal box

The NER 'Loop' or 'Curve' was crossed by the CKPR's single track by bridge No. 134, known to the NER as bridge No. 4. This bridge was infilled during 1939. Onward, the four LNWR cottages of Eamont Terrace were visible (and still are) across a field and main road; they stand with the NER road bridge (now south abutment only) to one side and the WCML (Lancaster & Carlisle Railway of old) with its Down loops (now one loop) behind them. Hereabouts, from the CKPR in fair weather, Cross Fell, premier summit in the Pennines, can be seen ahead. Bridge No. 135 (Mile End) crossed a by-road which has become busy since the A66 was redeveloped and this bridge was destroyed in 1983, its abutments replaced by landscaping. 'Redhills Cottages', a terrace of eight houses backing towards the CKPR, were a casualty of the A66 roadworks. We now complete our leisurely travels - and digressions - from Workington, Cockermouth, Keswick and many another place to descend beside the WCML and the southern approaches to Penrith.

Excitements on the bank

The runaway from Blencow to Penrith on December 26 1889 will be included in the later section devoted to mishaps. There were 'happenings' in later years too.

When the long section was made in 1938, between Blencow to Penrith No. 1 box, the risk of accident was clearly in mind. Near MP 28 1/4, a short portion of the old Down road was left in situ, with spring-controlled points

Above: A general view of the CKPR junction with West Coast Main Line, viewed from Penrith No. 1 signalbox as rebuilt 'Baby Scot' 4-6-0 No. 45527 *Southport* passes with the lightweight two-wagon Harrison's shunt, from near Shap. The picture was taken on July 31 1964. *Derek Cross.*

Left: Descending the CKPR route to Penrith No.1 (Keswick Junction) signalbox, which can be seen, the handsome LNWR bracket signal could offer alternatives of proceeding by the CKPR line (left), 'EV line '(Eden Valley - next right) or onto the Down main line. The ground signal would indicate a road set across to the Up main and so to Penrith yard or warehouse. August 15 1950. *E.S. Russell.*

normally set to divert a descending vehicle or train onto it and thence into a sand-drag. In order that a properly authorised descending train would not be diverted to the drag, the signalman at Blencow had first to secure the token for the section and then pull a lever which not only electrically set the catch points for safe downhill running, but also proved them set and locked before the train could be signalled down the bank. Notwithstanding these safeguards, there was an occasion when a goods train descending from Blencow to Penrith, with the driver duly in possession of the miniature staff, was put through the catch points onto the 'old road', heading for the sand-drag. It happened that the driver on duty that day was a cautious man – and not his 'high speed' colleague who often worked the turn - and he succeeded in stopping with minimum damage. It was never satisfactorily established how the Blencow signalman contrived to achieve this mis-setting of the catchpoints. He always insisted that a lightning storm at the time had upset the point motor so that the spring opened the turnout.

On another occasion, Tom Jackson was in the box, with the road set and authorised for a goods train from Flusco to run via the loop, behind the Up platform, bound down the bank for Penrith. The driver's pop-whistles alerted him to a 'runaway' situation. The 'Black 5' 4-6-0 locomotive had left

Above: Ivatt 'Mickey Mouse' 2-6-0 No. 46491 drifts past Penrith No. 1 box with six maroon-liveried LMS coaches comprising a Keswick-Manchester train of August 18 1962. This view clearly shows the track layout in the vicinity of the signalbox, and the CKPR connections to the WCML and the EV line. *Derek Cross.*

Flusco with a massive train of 40-loads of limestone products, but with no brakevan attached. The train ran by at speed - of course without picking up the token for the single line and with the driver and his mate preparing to jump off the locomotive. It just about negotiated the outlet from loop to running line and the crew stayed aboard. Tom knew that no ascending train would be due at Penrith No. 1 and reckoned that if he opened the electric catch points the inevitable pile-up at the sand drag would be on such a massive scale as to 'stop the job' for some days. He therefore sent 'train running away' on the bell to Penrith No. 1 box. His colleague there was noted for a propensity to argue points, and so it was on this occasion, but he was given no option: the runaway was coming! As it happened, the brakes on the engine and the tender began to take effect and the train came to a stand some two miles down the bank from Blencow, near Redhills and still about 3/4 mile from the junction at Penrith. Mr Jackson's judgment was commended by higher authority.

When Blencow box closed, in December 1967, and 'one engine' working applied, it was necessary to take out the electric points and sand-drag of 1938, but electrically operated points (leading to a sand-drag on the Up side) were installed only 475 yards short of Penrith No. 1 box and with control from that box, which by then had a track circuit on the branch near the new catchpoints. One Good Friday, after dark in the evening, the signalman was astounded and alarmed to see the track circuit light come on, indicating the approach of a train from Keswick - which was closed that day, with no known traffic. He raised the alarm and investigation was urgently set in motion: nothing was ever found.

Penrith station and its approaches
- as seen by the CKPR

Penrith station, on its sweeping curve, opened in 1846 as part of the Lancaster & Carlisle Railway and by early 1848 it was on the first through railway route from London (Euston) to Glasgow and Edinburgh. The LCR was leased to the LNWR in 1859 and vested in that Company in 1879 and - like the CKPR - became part of the LMS from 1923, and subsequently BR from 1948. The Eden Valley Railway (EVR) with running powers over the few miles from Eden Valley Junction (Clifton) to Penrith, fully opened in 1863, thus bringing the SDR (soon to be the NER) and later the LNER to Penrith. The CKPR opening, it may be recalled, was in late 1864 (minerals) and January 1865 (passengers).

The Penrith Joint Station Committee was established under Act of 1862 and its inaugural meeting was held in Penrith on July 24 1863, with powerful representation, namely:

LNWR: Richard Moon (Chairman); W.N. Hodgson (LNWR Director with special concern for the L&C district, also being a member of the CKPR Board); William Cawkwell (General Manager); S.B. Worthington (Engineer)

SDR (Strictly, **NER**): John Whitwell; Thomas MacNay (Secretary of the former SDR); Johnathan Dixon.

CKPR: Isaac Fletcher (Vice Chairman); Isaac Lowthian (Director); John Wood (then Resident Engineer on construction, under Thomas Bouch); Henry Cattle (Secretary and Manager).

Improvements at Penrith were planned and put in hand, and followed up at the ensuing meeting, at Euston, on March 16 1864, in anticipation of opening of the CKPR.

The Keswick line was provided with an entry to Penrith parallel with, but independent of, the LNWR main lines, so that CKPR passenger trains could run without hindrance to the back face of the Down platform. The NER secured its 'EVR bay' in the south end of that platform. This remained, broadly, the layout right through the years until the EVR passenger services ceased in 1962 and those from Keswick in 1972. Strictly, the EVR trains had an approach line of their own in due course.

More contentious were the arrangements for a running connection between the Keswick line and the main lines at the point where the routes came alongside one another, well to the south of the station. When Captain Rich, RE (for the Board of Trade) gave approval on December 22 1864 to the opening of the CKPR to passengers, he emphasised that the junction with the main line lacked adequate signalling and interlocking and must not be used by passenger trains. In particular, the Captain disapproved of "the two semaphores which control the CKPR's junction with the Up main line of the LNWR: one is at the junction signalman's box and one at the opposite side of the line, near the end of

the branch." The box was a pointsman's cabin on the Up (southbound) side of all tracks, fairly handy for access to the cattle sidings and the crossover between Up main and Keswick line, but remote from the signal for the protection of the junction against trains approaching from the Keswick line, on its descending grade. It took some 15 more years to achieve signalling at Penrith which gained Board of Trade approval and stood the test of time - right down to the coming of centralised power signalling in 1973.

Developments and improvements at Penrith station in the period 1865-1922 were normally on LNWR initiative and implemented according to its own plans and designs. The other Companies were consulted chiefly to obtain their often-reluctant contributions to the cost. Some examples:

February 1870: a scheme estimated at £1,120 for the concentrated control of points and signals was trimmed to one costed at £100 for connecting four pairs of points to the existing "raised signal box at the south end of the station.....to obviate the signalman going down to hold them." So far as one can judge, this was the box referred to in 1864, or one shown on early maps, a little to its north, also on the Up side of the main line. (Penrith No 3 box, by Saxby & Farmer, was built at the north end of the station in 1872, acquiring a replacement LNWR frame of 23 levers in 1884).

February 1876: The LNWR secured approval of £1,371 expenditure for the construction of a signal box "at the west end of the passenger station, to work the points and signals in that part." One is forced to conclude that the resultant signal box was Penrith No. 2, located just south of the station, on the Down side, near the turntable, and surviving to be rebuilt in 1950 and closed in 1968.

Below: An evocative view of the WCML platforms at Penrith station, looking south in 1925. Note the variety of trunks, suitcases and baskets awaiting collection by a Down train.
Real Photographs Company/Courtesy Ian Allan Ltd.

November 1878-February 1879: Discussion over this period produced approval of the LNWR plan, which was designed to meet BOT requirements, "for removal of the signal cabin from the proximity of the Up shunting siding to the Down side of the line, with locking of facing points and renewal and remodelling of signals for Penrith Junction and Station." Estimate £1,330. In August 1880, the work was reported recently completed. The new box, on the Down side, would be Penrith No. 1 - Keswick Junction', 1 mile 418 yards from Redhills Junction and 638 yards short of Penrith station. It was of standard LNWR pre-1903 type, with 64 levers and lasted until 1973 - and signalling every Keswick line train in and out of Penrith from 1880 until 1972. The box replaced in 1879-80 is thought to have been by Saxby & Farmer, dating from circa 1872 and itself replacing the pointsman's cabin mentioned in 1864. (cf. also the alterations which had been contemplated in 1870).

Other station improvements at Penrith

During the years 1866-72, various adjustments were made relating to the main Up platform, and the station staff were provided with rather more accommodation. A passenger subway under the main line tracks was put in hand in 1872. On the Down side, a request of the NER was met in 1875, by extending the platform at the south end so that its passengers would not have to board summer trains from ground level. Meanwhile, in December 1867, the LNWR was installing a boiler for hot water for carriage footwarmers,

the cost of this too being for joint account. The CKPR back platform road was snug but somewhat gloomy; it had the advantage of a through track, so that trains from Keswick could call there and then proceed to Carlisle.

Goods and coal at Penrith

There had been a contract for local cartage with Mr Dennison, but it was found unsatisfactory and from October 1879 the LNWR employed four horses of their own. Much later, in December 1914, six horses were stabled at Penrith yard, four employed on NER goods cartage and two on 'joint cartage'. The LNWR was providing new stables at that time. The Railway layout and buildings in the yard were elaborated in detail from time to time. Coal was handled on a substantial scale and at one time the coal agent was Robert Pearson, not a Company or Joint employee. He considered the local stationmaster's agency at Blencow station to represent unfair competition, but the CKPR board did not agree. In 1908, he addressed letters to individual Directors of the Keswick Company about " coal sales by the stationmasters at roadside stations," but he was rebuffed. Note that on the CKPR line, most station yards were provided with coal depots from early days. From January 1 1869, the rent for coal vaults (coal cells) at stations was to cease and in future 3d per ton was to be charged on all coal sold from the station depots and 1d per ton for all coal weighed by the Company's machine. This appeared to relate the fees paid by coal merchants (including, presumably, stationmas-

Above: At Penrith's Up main line platform, LMS No. 5068 _Miranda_ (a 'Jumbo' 2-4-0), and a 'Cauliflower' 0-6-0are doubtless working a through train from Glasgow or Carlisle to Keswick. Note the distinctive water tower at the southern end of the Up platform.
Howard Vogt Collection/Courtesy Preston Whiteley.

ters in some instances) to the turnover of their businesses.

After the once-busy goods yard at Penrith closed, wef January 7 1971, a rail-served coal concentration depot remained on part of the site, but this ceased to receive its deliveries by rail within a very few years.

The Penrith engine shed

It was evident that the stabling of locomotives at Penrith to work, or share the working of the CKPR line would be desirable. The subject was mentioned briefly in the first station agreement (April 24 1861) and more specifically in the fourth clause of the second agreement (September 11 1862). With the opening of the line imminent, the subject was raised at Euston during the meeting of July 14 1864. Mr Hoskins, the CKPR chairman, held that clause four of 1862 contemplated the CKPR providing steam sheds on its own line (one presumes for use by LNWR locomotives working CKPR traffic) but LNWR Chairman Richard Moon did not agree. Rather amusingly, David and Goliath appointed an arbitrator: Christopher Johnstone, General Manager of the Caledonian Railway, of the evocative address '302 Buchanan Street, Glasgow.' His handling of the reference was so delicate that he failed to clarify between the alternatives:

1. The LNWR are to build engine sheds, with the CKPR paying rent for the exclusive use of the premises; or
2. The CKPR are to build the sheds, for the free use of LNWR locomotives employed on the CKPR line;

He nevertheless appeared to show that the CKPR had some such obligation as outlined in Option No. 2. Mr

Above: An interesting scene at 'Penrith for Ullswater Lake' on August 13 1950. The Summer Sundays-Only evening train (note the express train headlamp code) is ready to leave the 'CKP' platform, bound for Darlington, via Stainmore. The double-heading suggests a heavy train which was probably too long to be accommodated at the NER bay (seen on the right). LNER (NER) Class J21 0-6-0s Nos. 65100 and 65038 are in charge. The track running to the left of the train shed was the CKPR run-round loop; once again, the water column is apparent. *Neville Fields.*

Hodgson, a director of both the LNWR and CKPR, suggested that the understanding was that the LNWR should build the shed at Penrith, "adjoining the engine turntable", the CKPR paying into the joint fund a rent for the land but the LNWR paying proportionately if the shed was used to some extent for its own purposes. In fact (September 1864), the LNWR expressed the intention of building the shed forthwith, with the CKPR paying interest at 6% on the outlay, with adjustment if the shed were used other than for solely CKPR purposes. This was agreed.

The shed was duly built by the LNWR - in 1865, it has been understood, but correspondence of 1869 implies that it was only in use from July 1 1868. The Keswick Company protested strongly that it had been led to expect a cost of £600, but was being asked (in January 1869) to pay more than five times this sum. The LNWR evidently resubmitted the actual cost at £1,440 and a compromise was then agreed, whereby the CKPR would pay interest on a notional £1,000, this arrangement to take account of some use of the shed by LNWR engines not wholly engaged on the CKPR line. Down the years, Penrith engines and men had daily duties to and from Carlisle with local passenger trains.

The SDR/NER had certain rights in the matter of a locomotive shed, dating from around 1865, and when they applied for use of its facilities in 1866, numerous excuses were received (from the LNWR?) and no accommodation was forthcoming. In February 1871, Mr Mackay wrote to the Keswick management asking for extension of the Penrith engine shed to permit stabling of one of their engines and to obviate its running through to Kirkby Stephen. The reply was that the CKPR did not propose to expend money on the LNWR premises but would consider favourably providing CKPR land on which the NER might build a shed. The NER did not let the matter drop and the emphasis shifted, to a financial arrangement. In February 1873, it was agreed (and minuted by the CKPR) that the Keswick Company allow £25 per annum to " the S&D Company'" in lieu of providing accommodation at Penrith for one of its engines working over the CKPR line, the allowance to apply from the time when the accommodation became available. The arithmetic emerges from NER records as -

The LNWR extended its Penrith shed, following NER pressure, at the cost of £750:

- on which sum the CKPR agreed to pay its usual 6%..£45 pa
- but with the NER contributing to this sum................. £20pa
- and the CKPR therefore having a net outgoing of.....£25 pa

There remains an element of mystery. So far as is known, the requirement of the NER (and LNER) was always to stable overnight a single passenger engine which had worked its last Down train in the evening and would work the early Up departure for the EVR line, until this stabling ceased in summer 1939. It is unclear why the CKPR should contribute, as the NER loco was not one engaged in mineral workings over the route to Cockermouth.

The need for the engine shed at Penrith was much reduced after diesel railcars took over most passenger duties on the Keswick road, in 1955, with Carlisle (Upperby) and Workington depots providing such steam power as was necessary, and the odd contribution from Oxenholme. The shed at Penrith therefore closed wef June 18 1962. This account of Penrith locomotive depot amplifies my story of its history in my book *Over Shap to Carlisle*, (Pub: Ian Allan, 1983).

Below: As this chapter started at the western end of the line, in Workington station, so we bring our leisurely journey to a close in the Down main line platform at Penrith. LNWR 'Cauliflower' 0-6-0s Nos. 58396 and 28555 are seen at rest after arriving with the 8.35am from Workington, on July 16 1949. Note the water tower, similar to that provided at the southeren end of the Up platform, and also visible in this view. *J.D.Darby.*

THE railway route through northern Lakeland, from Penrith to Workington, was founded on the demands of industry, so this history continues with the fascinating tale of the mineral and freight traffics before moving on to consider passenger traffic, which only developed to its peak as the iron and steel-based movements declined and largely disappeared.

Chapter 3

MINERAL & INDUSTRIAL TRAFFIC
and the economic see-saw, 1866-1914

Above: A down goods leaves Workington Bridge station in LMS days, bound for Derwent Junction, hauled by an LNWR 'Cauliflower' 0-6-0. Industrial activity in West Cumbria was the spur for the construction of the CWR and CKPR.
Richard L. Pattinson/CRA.

The iron and steel industry developed with incredible speed in Britain during the third quarter of the 19th century - as witnessed by the creation of Barrow-in-Furness and Middlesbrough and all they stood for. Even so, the industry was to was to have a very chequered career, owing to its susceptibility to 'boom and slump' from local and, even more, overseas causes.

The works which figured in West Cumberland, with blast furnaces and thus calling for iron ore, limestone and coke, are tabulated. It will be seen that their early development was mostly in the 1860s and the 1870s. During these decades, emphasis was on the export of pig iron produced in West Cumberland's blast furnaces, particularly across country to Tees-side and the east coast ports and to the earlier Bessemer steel manufacturing companies in the Sheffield district. As steel-making became established at the more technically advanced Cumbrian works, the pig iron was required for use in their own steelworks and their products were chiefly of steel, notably rails for the world's railways, manufactured and rolled at Workington. The table thus provides a pointer to the recipients of west-bound coke brought from County Durham by way of the CKPR and to the sources in West Cumberland of east-bound traffic (until about the end of the 1870s) in pig iron and (later) steel in various forms, rails in particular.

As early as 1866, the CKPR Board was complaining to Euston that pig iron was being sent from Workington to Sheffield by way of the FR to Carnforth and LNWR onwards to Preston (and thence maybe by LYR via Blackburn, Copy

Pit, Huddersfield and Penistone, finally via the MSLR into Sheffield). The CKPR contended that the LNWR's agreement on 'shortest routes' implied use of the CKPR and the LNWR's own Ingleton branch, to reach the Midland Railway, which would provide a direct route, from Ingleton via Leeds to Sheffield. In April 1867, LNWR General Manager William Cawkwell was at last writing - to say that routing to such destinations as Sheffield via CKPR and Ingleton "and so off their LNWR line" was never contemplated, the alternatives being the CKPR, Shap and Preston or by the Furness Railway and Preston. Methinks, he protesteth too much! The underlying reason would be to maximise LNWR revenue-earning train mileage and collaborate with friendly Companies such as the NER or LYR, but keeping the MR out of the picture at all costs. A compromise formula was arrived at in June 1867. Also in 1866, the CKPR failed to secure a share in iron ore traffic from West Cumberland to Consett ironworks; it was presumably lost to the LNWR, MCR and NER, via Carlisle. In 1868, the NER declined to reduce its rates for conveying coke on the axis from Durham to Stainmore, CKPR and West Cumberland, saying that the lower rates in force between Durham, Stainmore, Tebay and Barrow dated from agreements between the SDR and Schneider & Company, ironmasters at Barrow. In July

Right: This dramatic scene illustrates vehicles of a 'double' coke train from Mid Durham to West Cumberland, on November 1 1900. The wagons (tare weight 6 tons 15cwts to 6tons 19cwts, according to precise type) had a carrying capacity of 10.5 tons and were built specifically for the traffic from former SDR territory; note the NER lettering 'Central Division and West Cumberland'. The rear van, with double verandah and large central 'birdcage' is of a genuine SDR design, while the van with an end 'birdcage' was designed by the NER to diagram V1. The pile-up occurred at Blencow, during the period of widening works, between Redhills and Blencow, There was a derailment or run-back of a westbound loaded train, on the newly-formed embankment. *Ian G. Sadler Collection.*

1868, the LNWR sought, by rate adjustments, to influence the routing of traffic in pig iron coming off the Joint Line and bound via the CKPR for Hull, Goole and Grimsby. Presumably, at that date, the pig iron originated from Cleator Moor and was bound for shipment to the continent; it is said that Prussia provided a market for Cumbrian pig iron, used in making cannon, until the time of the Franco-Prussian war of 1870.

Further evidence of the existence of iron ore traffic eastward via CKPR metals and the NER Stainmore route - but also of slump - was provided when bad debts had to be written off. These resulted from failure of the South

Cleveland Iron Works Company Ltd (1875) and the Rosedale & Ferryhill Iron Company (1879). In the first case, the ore had moved from the Joint Line to Glaisdale furnaces, situated beside the NER's delightful Esk Valley line. In the latter, it would be ore transported to Ferryhill, north of Darlington on the Anglo-Scottish East Coast Main Line. The late 1870s were notable for depressed traffics in coke westward and iron ore eastward, and reduced rates for their conveyance. Import of Spanish ore from 1871, on an increasing scale, progressively ended the eastbound traffic in West Cumberland ore via Keswick. Nationally, January 1879 witnessed a cut in the bank rate, doubtless aimed at

Right: Goods trains and their traffics: A modest eastbound (Up) goods train comprised of three wagons and a standard BR 20-ton brake van leaves Keswick on August 14 1950, behind a 'Cauliflower' of 12C (Penrith) shed. *Neville Fields.*

COCKERMOUTH, KESWICK AND PENRITH RAILWAY.

PARCELS WAY BILL.

From *Braithwaite* to *Penrith* Train *9.37am* Date *Mch 19* 1875

M'Corquodale & Co., Printers, Glasgow and London.

No.	Description.	Name.	Destination.	Paid on	To Pay. £ s. d.	Paid £ s. d.
1	*Horse*	*Chas Ray Esq*				*6 11*

Horse Box No 475
Ticket No 236. Horse Box Labelled London Through to Euston & entered
per Jenny Bill referring to you for a/c

This Way-Bill must not be used for Fish, Game, Dead Rabbits, Poultry (Live or Dead, including Pigeons), Meat, Tripe, Butter, Cheese, Vegetables (including Watercress), Eggs, Fruit, or Ice, in quantities of 2 Cwt. and upwards.

Guards' Signatures.

COCKERMOUTH, KESWICK AND PENRITH RAILWAY.

PARCELS WAY-BILL. From PENRITH to *Keswick* via

Departure, _____ o'Clock Train, _____ day of _____ 189_

McCorquodale & Co. Limited, Printers, Glasgow and London.

No.	Description.	Name.	Destination.	Weight. Lb.	Paid on.	To Pay.	Paid.	Senders.
1	*10 Box Market J. M.*							
2								
3								
4								
5		*Keswick*						

N.B.—The Guard of the Train must see that the Entries on this Bill correspond with the Parcels delivered to and given up by him.

COCKERMOUTH, KESWICK AND PENRITH RAILWAY.

No. 183 HORSE, CARRIAGE AND DOG TICKET.

7.18 A.M. o'Clock Train *12th May* 1874

From *Embleton* to *Penrith*

AMOUNT PAID. £ s. d.

Horse, ... at ____
4-wheel Carriage, ...at ____
2-wheel Carriage, ...at ____
Dog, ... at ____

paid 1/-

Mr. *Passenger*

Booking Clerk.

NOTICE.—The Company will not be answerable for any damage done to any Horses conveyed by this Railway, although every precaution will be taken by the Company to ensure their safe conveyance.

☞ THIS TICKET MUST BE GIVEN UP WHEN REQUIRED.

This page: Representative consignment notes of the CKPR period 1874-1897. They include (top): Charles Ray's horse, in horsebox, sent from Braithwaite to Euston, by day service on March 19 1875. Presumably the horse travelled by passenger train on the CKPR but possibly by horse-and carriage train on the main line; the fare was 6/11d. Above: 10 boxes of kippers sent from the north via Penrith to Keswick on January 19 1897 and (left) a dog, conveyed from Embleton to Penrith on May 12 1874 for one shilling. *J.M. Hammond Collection.*

stimulating reluctant exports, whilst locally a squeeze was applied to wages by the CKPR, mainly in the traffic and permanent way departments.

In 1880-83 the tale was different. West Cumberland achieved its maximum output of iron ore during the years 1881-83. Already, in February 1880, the NER had requested night opening of the CKPR to accommodate the increased,

and heavy coke traffic westbound over the line and to eliminate the working of 'double trains' - that is, double loads with two engines - which the NER was finding "dangerous and productive of delays". The CKPR agreed promptly, in February 1880, and a limited period of night opening was instituted. A similar request was made and agreed in December 1881, the night working commencing from January 1 1882. Again, wef March 1883, night working was introduced, to meet pressure of peak coke traffic. These spells would put great pressure on staff of the CKPR, especially the signalmen and other traffic men, who would find themselves working 12-hours turns of duty,

From 1883, slump set in with a vengeance and continued for several years. By January 1884, the ironmasters of West Cumberland were combining to press the Railway Companies for reduced coke rates from Durham and

Newcastle districts; the NER, MCR and CKPR agreed, while the LNWR, grudgingly, offered only a partial concession. Even at Threlkeld quarries, whose output was granite, not limestone for blast furnaces, poor trade was evident in their dealings with the Railway in 1883 and 1884. It is recorded that nearly half the furnaces in West Cumberland were 'out of blast' by August 1886. In sympathy with decreased levels of trade, the CKPR's annual rate of dividend declared showed fluctuations in the range 3% to 6% during most of the 1870s, falling to 2 1/2% at the close of the last half-year of 1879 but rising to 5% to 6 3/4% in the period 1880-81. This was accompanied by stirrings for increased salaries among the Company's staff. Dividends were notably low in 1886, up again in 1889 and also for a year or two after, while the years 1888-89 witnessed the nearest approach to 1881-82 levels of production from the Cumberland iron ore mines. In the winter of 1890-91, the LNWR offered to buy the CKPR, at 5% on the ordinary capital; the Board hesitated and the propitious moment passed, never to recur.

A coal strike in 1892 depressed trade and the import of coke from County Durham to West Cumberland was suspended for some months.

In the new century (January 1904) the ironmasters (now formally represented by the West Cumberland Ironmasters' Association, with F.W.Jackson as Secretary) sought reduced through-rates for coke from Newcastle and Durham districts to the iron furnaces of West Cumberland. A meeting between the Association and the Railway Companies, at Carlisle, March 1904, was inconclusive. In May, the CKPR agreed with Mr Burtt, the NER traffic manager, to allow a rebate of 10% off the through coke rates for the period April 1 1904-December 31 1904. The interested Companies met at Euston on August 2 1904; the agreement was ratified, and

subsequently extended to March 31 1905 and then June 30 1905. Then, in August 1905, the Railway Companies again met at Euston and agreed a 'permanent' allowance off Durham-West Coast coke rates: 5d off 5/- and under, 6d off rates over 5/- per ton. The Companies shared the sacrifice proportionally, according to their coke train mileages. In 1910, Mr T. Ainsworth, of the Cleator Moor Company, with extensive iron ore mining interests, sought from the CKPR a reduction in the eastward rates for iron ore from Eskett Junction (on the Joint Line) to Middlesbrough. The CKPR was prepared to accept 6/- per ton on a confirmed order of 10,000 tons if the LNWR and NER would agree (the outcome is not recorded).

The members of the CKPR Board noted, in May 1911, that revenue "is in a low condition." They each agreed to deduct £100 per annum from their fees while this continued and decided on various redefinitions of staff duties; one might describe this as 'cheese-paring.' Thus, the junior fencer and Mr Black, the quarryman at the Company's Flusco ballast quarry, were to be given notice, likewise (wef from the end of September 1911) William Richardson, the Company's canvasser. The gardener's pay was to be cut to the rate of £40 a year after the end of October. The painting staff was to be reduced from the spring of 1912, to one man and an apprentice and major painting work was to be entrusted to contractors.

There was a countrywide railway strike on August 18-19 1911 and a miners' strike in March-April 1912. However, from August 1912, and during the years 1912-14, progressive increases of pay for staff, negotiated sectionally, reflected better trade and traffics. Some rates increased by 4% from July 1 1913 - although the Company's declared dividends were minimal.

IRON WORKS OF WEST CUMBERLAND HAVING BLAST FURNACES – PRODUCING PIG IRON AND DEMANDING COKE

1) The works which were located south of the railway route from Cockermouth to Derwent Junction and Workington - these were most likely to import coke from County Durham by way of the Stainmore route and Keswick:

TITLE	FIRST PRODUCTION (Circa)	SUBSTANTIALLY ENLARGED (Circa)	DECLINE COMMENCED (circa)	FINAL DEMISE
Cleator Moor	1841	1862-82	1920	1929
Harrington	1857	1872-82	1909	1926
Lonsdale (Whitehaven)	1872	1873-83	1890s	1902
Moss Bay (Workington)	1872	1872-77 1934 1949-66	1974	1981* *Steel also made from 1877*
Derwent (Workington)	1873	1873-79 1883 1893-97	1974	1981* *Steel also made from 1883*
Parton	1874	Soon in decline		1889
Distington	1878	1878-82	1921	1922

The creation of Workington Iron & Steel Co. Ltd in 1910 led to most of future investment being in the adjoining Moss Bay and Derwent works, with their progressively closer working and virtual integration from 1934.
After cessation in 1981 of production of iron and steel, the rail rolling mills continue to operate but using steel from Teesside.

In general, substantial production of pig iron was achieved by circa 1880, with Cleator Moor, Harrington, Distington, Moss Bay and Derwent works continuing into the 20th centuary and only the progressively merging Moss Bay and Derwent works surviving effectively beyond 1920. These were the two iron *and steel* works in West Cumberland (apart from limited production at one works mentioned below) and have rolled steel rails ever since 1877-83 period.

2) Those works located north of the river Derwent, being those most likely to import coke from the Durham coalfield by way of Carlisle:

TITLE	FIRST PRODUCTION	SUBSTANTIALLY ENLARGED	DECLINE COMMENCED	FINAL DEMISE
Oldside (Workington)	1841	1879-80	progressive	1930
West Cumberland (Workington)	1862	1862-72 1899	1885	1900 *Steel from 1870 -72 until demise*
Lowther (Workington)	1873	1873-82	1897-1905	1911
Maryport	1868	1868-82	1883	1892
Solway (at Maryport)	1871	1871-72	1921	1927 (or earlier)

Right: This table details coke conveyed by rail from collieries in NE England to West Cumberland. It opens in the high-production period (1888-89), when the all-time peak of 1881-82 in West Cumberland iron and steel industry was most nearly approached. It ignores the substantial tonnages travelling by Stainmore and Tebay to Carnforth and Furness ironworks.

When examining the table on the right it is interesting to note that the figures for 1892-93 are curtailed by the coal strike of 1892 but increased by traffic diversion from the Furness Railway for some months after the subsidence disaster at Lindal of October 1892. Numbers of trains quoted (daily average) assume that during the period covered by the table the traffic via Keswick was usually made up by the NER/LNER in 'double loads'. The use of two NER locomotives on each train of coke, with corresponding balancing workings, as between Kirkby Stephen and Cockermouth, is the pattern generally recalled or passed down the generations. The figures have been deduced from the tonnages but are also supported by spot-checking of working timetables.

It is also interesting to observe that the tonnage routed via Carlisle was usually double that sent via Keswick between the mid-1880s and 1902. the ratio moving to three and four times and by 1911-13 to more like 10 times. There was a temporary recovery in Keswick route traffic during the war of 1914-18 and for a year or two afterwards. The Keswick traffic (via the Redhills link) became intermittent and ended in 1926. However, there is evidence of a revival in 1928-29; McGowan Gradon referred to reversal at Penrith in 1928 and D.S.Barrie photographed a double-headed coke train near Eamont Junction in, seemingly, 1929.

Coking of coal at West Cumberland sites for use in the district's iron industry only commenced on a significant scale about 1908, but it quickly became the policy of the Workington Iron & Steel Co. Ltd., from its formation in 1909-10, to be self-sufficient in coke from plants at selected collieries in West Cumberland and from batteries of ovens at the integrated iron and steel works at Moss Bay/Derwent, from 1936: this was the factor which finally killed the traffic.

YEAR	TONNAGE VIA KESWICK	NUMBER OF TRAINS DAILY VIA KESWICK (Approximately)	TONNAGE VIA CARLISLE
1887-89	228,436*	4	483,510*
1890-94	185,173*	3-4	323,272*
1895-99	200,853*	4	397,620*
1900	219,334	4 (+1conditional)	462,616
1901	192,388	3	422,262
1902	201,622	3	450,861
1903	156,779	2	438,880
1904	133,753	2	411,362
1905	109,262	2	489,658
1906	121,603	2	552,976
1907	123,818	2	589,730
1908	96,207	1 - 2	384,668
1909	116,482	2	389,079
1910	74,489	1	385,523
1911	20,852	1	232,624
1912	17,541	1 (and not daily)	165,549
1913	16,422	1 (conditional)	215,656
1914	27,088	1	110,765
1915	61,440	1 - 2	147,388
1916	93,116	2	196,736
1917	74,637	1 - 2	290,424
1918	111,935	2 (alt: 1 + 2 Cond.)	289,087
1920		2	
1921		1 (+ 1 conditional)	
1922		1 (+ 1 conditional)	
1925		2 (conditional)	
Indicates yearly averages during 1887-1899			

Routing of block trains of coke from the North East.

While the accompanying table and notes give a good indication of the scale of the coke traffic which passed over the CKPR from the 1880s until the traffic faded away in the early and mid-1920s, the question of how this traffic was handled west of Cockermouth is obscure. The LNWR clearly treated this as 'trip' working and did not include it in its working timetables. The Company would have an incentive to run, using its own locomotives and train crews, via Derwent Junction through to the ironworks, but there are indications that the 'johnny-come-lately' Cleator &

Workington Junction Railway contrived to take over much of the coke at Workington Bridge and run it over its own metals to Harrington Junction and thence by its branch lines to Moss Bay and Derwent Works, as well as over the length of the CWJR 'main line' to Cleator Moor works. In addition, some of the coke coming via Carlisle and the MCR was probably routed via Linefoot to Harrington Junction.

GOODS TRAINS ON THE KESWICK ROUTE

Basic freight services in the 20th century, including early LMS days

The importance of the CKPR route for through conveyance of coke between West Durham and West Cumberland - and some balancing eastward movement of iron ore and pig iron - has already been discussed.

Beyond these traffics, there was, in general, little use in peacetime of the route for through transit and no services which could be styled express goods trains. The LNWR term 'fast goods' was misnomer when applied to a CKPR working, one might kindly say that it was relative rather than definitive!

From the LNWR/CKPR of the early 20th century to the combined LMS of the 1920s, the pattern of freight trains was remarkably constant, and can be summarised thus:

Up direction, Cockermouth-Keswick-Penrith

1. Morning goods, originating at Cockermouth Yard and leaving the Junction at 9.40am (1906), 10.25am (1918), 9.20 (1921), 9.55am (1925) and bound, with many calls, for Penrith, where it was due variously, between 12.55pm and 2.35pm, according to the schedule in force. Arrival intermediately at Keswick ranged between 10.50am and 12.5pm but the stay there was never booked (in tables studied) to exceed 20min, implying that traffic collected there had already been assembled and placed ready for attachment.
2. Mid-day 'fast goods' from Workington, leaving or passing the 'Main' station at 12.00 noon to 2.55pm (timings varying down the years) and making calls through to Penrith, due 4.20pm in early century, but by 1914 (et seq) terminating at Keswick, around 4.30 -5.30pm. Among calls, that at Cockermouth Junction (and Yard) was usually allowed about one hour.
3. Early evening local goods train from Keswick (or Threlkeld) to Penrith, with intermediate calls. Until at least 1918, the light engine (or engine and van) left Keswick at 5.55pm (6.40pm by 1918) for Threlkeld and the goods was booked to start at Threlkeld at 6.20pm (7.7pm by 1918) for Penrith (due 7.45pm). In 1921, and into LMS days, the goods officially originated at Keswick (at 6.00pm) with calls to Penrith (due around 7.40 pm).

There were also workings which, while booked daily, were clearly provided to offer relief from overloading of those already tabulated, namely:-

1) From 1914, or rather earlier, a 'teatime' goods was booked from Threlkeld (departing variously at 4.40pm, 4.45pm and 4.50pm) to Penrith (due 6.00pm or thereabouts). Note that by 1921 onwards, the early evening goods was starting with a load from Keswick - as, one suspects, it may well have done informally even before that - and barely pausing at Threlkeld. Nevertheless, in the 1920s and in the earlier 1930s, there were periods when Threlkeld quarries loaded the available 18in goods ('Cauliflower')

0-6-0 engine to its maximum of about 11 wagons of granite for the climb from Threlkeld to Troutbeck. Alternatively, the locomotive would often make two trips with loads up the bank to Troutbeck, finally assembling its train there for the onward run to Penrith.

2) In the last year (1918) of the war, a 'mineral train' was booked from Workington at 9.25am, with a conditional call at Close Quarry Siding and brief stops at Bassenthwaite Lake and Keswick, to Redhills Junction and onwards, evidently using the NER Redhills cut-off, to reach Ingleton. While this train could have continued to a destination on the Midland Railway, it could also have connection with Ingleton Quarries or the New Ingleton Colliery, the latter developing, with rail connection, from about 1912 and operating until 1925.

3) In the 1920s, a 10.50am Workington-Keswick (due 2.6pm) goods appears, calling at Brigham (for 30min), Cockermouth Junction (one hour) and briefly onwards, including Close Quarry Siding.

Some of the Monday and Saturday times differed from those listed here, but the 'pattern' was little different.

Down direction, Penrith-Keswick-Cockermouth.

1. 'The mail': This was the early goods, leaving Penrith at times between 5.30am and 5.45am, for Cockermouth Junction (reached variously between 8.38am and 9.15am) and conveying mails as far as Keswick. Many of its calls were brief but it spent about an hour at Keswick, detaching a van containing newspapers, and wagonload traffic, also goods for early delivery around the town and environs, while empties were placed by the engine, ready for an Up working.
2. 'The Keswick goods': the mid-morning local goods, leaving Penrith Yard at between 10.40am and 11.15am and due into Keswick between 1.0pm and 1.20pm, with fairly brief roadside calls except at Threlkeld. Typically, a half-hour was allowed here for traffic purposes, although this was liable to be extended on Saturdays to enable the engine and guard to take the quarry-workers' passenger train from Threlkeld to Keswick, and return 'light' to complete their duties before continuing with the goods to Keswick. This goods train was scheduled to call at Briery Siding to attach and detach traffic, at dates as far apart as 1906 and 1925, although in 1914 that service was performed by the preceding NER mineral train.
3. The afternoon Keswick goods and its onward connection westward; in 1906, this was a through working, at 5.20 pm ex-Penrith, to Cockermouth Goods (due 8.40pm), with calls on the road, including 6.55pm - 7.20pm at Keswick. In the years 1914-18 it left Penrith about 3.40pm or 3.55pm, but the departure time crept forward over the years, to 2.40pm by 1925. The intermediate calls progressively lengthened and booked arrival at Keswick fell back progressively from 5.15pm towards 5.40pm. The onwards goods train left Keswick at times between 6.45pm and 7.50pm and made various calls to Cockermouth Junction, inclusive, then ran fast to Workington, due between 9.0pm and 9.30pm, or thereabouts. In 1921, maybe generally, it was the train used to convey coal for Cockermouth line stations west of Keswick.

By early LMS days an additional service was scheduled at 3.8pm daily, from Keswick to Workington (5.40pm), with traffic calls which included about 30min at both Cockermouth Junction and Brigham.

Subsidiary freight services for the same period

On the CKPR line proper, the odd 'short' working was run from Keswick to Threlkeld and/or Troutbeck, for example, the 2.15pm Troutbeck goods was booked daily for many years in the period 1914-25 (at least), also 'conditional' trips. Calls at Briery Siding by the Down goods or mineral trains have already been mentioned, but additionally, 'trip' workings from Keswick to the Siding and back have also been recalled.

At the western end, on the CWR line, the Monday cattle market at Cockermouth was a great source of traffic; note the extensive cattle pen facilities provided adjoining Cockermouth passenger station. The MCR's link at Brigham to such places as Aspatria and Wigton and its running powers to and from Cockermouth produced both general goods and livestock traffic, with Mondays the busiest day by far. There was clear cause for congestion on the single line between Cockermouth Junction and the passenger station, which was also traversed by MCR passenger shuttle trains, as well as the basic Workington-Keswick passenger and freight service, not forgetting the fluctuating pattern of NER through mineral working.

There were typically two early morning trains from Workington to Cockermouth Goods, one being a mineral train from Derwent Iron Works, whilst on Mondays, cattle trains had to run from Workington to Cockermouth passenger station and its yard. In early century, a 'mixed; train ran from Moor Row by the Joint Line to Marron Junction and was liable to be combined there with the 8.10am goods from Workington, which thus conveyed passengers and freight onwards. Accordingly, it had to run through to Cockermouth passenger station. In the same period, the Down working of the goods and mineral train from Cockermouth Goods to Workington was at 11.0am and it had to detach coke (doubtless derived via the NER and CKPR from Durham) at Marron Junction for the LNWR's 11.25am mineral duty to Ullock and Distington Iron Works. Clearly, the LNWR was maintaining its connection with Distington Works, against potential competition from the newer route created by the CWJR. Another working by the (former) LNWR/FR Joint Line was evident in 1925; this was 7.40am MO express goods from Drigg (Furness line) to Cockermouth Passenger (due 10.50am), with return at 4.7pm MO Cockermouth Passenger-Drigg, angled at cattle traffic from/to Egremont and neighbourhood.

Papcastle quarry was served by a shuttle working from Brigham, formed by the engine and brake of an Up CWR goods, a member of Brigham station staff accompanying the trip. The working continued nearly to the end of the LMS era. In earlier times, a mineral train was run as required at 9.55am from Workington to Papcastle, returning at 12.35pm from Papcastle.

A relic of early CWR days survived (just) in 1906, when the 'conditional' train from Papcastle to Workington was booked at Marron Junction from 1.48pm to 3.10pm. It shunted at Lowther Pit from 2.0pm to 2.55pm, but this had declined with the fading fortunes of the pit, by 1914.

William Pit Sidings, between Workington Bridge and Camerton stations, provided the junction and exchange point for the colliery branch line, worked by the Allerdale Coal Company's locomotives. This signal box figured in calls between Cockermouth and Workington, also in a specific 'trip' working from/to Workington. The pit dated from the 1880s and produced traffic until 1959, with subsequent dismantling of the colliery and branch line in 1961.

One may also mention traffic between the Joint Line and Workington via Marron Junction and Derwent Junction, associated with the many private sidings and branch lines served - the output of iron ore mines being for many years the main source of traffic from the Joint Line's territory. A latter-day traffic was limestone from the United Steel Companies' Rowrah Hall quarries, routed via Marron to the iron and steel works at Moss Bay. This operated from August 1938 until (probably) November 1953, when the old Joint route effectively ceased to be used - apart from the northward passage on September 5 1954 of the 'West Cumberland Rail Tour' train of the Stephenson Locomotive Society and the Manchester Locomotive Society.

Freight in later times

The disappearance of the Durham-West Cumberland coke traffic, which essentially ended in 1926, has been described. The 'great depression' of the early 1930s, following the Wall Street financial 'crash' of 1929, was particularly severe in West Cumberland and caused the final demise of much long-established industry. This was obviously detrimental to traffic associated with Maryport and Workington and their immediate hinterland. The former 'Joint Line' declined with its industries and with the developing hold of motor traffic on goods and livestock movements. The Bullgill-Brigham (formerly MCR) line closed from April 29 1935, finally ending the Monday mornings of bustle at Cockermouth passenger station and its cattle sidings.

However, the LMS did its best and kept up much of the 'traditional' pattern of freight on the CKPR route, helped by virtual removal of competition in the war years from 1939 to 1945 and for a very few years afterwards. ASLEF (the footplatemens trade union) called its incredibly foolhardy strike from May 29 to June 14 1955 with the result that many freight and mineral traffics were lost for ever by the railways. BR's Modernisation Plan of March 1955 received close scrutiny and generally favourable endorsement from a powerful parliamentary committee. However, the Macmillan government chose to ignore this and appointed Richard Beeching and Ivan Stedteford from outside industry to make a quite different appraisal. From this emerged the infamous 'Beeching plan' of 1963, and the subsequent decision wilfully to throw to the wolves almost all of BR's then still extensive freight traffic - an objective achieved with great rapidity. The CKPR stations at that time retaining layout, accommodation and staff for handling freight traffic were: Brigham, Cockermouth Goods, Bassenthwaite Lake, Braithwaite, Keswick, Threlkeld, Troutbeck, Penruddock and Blencow. Goods facilities were withdrawn from all stations at a stroke, with effect from June 1 1964. Only Flusco and Blencowe quarries, at the eastern end of the line, retained connections through which to despatch stone by rail - until June 16 1972.

The years 1952-55 may be said to represent the final era of post-war freight working, before disaster overtook it. The basic provisions of that period on the Keswick route comprised:

UP

7.25am: Daily, (becoming 7.18am) Workington-Cockermouth Junction (8.0am) and Yard.
9.25am: Cockermouth Junction-Penrith Goods, due 2.20pm (later 1,5pm) with calls including Keswick (10.47am-11.26am), Threlkeld (11.38am-11.52am), Penruddock

(12.15pm-12.55pm), Blencow (1.7pm-2.5pm in 1952, but omitted by 1955).

1.5pm: SX Workington-Keswick goods, due 4.52pm, with calls.

5.l5pm: Daily (4.55pm SX by 1955), Keswick-Penrith goods, due at 6.48 pm (due 6.15pm, SX by 1955), with only a few calls.

DOWN

6.10am: SX Penrith-Cockermouth Junction 'goods and mails', due 8.46am, with various brief calls but typically at Keswick 7.1am-7.54am. On SO in 1952, it ran only between Keswick and Cockermouth, in the same times, with no mails conveyed - and in 1955 it ran daily throughout from Penrith, but no mails are mentioned.

l.51pm: Daily (SX by 1955) Penrith-Keswick goods, due 4.22pm, with calls.

6.25pm: SX (6.14pm SX by 1955) Keswick-Workington goods, with some calls.

Thus, taking account also of the 11.44am (see below) there were effectively two goods workings each way over the whole route, to be compared with, in general, three in times past. Subsidiary workings of 1952-55 were:

9.0am: Cockermouth Junction-Cockermouth Passenger goods train.

9.45am: Cockermouth Passenger-Cockermouth Junction, calling Gas Works Siding, 9.48am-10.00am

11.44am: Cockermouth Junction-Workington, due at 1.13pm, with calls including William Pit (and it was preced-ed by a 'trip' working, William Pit-Workington). NB: The Pit closed in March 1959

Two afternoon SX 'conditional' workings (one for 1955) for engine and brake, Workington-Cockermouth passenger station, were balanced by conditional freight paths at 4.0pm (not in 1955) and 5.16pm from Cockermouth Passenger station to Workington Dock and Maryport (Workington Main by 1955).

The junction for the 'Joint Line' figured with one trip (SX) in September 1952 (vanished by 1955), namely Workington 2.55pm to Marron Junction, due 3.35pm - with empties, calling William Pit Sidings. Its return was from Marron Junction (3.45pm) to Workington (due 4.20pm) calling once more at William Pit Sidings.

At the eastern end, the continued significant stone traffic from the private quarry connections at Blencow and Flusco called for a 'trip' working, namely 10.42am daily (10.37am in 1955) from Penrith to Blencow (11.00am-11.45am) - Flusco Siding (due 11.50am), returning at 12.32pm to Penrith (booked arrival 1.20pm).

Below: On July 26 1963, a Keswick-Penrith goods train including sheeted limestone wagons, drifts down the gradient off the CKPR line near No.1 signalbox, converging directly to the Down WCML, bound for Penrith yard. *Derek Cross.*

Chapter 4:

PASSENGER TRAFFIC

Above: A sylvan setting near Keswick, in May 1936, as a 'Cauliflower' 0-6-0 steams through the countryside with an Up passenger train.
Locomotive & General Railway Photographs.

PASSENGER TRAINS: THE COCKERMOUTH & WORKINGTON RAILWAY, 1847-1866

The passenger trains introduced between Cockermouth and Workington (8 1/2 miles), from April 28 1847, assumed a fairly logical pattern by the end of that summer:

Cockermouth: depart for Workington: 6.55am, 10.10am, 2.10pm, 5.50pm, 6.30pm.
Workington: depart for Cockermouth: 8.10am, 10.55am, 2.55pm, 6.35pm, 7.30pm.

Thus, there were five trips each way on weekdays with four each way on Sundays. Calls were at Brigham, Broughton and Camerton and the fare throughout was 1/6, 1/- and 8d for first, second and third class single tickets. Clearly, one passenger engine and set of carriages could cover this timetable.

In 1850, weekdays trains were (seemingly) unbalanced, with four advertised from Cockermouth but six out of Workington. However, the timings still permitted operation by one engine - and maybe one train crew, bearing in mind the long working hours of those days on a rural railway. The Sunday service had been reduced by this time to two trains each way. Fares had risen to 1/8, 1/2 and 8 1/2d, for the respective first, second and third Class rates.

By 1855, there were five advertised trips in each direction, with two trips on Sundays, and one locomotive could work them all. In January 1855, the working day extended from 7.20am from Cockermouth, until the final arrival back at 9.15pm. By August, the day was curtailed to 8.0am-9.15pm.

In 1856, it was remarked deprecatingly at a Board meeting that the Company's carriage accommodation was insufficient and "the practice of carrying passengers in trucks is dangerous." It was not stated whether this referred to passengers riding on the goods train, or to the reinforcing of passenger trains by the attachment of goods vehicles. However, the Company's stock remained at eight carriages (two first, two second and four third class vehicles, all four-wheeled) through to 1864; in that year £375 was spent on a new (replacement?) carriage from builders Brown Marshall & Company. In 1865, the same company secured an order, at £379.10.0, for a composite carriage with two central first class compartments and a second class compartment at each end.

From August 25 1857, the service was reduced, but the January 1860 timetable shows overall times of operation from 7.0am ex-Cockermouth until 9.35pm at night, with five trains each way. The situation was much the same in August 1860, apart from returning one hour earlier with the last train from Workington to Cockermouth, arriving at 8.30pm, with three trains on Sundays.

The CWR operated a through engine working to Whitehaven as early as 1852. Commencing in the spring of 1858, a Whitehaven Junction Railway engine and carriages ran through to Cockermouth from Whitehaven at 8.15am, returning at 9.50am from Cockermouth to Whitehaven. A

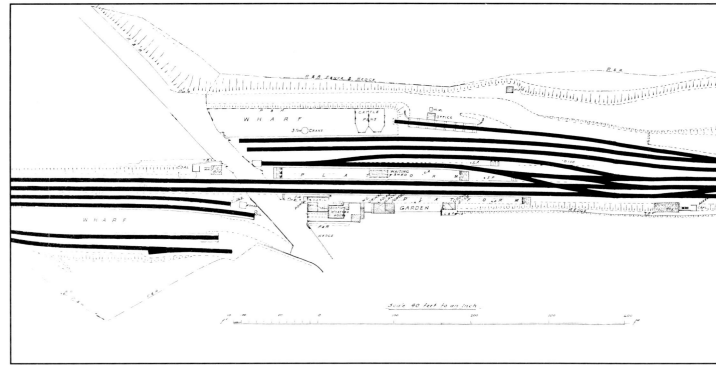

Right: The CKPR winter passenger timetable of January 1885, 20 years after the opening of the line.

WORKINGTON	(dep)	6.25am	8.15am MO	8.30am	10.52am	3.8pm	5.40pm	8.24pm	9.40pm
COCKERMOUTH	(arr)	6.48am	8.45am MO	9.0am	11.19am	3.38pm	6.10pm	8.52pm	10.8pm
"	(dep)	6.55am		9.10am	11.22am	3.40pm	6.15pm		
KESWICK	(dep)	7.30am		9.45am	11.55am	4.12pm	6.55pm		
PENRITH	(arr)	8.20am		10.35am	12.45pm	5.0pm	8.0 pm		

PENRITH	(dep)	6.30am		9.55am		1.40pm	5.30pm	7.20pm
KESWICK		7.45am		10.43am		2.30pm	6.15pm	8.10pm
COCKERMOUTH	(arr)	8.19am		11.13am		3.0 pm	6.42pm	8.40pm
COCKERMOUTH	(dep)	8.48am	10.15am	11.14am	1.55pm MO	3.5 pm	6.45pm	8.45pm
WORKINGTON	(arr)	9.11am	10.42am	11.41am	2.35pm MO	3.33pm	7.13pm	9.13pm

4.00pm and 6.25pm, all except the first running through from Whitehaven. In the Down direction, departures from Penrith were at: 7.45am, 9.55am, 1.30pm, 2.30pm and 7.00pm - again, five advertised, all running to Workington, indeed four through to Whitehaven. By summer 1877, two significant changes had emerged: the 5.30am 'mixed' from Penrith to Cockermouth (with connecting passenger service to Whitehaven) was acknowledged as such, whilst the 2.30pm ex-Penrith had been retimed to leave, probably more helpfully, at 5.10pm. By summer 1885, the 5.30am Down admitted to being 'mixed', the 5.10pm Down service ran at 5.45pm and the 7.00pm Down at 7.20pm.

The coming of through carriages, from 1886.

During the 1870s, the CKPR Board received complaints about delays and other problems involved in changing trains at Penrith. Eventually, in August 1879, the Directors asked the LNWR to operate through passenger carriages, also a luggage van, for the carriage of holiday-makers' heavy trunks, cumbersome hat boxes, and other bulky possessions. They suggested running through vehicles on the 10.00am train from Euston, for the CKPR to convey to Keswick and Cockermouth, with a balancing working by the midday connection, for London. The LNWR response was to provide a better southbound *connection* with effect

from July 1 1880; the 12.55pm from Carlisle (the 1.25pm from Penrith) seemingly an Up train for Manchester and Liverpool, would be extended to London, with arrival due at 8.30pm. George Findlay wrote to say that his Board did not wish to provide through carriages to and from the CKPR. Other improved *connections* were however introduced about this time. From June 1 1880, a daily summer service of trains was run between the MR's station at Appleby and Penrith, using the NER Eden Valley Railway route and timed to connect with the CKPR trains. The Keswick Company had been seeking through bookings between their line and the MR by this link and presumably the bookings were introduced at this time. The LNWR also provided additional trains from Penrith to Carlisle in the mid-morning period, with a return working towards 5.00pm, timed in conjunction with convenient CKPR trains.

More discussion followed. The CKPR asked the NER and the MR about through carriages and Manager Peter Thompson met G.P. Neele (around July 1880), when the LNWR Superintendent expressed himself in favour of through vehicles. However, he shortly retracted, doubtless overruled either by his General Manager or the LNWR Board. Pressure was maintained by the determined CKPR Board and, at last, in March 1886, came inklings that the LNWR proposed changes in the passenger service from June 1 1886.

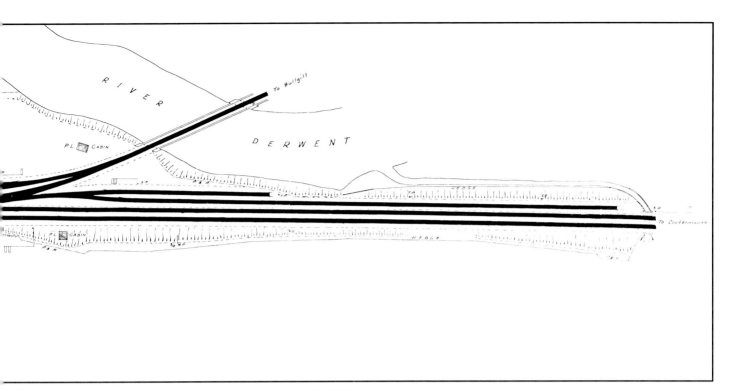

Above: Brigham level crossing and station are shown on this LMS plan, with two signalboxes still in use: No. 1 is to the east (opposite the junction) and No. 2 is westerly, by the level crossing. Note the MCR back platform road and loop, on the north side of the passenger station, also the MCR Derwent branch to Bullgill, with the bridge which collapsed on December 16 1936.

The timetable for the period July-September 1886 included extra trains:

9.20am Penrith-Keswick
11.00am Keswick-Penrith,

The CKPR had won the argument, at least for a trial period, for the 11.0am from Keswick was actually a through train to Euston, due to arrive in the capital about 7.0pm, "to run as an experiment during those months, at an extra payment to the LNWR of 6d per mile." In the corresponding months of 1887, the LNWR ran a 9.18am Penrith-Keswick service (described as a"a short train") and an 11.0am Keswick-Euston ("an express"). Between July and September 1888, additional trains comprised: 9.18am Penrith-Keswick and 12.50pm Keswick-Penrith, while the 11.20am ex-Cockermouth was run as a through express, between Keswick and Euston,where it was booked to arrive at 8.00pm; presumably the through carriages were attached at Keswick. Once again, the CKPR paid 6d per mile extra.

The through carriages officially advertised from Keswick during the high summer months of 1886-88 were in the Up direction (to Euston) and in the last of these years (1888) were seemingly associated with a service (also with through carriages from Keswick?) due to arrive at Manchester Exchange (via Hindley Curve) at 3.40pm. The corresponding Down main line timetables show an express leaving Euston at 10.30am (1886 and 1887) and 10.40am (1888) and nominally terminating at Penrith at 5.40pm, 5.45pm and 5.35pm, in the successive years. Departure for Keswick and the CKPR line was 10-15 minutes later - thus hinting strongly at through Down workings.

In 1888, the same Down main line service gave excellent times from, alternatively, Manchester Exchange (2.25pm) and Manchester Victoria (2.35pm); it is thus possible that both Up and Down through carriages connected Keswick with Manchester in the summer of 1888.

Encouraged by the developments of 1886-88, in early in 1889 the CKPR Board proposed a revision of their original 1864 working agreement with the LNWR, in order to develop traffic. The original agreement called for payment of 33 1/3% of coaching receipts, in return for which the LNWR provided a basic service of three trains each way daily. The Keswick Company now proposed to pay 35% - but to fix the number of trains operated. The resulting new agreement (January 31 1889) provided for 35% payment (and not less than 1/- per train mile for goods and passenger trains combined) but with 'the number limited as before *but by mutual agreement'*. Presumably, this drafting was intentionally vague.

Thus, after 25 years of working experience, the pattern of summertime operation on the Keswick road was taking a rather more evolutionary and enterprising shape.

PASSENGER TRAINS OF THE CKPR IN ITS DAYS OF MATURITY, 1890-1922

Basic services

The winter service of January 1885 has already been outlined. The basic pattern of five trains each way over the CKPR during 'out of season' months continued for some 15 further years. During the 1890s, the last Down train's departure time from Penrith was helpfully put back by about an hour - to around 8.25pm. From the early 1900s, there was also a strengthening of the basic service to six trains each each way. This continued until 1917-18, when wartime stringencies forced a reduction of the service to five trains in each direction, further reduced to four trains each way from April 1918.

SUMMER SERVICES; 1892					Express	SO					$ Thu SO
WORKINGTON (Dep):	6.42am	8.27am	9.12am	10.41am	11.51am	1.35pm	2.55pm		5.30pm		
COCKERMOUTH (arr)	7.01am	8.55am	9.29am	1108am	12.08pm	2.00pm	3.22pm		5.58pm		
COCKERMOUTH (dep)	7.02am		9.30am	11.10am	12.10pm	2.08pm	3.25pm		6.00pm		
KESWICK	7.30am		10.00am*	11.40am	12.35*pm	2.55pm	3.55pm	4.50pm $	6.30pm	7.10pm	8.15pm
PENRITH (arr)	8.20am		10.45am	12.30pm	1.15pm		4.45pm	5.33pm		7.57pm	8.57pm

	SX	SO
WORKINGTON (Dep)	8.7pm	10.12pm
COCKERMOUTH	8.33pm	10.40pm

					ThuSO$		SO	Express**		
PENRITH (Dep):	7.30am	9.20am		1.15pm	1.55pm	2.50pm		5.45pm	6.20pm	8.25pm
KESWICK	8.15am	10.0 am		2.0 pm	2.40pm	3.35pm	5.55pm	6.25pm	7.10pm	9.10pm
COCKERMOUTH					**					
(arr)	8.45am	10.33am MO		2.32pm			6.25pm	6.55pm	7.43pm	9.42pm
COCKERMOUTH										
(dep) 7.40am	8.48am	10.34am	1.50am	2.34am			6.27pm	6.57pm	7.46pm	9.45pm
Workington (arr) 8.8 am	9.13am	10.58am	2.17pm	2.59pm			6.49pm	7.19pm	8.12pm	10.2 pm

* Through carriages left Keswick at 10.0am for Euston (due 6.10pm) and for Manchester Exchange (due 2.0pm); also Keswick 12.35 pm for Euston (due 8.40pm).

** The first portion (from Preston) of the 10.40am Euston-Carlisle conveyed through carriages from Euston to Keswick, also from Manchester Exchange (dep.2.30pm) to Keswick - the Keswick vehicles from both London and Manchester being attached to the 5.45pm express over the CKPR, from Penrith.

$ indicates through trains between Keswick and Carlisle or vice versa.

Most trains shown above from and to Workington came through from, or ran to, Whitehaven at this period.
There was a passenger train into Cockermouth at 8.40am MO, which came from Whitehaven via Moor Row, Rowrah and the direct eastern curve at Marron Junction. Return was at 3.30pm MO from Cockermouth to Rowrah.
On the CKPR, there were two trains each way on Sundays.

Around this time, 'colliers trains' were running, departing at 5.00am from Workington to William Pit Siding and leaving William Pit Siding for Workington at 5.50am. There was also a 1.5pm SX Workington-William Pit Siding (on SO it ran as 1.5pm Workington-Cockermouth passenger). 'workmen's trains' ran: 8.55pm Workington-Cockermouth and 9.40pm Cockermouth-Workington, also Sundays, 5.15am Cockermouth-Workington - and 5.35am Workington-Cockermouth passenger. Keswick offered a quarry workers' train at 7.05am to Threlkeld, with a return working from Threlkeld at 5.40pm SX (l2.45pm SO).

The MCR ran several passenger daily services between Cockermouth via Brigham (reverse) and the Derwent Branch, thence to Bullgill. West of Cockermouth, it is interesting to note three trains daily from Whitehaven to Workington by 'the long way round' via Cleator Moor, the Joint Line and Marron Junction (taking 1hr 15min to 1hr 21min). Southbound over the Joint Line there were two trains:

1)7.50am ex Workington
2)The interesting 3.20pm ex-Cockermouth, which reversed at Marron Junction (3.33-3.38pm). By this time, the direct east-south chord at Marron had been severed.

A basic six trains (each way) were reinstated after the war and this was the pattern in both1921 and 1922, as the CKPR's days of 'independence' ran out. No evidence has been found of 'mixed' trains in the period from the 1890s onward.

The MCR showed modest enterprise in the period discussed. Its 'Derwent Branch' from Bullgill to Brigham, which linked the MCR main line with the CWR, had been opened during 1867 (just after the CWR became part of the LNWR,) and from November 1 1867 they were to run to Cockermouth passenger station, exercising running powers under an agreement with the LNWR and CKPR, concluded at Euston on October 17 1867. They duly ran passenger trains (which reversed at Brigham) to Cockermouth on weekdays. In Spring 1920, the Company arranged to run a Sunday train from Carlisle to Cockermouth and return, with its own engine and carriages. The MCR wished to run forward to Keswick on Sundays, but the LNWR declined either to permit this, or to do it themselves. On weekdays from 1919 the MCR had been allowed to run empty stock between Cockermouth and Keswick in order to form a 9.45am passenger service from Keswick to Cockermouth and the MCR line. By November 1920, the MCR engine and carriage was enabled to convey passengers into Keswick (at 8.48am) and out again, the jealous guardians at (Euston) of the CKPR justifying their 'concession' as a help to children from Cockermouth travelling to Keswick School. The single to-and-fro working continued during 1921-22 and by Spring 1922 had been joined by a 'teatime' working, due into Keswick at 6.05pm and out again at 6.30pm, to the MCR. Cecil J. Allen (in *The Railway Magazine* of 1921) recorded the 9.45am ex-Keswick as comprising a single LNWR corridor composite coach, lettered 'on loan to Maryport and Carlisle Railway' and running through to Carlisle all year round. Its locomotive was provided by the MCR.

In summer season

Summer services (primarily July-September) continued to produce interesting changes and improvements during the period 1890-1914. The version for 1892 is shown in the table below. During the 1890s, the summer pattern of passenger services on the line continued to provide:

1) Five Up passenger trains daily over the full length of the CKPR , also one Up service from the west, terminating at Keswick. Two trains started from Keswick to proceed eastward.

2) Six Down services from Penrith over the CKPR, plus one other which ran from Penrith to Keswick.

In simple terms, the service could be summarised as providing 6 1/2 trains each way!

From 1900, the CKPR service was developed to seven trains each way in Summer. An extra working in and out of Keswick from/to Workington raised the figure to 7 1/2 each way from 1903. From January 1904, by agreement with LNWR Superintendent of the Line Robert Turnbull, day return tickets were issued on one day weekly from Cockermouth (11/-) and Keswick (10/-) to Liverpool and Manchester in order to encourage out-and-back travel. There were also tentative experiments with residential travel, which had been a successful feature of the Windermere line since 1875. An experiment in summer 1902 with a Keswick-Manchester (and Liverpool) train (departing at about 7.15am MO) was however a dismal failure and in May 1906 Mr. Turnbull told the CKPR Board that there was no thought of repeating it - although, in 1910-11, a 7.10am MO Keswick-Oxenholme was tried, connecting with the Windermere-Manchester residential train.

Summer 1906 witnessed further improvement. In the Up direction, there was an additional train at 8.30am (ex-Workington) due into Penrith 10.25am, but no 'short' workings on the CKPR proper; thus, there were eight Up trains. In the Down direction, there were seven through trains, with a further train running only as far as Keswick, and another which started there. Thus, effectively there were eight down services. The summers of 1907-09 were served very similarly.

During the summers of 1910-14, the level of service was the equivalent of nine Up and '8 1/2' Down, eight trains each way actually running over the whole of the CKPR, the remainder representing workings on the eastern (Keswick-Penrith) portion of the line only.

There were some Keswick-Penrith-Carlisle through workings. However, the long-range through carriages were mainly between Keswick and Euston (tending, as time passed, to run from Whitehaven or Workington, via Keswick, to Euston, and return). In 1898, they were seemingly included in the 9.45am Up train from Keswick (arrive Euston 6.00pm) and the1.30pm Up service (arr Euston 9.20pm). The first of these services, on the LNWR main line, was styled the 'Keswick and Windermere Express' whilst the second was titled 'Lakes Express', a name which became very familiar indeed much later. The same year, through carriages ran to Keswick in the 10.25am departure from Euston, a train grandly known as the 'Cambrian, Central Wales and English Lakes Express'; departure was at 5.3pm from Penrith, due into Keswick at 5.50pm. It is not clear whether Manchester-Keswick through carriages were run at this time.

By 1905, the London carriages were included in the 9.00am Up train from Keswick. In 1906, the favoured train was the 9.00am Up service (arr Euston 5.5pm) and probably also the 11.45am Up duty (attached to the Up Perth train, due at Euston at 7.10pm) In the Down direction in 1906, a 10.10am ex-Euston train served Morecambe, the Furness line, Windermere and Keswick; there was a non-stop run from Stafford to Lancaster calling at Penrith (5.4pm-5.10pm, involving reversal), reaching Keswick at 5.55pm.

From Manchester Exchange, the first portion of a 3.3pm departure reached Penrith at 5.37pm and clearly proceeded as the 5.45pm express over the CKPR line, due to arrive at Keswick at 6.28pm. In 1907, the 3.3pm from Manchester Exchange ran to Morecambe, also to the FR line, and not apparently to Keswick. At that time, Keswick had Euston carriages in the 9.0am Up and 1.45pm Up trains, and also had two Down services from Euston - at 10.10am (arr Keswick 5.55pm, as in the previous year) and 11.30am (second portion from Preston, off a Scots express, reaching Keswick at 6.35pm). The same two Up through services operated in 1908, leaving Keswick 9.0am and 1.45pm, and the through vehicles probably came down with the 10.10am and in rear of the 11.30am Scots train, being included in the CKPR's 5.10pm and 5.45pm trains, respectively (from Penrith). In 1909, the two Up workings ran in the same paths. In the Down direction, the through carriages were clearly included in the 5.10pm from Penrith, less clearly in the 5.45pm.

It was the expansion of through carriage workings which stepped-up the summer service from 1910. In this year, Keswick enjoyed the services of Up through carriages to Euston (two services), Manchester Exchange, Manchester Victoria and Liverpool Exchange. Vehicles for Euston were attached at Keswick at 9.0am, for arrival in London at 5.5pm as part of the up 'Keswick and Windermere Express'. The 1.45pm working at Keswick (12.2Opm ex-Whitehaven) conveyed through carriages from Keswick for attachment at Penrith to the 12.0 noon Glasgow/Edinburgh-Euston, due 8.30pm. In addition to the Keswick-Euston 57ft brake tri-composite carriage, there were two vehicles for Manchester Exchange and one for Manchester Victoria; these three were detached at Preston from the same main line express. A 6.5pm departure from Keswick was run to take a through carriage for Liverpool Exchange, which formed part of the 4.30pm Glasgow-Manchester/Liverpool express as between Penrith and Preston.

In the Down direction, the 10.10am Euston-Blackpool and the Lakes conveyed a carriage from London to Keswick and (from Stafford north) through vehicles from Birmingham to Keswick. The 11.30am Down service for Scotland included two carriages for Keswick, coming off at Preston and going north along with through carriages for Keswick from the 2.35pm ex-Manchester Victoria and 2.52pm ex-Liverpool Exchange (as well as London Euston/Manchester Exchange-Windermere through vehicles, to be left behind at Oxenholme). At this time, a move was apparent to develop 'day return' traffic inwards to the Keswick line, as witnessed by an arrival from the south at Penrith at 9.7am, with a 9.30am Penrith-CKPR line train in connection. The 6.5pm train, originating at Keswick and calling only at Troutbeck en route to Penrith, connected into the evening Glasgow-Manchester/Liverpool and (as explained above) two vehicles ran through from Keswick to Liverpool. It is not too clear whether the Liverpool through carriages continued as such in later years but in 1914 the 6.5pm train was specifically advertised as running from Keswick to Preston.

The North Eastern Railway

The NER had been prominent in the development of day excursion trips, via Stainmore, the Eden Valley line and the Eamont-Redhills NER link, to Keswick, with very early starts from Hull, York or Durham colliery districts. An intriguing item in the history of NER coaching stock was their vehicle

No. 104, built in 1896. It was a bogie lavatory composite with four first class and two third class compartments, on record as being intended for a Kings Cross and Penrith service. If this ever ran, it would surely be operated primarily in summer and extended to Keswick. There was a companion vehicle, perhaps intended for a balancing working.

A daily Darlington-Keswick train service ran first, it is believed, in the summer of 1906 and could account for the 11.5am Penrith-Keswick (terminating 11.43am),introduced that year. During following years, the 11.43am ex-Penrith ran through to Whitehaven. In the summers between 1911 and 1914, through carriages operated from York and Newcastle upon Tyne, both via Stainmore to/from Keswick, and would be designed to encourage period ('tourist') return travel.

The Midland Railway

The Midland Railway came into the picture too. From the summer of 1910 - and likewise in 1911 and 1912 - there were through carriages from Leeds to Keswick, in the 10.0am Leeds Midland-Glasgow St Enoch train, which was purposely diverted to run via Ingleton and Penrith. The through vehicles used the new 12.15pm Penrith-Keswick train, terminating at 12.50pm, which was indeed a conveniently-timed tourist service. The new Up express on the CKPR started from Keswick at 12.35pm and included Keswick-Leeds coaches for transfer at Penrith to the 10.30am Edinburgh Waverley-Leeds-St Pancras train, routed via Ingleton. During 1913 and 1914, the MR service in question was somewhat curtailed; it ran four days weekly in high summer (Monday, Tuesday, Friday and Saturday) , at 9.35am from Leeds. The Up working remained around midday - in July 1914, the express started from Keswick at 12.35pm for Leeds. The CKPR favoured restoration of the Leeds-Keswick through workings after the war years but in summer 1920 the LNWR and MR combined to refuse the facility. Note, however, that a Leeds-Keswick summer service was run, via Carnforth, and (in LMS period) it ran each Summer from 1923 to 1926 (inclusive) via the Ingleton route, at first on four days weekly but later on Saturdays only. And there was a revival during the peak period of the Summers 1922-39 (inclusive) on FSO, subsequently moving to SO.

The 1914 peak

In summer 1914, booked through workings from Keswick reached their peak:

1) The 7.10am MO Keswick-Oxenholme connected into the Windermere-Manchester 'club' residential train and was aimed at business men, who might join their families for the weekend before returning to town on Monday morning.

2) The 8.30am from Workington (9.0am ex-Cockermouth; 9.38am ex-Keswick) ran through to Euston (arr 5.7pm).

3) The 8.15am from Whitehaven (9.15 from Cockermouth; 9.52am from Keswick) included through carriages to Carlisle (arr 11.20am)

4) The 12.35pm (Monday, Tuesday, Friday, Saturday) from Keswick was the through express (via Ingleton) to Leeds (arr 4.10pm)

5) The12.20pm from Whitehaven (1.45pm ex-Keswick) may well have conveyed through carriages into the 12.0 noon Glasgow/Edinburgh-Euston (8.30pm), and for Manchester too.

6) The 2.47pm from Workington (3.55pm ex-Keswick) was a through train to Carlisle (arr 5.7pm).

7) The 6.10pm from Keswick was a through train to Preston.

A Down working at 6.45am (MSO) from Manchester Victoria in that summer was seemingly run through to Keswick, where it was booked to arrive at 11.00am. Certainly, the 2.55pm from Manchester Exchange (due to arrive at Keswick at 6.28pm and Whitehaven at 7.58pm) was a through train, with a portion for Windermere, detached en route. There was also the 9.35am service from Leeds (Monday, Tuesday, Friday, Saturday) to Keswick. The Down Euston through service is a little obscure, but Bletchley originated a through carriage at 11.3am for Keswick, leaving Penrith at 5.10pm and reaching its destination at 5.55pm. A portion from Birmingham was probably included in the same main line train. The 5.45pm from Penrith conveyed a Carlisle-Workington carriage.

Wartime Summers, 1914-1918

The wartime summer service on the Keswick road was reduced by 1917 to the five passenger trains operated each way over the CKPR, as in corresponding winters, with no 'short' or long-range passenger workings anywhere between Penrith and Cockermouth. The Cockermouth-Workington line of the LNWR only benefitted from the same five trains, accompanied by the all-year 7.40am train from Cockermouth-Workington and 1.5pm SO Workington-Cockermouth, both intended for such folk as shop workers. There were also the workmens and colliers' trains and the all-year trains to and from the Joint Line, and five MCR trains each way to and from Cockermouth, with extra services on Monday, for the market traffic. From April 1 1918, a further 'squeeze' was apparent.

Latterday summers of the CKPR, 1919-22

In the spring of 1919, there were slight improvements, and during that summer the basic service on the CKPR reverted to six trains each way. In addition, a 10.0am Keswick-Euston through train appeared (to run until the end of September), combining with a Windermere portion and restaurant car at Oxenholme. Down through carriages for Keswick were provided in the 11.15am Euston-Windermere train, these being worked to Penrith and run in the 6.25pm daily CKPR train, from which they were detached at Keswick at 7.8pm.

There was no basic change by the summer of 1921, but the through carriages were run from both Workington and Keswick and ran at 9.15am from Workington (Cockermouth at 9.35am; Keswick 10.10am), so providing a seventh Up train throughout - and they reached Euston at 6.5pm. These coaches probably came down in the 10.40am train from Euston - and were attached to the 6.0pm departure from Penrith to Workington.

There were still no booked Sunday trains at this time, even in summer.

This page: A selection of tickets, illustrating some of the styles employed. The bicycle tickets of 1899 and 1907 were white. The LMS tickets shown are green; the one from Penruddock is dated 17 NO 49 and the 'Tourist' ticket is from early days of the LMS, as witness the style of the serial numbers (as used also on the CKPR.)
Courtesy C.C. Green, G. Lord, Denis R. Perriam, Mrs M. Ridley.

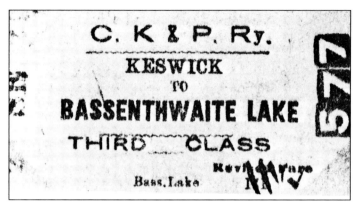

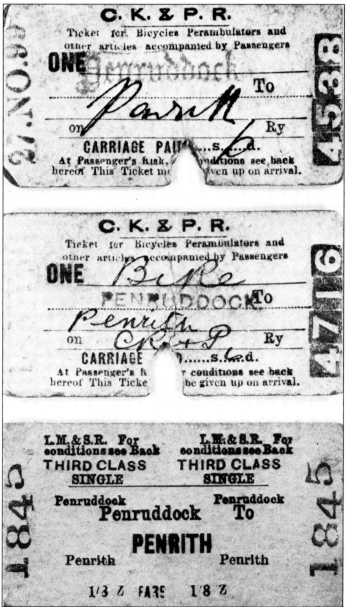

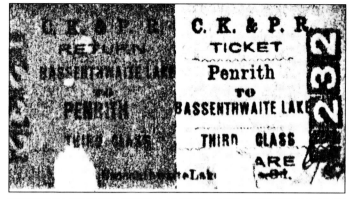

PASSENGER TRAINS IN THE LMS ERA, 1923-1945

Basic Services

The basic service continued at six trains each way (as in much of the 1904-1922 period) through to 1939. Their departure times from Cockermouth (Up) and Penrith (Down) continued to vary a little from year to year but, in general, remained incredibly close to those applying early in the 20th century.

A 'short' working worthy of comment was derived from MCR practice of 1920; it ran into Cockermouth from the west and through to Keswick, where it arrived at 8.47am. Departure was at 10.0am. It then returned at 6.8pm, leaving again at 6.30pm. With variants in some years, these workings conveyed a through carriage from Carlisle (via Bullgill) and Brigham (reverse). This obviously provided a valuable link between Cockermouth and Carlisle. One might doubt whether the same would be true round the western end of Skiddaw mountain barrier. It is revealing to see their value, even from Keswick to Carlisle and back, demonstrated on typical a weekday in 1934:

Outward by 'conventional' route via Penrith and WCML
Keswick: dep 9.39am, due at Carlisle 11.35am - with 50 minutes to wait at Penrith. The alternative was
Keswick: dep 9.56am, due at Carlisle 11.43am - via Brigham, snug in a through carriage!

Returning:
Carlisle: dep 4.35pm, due at Keswick at 7.00pm - with 64 minutes wait at Penrith, or
Carlisle: dep 4.20pm, due at Keswick at 6.09pm - in the through carriage, via Brigham.

In each case, the overall time between Keswick and Carlisle much exceeded that taken by a motor car of 1934 on the roads of that day, but the through carriage by the former MCR's Brigham route was a comfortable corridor

Above: LMS-built non-corridor coaching stock is headed by 'Cauliflower' No. 28589, still lettered 'LMS', climbing away from the WCML at Penrith No.1 box in August 1950 - a scene typical of the 1930s-1950s period. *E.S. Russell.*

Right: With 'express lamps', a 'Cauliflower' (No. 8358, of Workington shed, withdrawn in 1930) and a 'Jumbo' 2-4-0 leave the Up back platform at Keswick in the later 1920s. The LNWR and early LMS-built coaching stock is painted in LMS red livery and a wagon stabled in the bay is fitted with gas containers for recharging the cylinders of gas-lit rolling stock.
Roy Anderson Collection

coach 'cascaded' (in present-day parlance) from former main line duties and the times were not unreasonable. The poor link provided at Penrith in each direction reflects not only the problems of connecting with both Up and Down main line trains, but also the prevailing disregard for the economics of secondary routes such as the CKPR. The former MCR Brigham-Bullgill line closed entirely from April 29 1935; a morning school-time train into Keswick from the west and out again, also a late afternoon trip in and out, were run for a few years at times akin to the 'MCR trips,' but they were from/to Workington and did not provide Keswick with a Carlisle service.

Wartime again curtailed the basic services from six to five each way daily, in the years from 1939 to 1945. Typically,

through Workington-Penrith trains of January 1944 appeared thus on the CKPR section:
Cockermouth: dep for Penrith at 7.12am, 11.27am, 2.38pm, 5.48pm and 6.43pm.
Penrith: dep for Cockermouth at 7.35am, 10.07am, 1.25pm, 4.53pmSX, 6.23pm SO and 8.10pm. and with also:
8.25am Workington-Cockermouth (arr 8.52am)
11.50am SO Workington-Keswick (arr 12.45)
8.55pm SX (10.30am SO) Workington-Cockermouth
7.25am Cockermouth-Whitehaven
1.05pm SO Keswick-Workington
4.15pm SO Cockermouth-Workington
This represented a more enlightened spread than was provided in the depths of the First World War.

Left: The through train from Glasgow has arrived at Keswick behind 'Cauliflower' 0-6-0 No. 8318, on Sunday August 20 1939. LNER corridor stock is also prominent, likely to return to Newcastle upon Tyne or another NE destination during the evening.
Herbert Gelder/Courtesy Frank Alcock.

Summer services of the main LMS era

In general, Summer services featured six weekday trains in each direction on the CK&P section, also two long-distance trains, one to/from Euston, the other to/from Manchester Victoria; in each case, Workington was the western terminal point. No original Saturday extras appeared in the timetables. Taking summer 1930, this pattern of six 'local' trains each way applied, plus:-

11.35amSO: Keswick-Carlisle
5.5pm: Keswick-Penrith
9.40am: Penrith-Workington semi-fast
2.13pm: Penrith-Keswick
5.43pm: Penrith-Keswick express (with connection out of the 10.40am Euston-Carlisle)

9.5am: - from Workington (calling at Keswick from 9.56am-10.8am) to Euston (5.20pm) styled 'The Lakes Express' and with through carriages from Workington, Keswick, Windermere and Blackpool Talbot Road to Euston (and Blackpool-Birmingham on SX), the restaurant car being from Windermere,
11.35am: 'The Lakes Express' from Euston, conveying a portion for the CKP line to Keswick (6.51pm) and Workington (7.42pm).

11.45am: Workington (Keswick - dep 12.36pm) - Penrith express, with through carriages from Workington and Keswick to Manchester Victoria - attached at Preston to the 10.45am Glasgow-Manchester/Liverpool restaurant car express, due at Victoria at 4.27pm.
9.40am: Manchester Victoria-Keswick and Workington through carriages were attached between Preston and Penrith to the long-lived 9.25am Crewe-Perth service.

The end of the 1930s provided eight Monday-Friday trains over the CK&P road but only one was a long-distance service: 9.05am Workington-Euston (due 4.50pm), being 'The Lakes Express'. On Saturdays in July and August 1939, the 'Lakes' ran at 9.05am ex Workington and 12.00noon ex Euston (the latter due into Keswick at 6.27pm, then through to Workington) and there were also:-

10.52amSO: Liverpool Exchange (not Manchester) - Keswick (due 2.48pm) but with no corresponding Up

through working advertised.
12.47SO: Leeds City-Keswick (due at 4.53pm) routed via Ingleton
10.10amSO: Keswick-Leeds City (due 2.5pm) routed via Ingleton

Incidentally, there was a history of Leeds-Keswick-Workington running back in 1923, as well as in pre-1914 years.

Sunday trains had generally been notable by their absence from the Keswick line since April 15 1917 but a remarkable development of the later 1920s was a restaurant car express on Sundays in summer from Glasgow St. Enoch (9.55am), calling at Kilmarnock, Dumfries, Annan, Carlisle and Penrith, then due at Keswick at 1.52pm. The train returned at 6.55pm from Keswick, with the same calls to St Enoch, where arrival was due at 10.46pm. The times quoted are those of 1939. This service probably originated in 1927. In August 1929 David L. Smith (GSWR historian) travelled with nine carriages (277 tons) behind 'Compound' 4-4-0 No. 1179 of Glasgow (Corkerhill) shed to Carlisle, whence an LNWR 'Cauliflower' 0-6-0 and an LNWR 'Jumbo' 2-4-0 combined to run briskly to Keswick, and later, back again to Carlisle. The train was aimed principally at excursion passengers; out-and-back travel within the day at a 'bargain' rate. Likewise, each Sunday in summer, a Newcastle upon Tyne-Keswick train was operated, via Carlisle (reverse), reaching Keswick at 1.06pm and departing homeward at 7.10pm; this too was essentially a day excursion service. Sunday local trains were limited, in 1939, to one working into Keswick from the west and out again in the evening - directed at 'half-day' trippers.

The August 1944 service followed closely that already quoted for January 1944 with, additionally:

12.30pmSO Keswick-Penrith
3.35pmSO Workington-Cockermouth

These trains were accompanied by a single (one way only) long-range through service, namely: through carriages leaving Liverpool Exchange at 8.10amSO for Keswick, completing their journey as the 11.13amSO Penrith-Keswick service, which arrived at 11.55am and terminated.

It is interesting that Liverpool now figured, privileged in place of Manchester and London. Had this some social reason, perhaps a number of Merseyside families still billeted in northern Lakeland due to earlier air attacks on Liverpool?

LMS AND BRITISH RAILWAYS PASSENGER SERVICES, 1946-1972.

LMS,1946-47

From October 7 1946, the LMS attempted to restore many train services and timings to something approaching their 1938-39 standards. The results were praiseworthy on principal main lines, but, sadly, 'nothing to write home about' on secondary and branch routes such as the Penrith-Workington line. The timetable of October 7 1946, intended to operate until May 4 1947 (but not helped by the coal shortage of 1947) showed a basic seven trains each way, accompanied by a few 'short' workings. The starting times differed considerably from the remarkably stable pattern of the1904-39 period. No serious attempt was made to connect passengers with Carlisle, at Penrith, and there were similarly few useful southerly main line connections. The total train mileage advertised on the Keswick line was clearly adequate for all needs, but when the train times are examined in detail, one wonders who was expected to travel, as neither workers nor shopping outings were neatly provided for - and not even scholars. The tale is all too typical of railway management, and not only in 1946.

By 1947-48, there was a curtailment, to six trains in each direction – and still no attempt to run to or from Carlisle, nor to connect with that county town. At the west end of the route, the unbalanced 7.25am Cockermouth-Workington (due 7.51am) was withdrawn mid-term, in April 1948, thus permitting no arrival in Workington before 9.18am.

British Railways, from January 1 1948

In the first summer of the new British Railways regime's operations, (1948) the six trains each way basic service was supplemented by three Up (two SO and one running three days weekly) and one Down (SO). However, long-range through carriages operated, in some cases attached to basic all-year trains:

9.10am Keswick-Manchester Victoria (due 1.16pm) SO.
10.20am Manchester Victoria-Keswick,SO.

10.0am Workington(Keswick 11.8am)-Liverpool Exchange (2.35pm) -SO

8.35am Workington (Keswick 9.38am)-Euston (5.25pmSX, 5.10pmSO) Mon/Fri/Sat
11.55am Euston Workington, Mon/Fri/Sat.

Below: Three LMS coaches forming the Up 'Lakes Express', with Ivatt Class 2MT No. 46491 at its head, coasts downhill towards Penrith No. 1 signalbox in June 1963, whilst Stanier 'Black 5' 4-6-0 No. 45135 stands in the down loop with a mixed freight, awiting a clear road north. The train is carrying Ford *Anglia* and *Classic* models on a pair of flat bolster wagons. *Derek Cross.*

With the bridge-strengthening complete and the new, large turntable in use at Keswick by the summer of 1939, large tender engines could work the line. Above: On Sunday July 17 1960, the 'Newcastle' is about to leave Keswick at 6.30pm: 10 corridors, worked by '5XP' No. 45738 *Samson* and '5MT' 45286, of Upperby shed. *Harold D. Bowtell.*

Left: No. 46136 *The Border Regiment*, a 'Rebuilt Scot' 4-6-0, climbs out of Penrith with 11 mixed LNER (Gresley) and BR-built coaches, forming the 10.0am Newcastle-Keswick train of Sunday 1 September 1957. *Robert Leslie.*

Below: The large vacuum-operated turntable at Keswick dated from the summer of 1939. *Roy Anderson Collection.*

The Coming of diesel trains - from 1955

Diesel multiple unit (DMU) train sets were introduced to the Keswick route from January 3 1955, among the first examples of this innovation anywhere on BR. They soon took over the basic all-year workings and, by spring 1956, there were eight trains in each direction between Workington, Cockermouth, Keswick and Penrith, of which four Up and three Down services were through to/from Carlisle, a long-needed reform. Moreover, the journey times were much reduced. The pattern of eight DMUs each way (plus two or three longer-range steam-hauled corridor trains which ran for a summer season) became established and is seen in 1957 (June 17-September 15) and 1961 (June 12-September 10). In 1961, the basic summer departures were:

1) From Cockermouth (Up): 7.25am (C), 10.10am (C), 11.48am, 12.44pm (C), 1.48pm, 3.26pm, 5.49pm(C), 7.31pm (C),
('C'- now running to Carlisle)

2) From Penrith (Down): 7.18am, 10.20am(C), 11.38am(C), 12.07pmSO,
1.30pm, 3.25pm, 5.00pm, 6.08pm(C), 8.32pm(C),
('C' - started from Carlisle)

The 'dated' trains operated -
8.20am: Workington - Manchester Victoria (1.24pm)/Crewe (1.36pm) SO.
10.15am: Manchester Victoria-Keswick TC on a Workington train SO.

Above: A two-car 'Derby lightweight' DMU, led by Driving Trailer Composite No. M79607, leaves Penrith, en route for Workington, probably in 1955 when these units were first introduced on the route. The train is painted in BR green livery, with yellow lining, and featuring the BR 'lion and wheel' emblem. *National Railway Museum.*

8.55am*: Workington-Euston (5.45pm) (combining with a Windermere portion
11.35am*: Euston-Workington
(* SX, with variation on SO.)

Sunday workings included Newcastle-Keswick and back, but not the Glasgow-Keswick train of 1939.

Very similar arrangements continued during the 1962-65 period, inclusive, DMUs being supplemented by 'The Lakes Express' (Keswick and Workington portion) and the Manchester train. By 1964, the summer service of DMU trains was marginally expanded and the Newcastle-Keswick (and back) working on Sunday had become a DMU from 1961 and was still such in 1964.

Decline and withdrawal of services 1966-72.

When the timetable for the period April 18 1966 to March 5 1967 was published, it showed an all-DMU service equivalent to 6 1/2 trains SX (5 1/2 SO), primarily to and from Carlisle, but with no 'Lakes Express' or other long-range trains, even on summer Saturdays. A Sunday service was to run from June 19 1966 until September 4 1966 but with the few Sunday trains notably including the Newcastle-Keswick

DMU (due in at 12.53pm) and its return working (at 18.50 from Keswick).

In the event, this half-hearted proposition was stillborn, as from April 18 1966 the whole route west of Keswick, through Cockermouth to Derwent Junction (Workington) was closed to traffic and only a truncated service could be continued, on the eastern end of the line, namely between Keswick and Penrith, and to/from Carlisle.

The timetable from March 6 1967 (nominally effective until May 5 1968) acknowledged these limitations and offered a basic service of five trains each way, all but one to/from Carlisle, and six trains during the summer (mid-June to September 2 1967), plus a seventh service coming Up from Keswick on summer Saturdays. No long-range trains were advertised, nor were there any through carriage workings. The winter arrangements called for no crossings of Up and Down passenger trains on the CKP line and so pointed to the pattern of December 4 1967, from which date the double track sections, most of Keswick's surviving track layout and the signal boxes were taken out of use, leaving a single track route from Keswick to Penrith No.1 box, with only one train allowed to operate at a time. The line had become, effectively, a long siding. This extremely basic form was displayed in, for example, the timetables of 1970 (May 4) - 1971 (May 2), providing:

Six DMUs from Keswick to Penrith, of which two ran through to Carlisle
Six DMUs from Penrith to Keswick, of which two came through from Carlisle,

There were no advertised extra trains in summer and no trains on Sundays. Not surprisingly in these circumstances, the service was finally abandoned before the 1971-72

timetable year was completed, with effect from March 6 1972. So, with two-car DMUs ill-supported in winter and sometimes disgracefully overcrowded in summer, Lakeland's delightful northern railway route ended its days - apart from a little residual stone traffic at its eastern end, which itself did not long continue - and one known special working. This last train ran on Thursday April 22 1972, when at about 5.20am a special passenger train of four vehicles was hauled by a Class 25 diesel electric locomotive (with steam heating van attached) from Penrith No.1 box onto the branch and stabled on the gradient with all handbrakes secured and scotches placed under the carriage wheels. This was a Royal train, which had come overnight from Euston and was thus stabled until departure at 9.45am for Carlisle, where the Princess being conveyed had duties to perform.

The actual time taken by a stopping passenger train from Penrith to Workington in the 1870s (inclusive of some 8min standing time at Keswick and Cockermouth combined) was 115-118 minutes, reduced to about 110 minutes in the late 1940s. The Up journey, from Workington-Penrith, occupied 121-127min in the 1870s and 112min in the late 1940s. Two

Below: A sunny day at Penruddock finds another two-car 'Derby lightweight' DMU leaving the Up platform, bound for Penrith. The staggered platforms are clearly seen.Note that by this time the livery had beem modified to include a yellow warning panel between the buffer beam and the drivers windows. This followed complaints by permanent way men and other railway staff that these units were not easily visible when approaching. In later days, all-over yellow ends were standardised for all multiple units and locomotives, although in recent years warning panels have once again become smaller and incorporated with more subtlety with changing BR liveries. *David Tee.*

stations, Marron and Broughton Cross (both on the Cockermouth and Workington section) had been closed in the meantime, so the figures were closely comparable, some 70 years apart. Aided by relaxation of speed restrictions over bridges which still applied to steam-hauled trains, the introduction of DMU working effected a remarkable overall acceleration in the 1950s to (typically) 75-78 minutes, further tightened to 69-73min by 1961 for Down (westbound) trains and 81-86min, tightened again to 79min in the Up (eastbound) direction. The overall time, Penrith-Workington, for the steam-hauled 'Lakes Express' of summer 1961, was 93min (SX) 107min (SO): there were fewer stops than in the foregoing examples of DMU timings, but considerably heavier loadings on Saturdays.

THE PROMOTION OF PASSENGER TRAVEL ON THE CKPR

In good time for the opening of the CKPR to passengers (effective January 1865), its representatives had met with those of the LNWR and NER (SDR) in June-July 1864 and agreed that passengers would in general have the alternatives of first and second class carriages. However, there would also be 'Government class' - popularly known as 'parliamentary' - on the first and last trains daily. Through bookings were to be given for passengers, parcels, horse and carriage traffic, dogs - and goods generally - but not all stations on the three Companies' lines were included in the

bookings at first. 'Tourist fares' were to be available from LNWR stations south of Preston through to Keswick, with break of journey permitted at any station between Penrith and Keswick - and passengers had the option of returning by way of Windermere, if they wished. This last provision implies the existence of commercial arrangements with the proprietors of coaches running from Keswick to Windermere station, via the road (now the A591) over Dunmail Raise, 'The Swan' (Grasmere) and Ambleside. The LNWR and the coach operators had probably provided a service from the south to Keswick by this route before the CKPR was promoted. The title 'circular tour tickets' was soon adopted. In 1870, the CKPR and LNWR were arranging to share the cost of the coach fare between Windermere and Keswick in agreed proportions. From 1878, Messrs Cook &Sons' 'coupon tourist tickets' were accepted, with Cooks permitted to retain 10% of the fares as commission.

After a couple of years of operation, the CKPR's Board heard in 1867 that the LNWR's district manager had received instructions from his headquarters 'to take all the good carriages from this line and substitute inferior ones.' Remonstrances followed, pointing to the working agreement, and presumably the LNWR thought better of its plan to downrate CKPR facilities..

There was some passenger travel in goods trains and, in 1868, it was agreed to discourage this. Where this practice was allowed, passengers were to sign an indemnity form, relieving the Company of responsibility, much as has

Above: A pleasant scene at the east end of Keswick station as a two-car 'Derby lightweight' DMU coasts into the platform, *en route* from Penrith to Workington, probably during 1955. The replacement No. 1 signalbox, built by the LMS, was fitted with a Midland Railway-style lever frame at the back of the box, which meant that the signalman had to work the levers (most illogically and very inconveniently) with his back to the passing traffic. *National Railway Museum.*

Above: The last day on Lakeland's northern railway. In suitably mournful conditions, a seven car DMU rolls through the Cumberland countryside near Penruddock on March 6 1972, providing one of the last passenger links on the truncated 'long siding' between Penrith and Keswick. *Peter W. Robinson.*

applied in Scotland to recent years. Goods brake vans would provide spartan, but cosy, travel in winter. It was not so in passenger compartments, and in November 1872 the decision was taken to provide footwarmers in first and second class carriages.

The classes of accommodation constantly preoccupied the railway companies. In May 1872, the CKPR decided to book third class by all trains on its line, but a year later it was ruled that, as from June 1 1873, 'third' tickets would only be issued for the first morning train from Penrith or Cockermouth, as during an earlier period. At the same time, the 'second' single rate was reduced from one and three quarters of penny to one and a half pennies per mile ('first' being 2 1/2d per mile, unchanged). At this period, a government duty was still payable by railway companies on some third class fares and, in November 1874, the CKPR proposed to pass on the charge to travellers by adding 5% to the relevant fares. The Midland Railway, looking to the impending opening of their newly engineered Settle & Carlisle main line, also expansion of their Scottish business as result, publicised a Board resolution of October 7 1874 to discontinue second class carriages and reduce first class fares - but at the same time abolishing return tickets at reduced fares on their system - from January 1 1875. Incidentally, an exception to this was the Tilbury boat trains, which retained second class until much later times.

From January 1 1878, the CKPR offered third class fares between all stations, by all trains; but this was not the end of the debate as, from the beginning of 1881, the LNWR and MCR reduced passenger fares and the CKPR determined to adopt a new scale:

First: one and five eighths penny per mile, with return at double
Second: one and a quarter penny per mile, also with return at double the single fare.
Third: restricted to 'parliamentary' bookings (this restriction was abandoned in course of time).

Much later, from January 1 1912, the LNWR was the leader of a group of companies which followed the MR's example of 1875 and abolished second class travel (apart from some inner London suburban services). The CKPR's Board promptly adopted the traditional stance of King Canute; the LNWR's decision had nothing to do with them and the waves could wash around them. Frank Ree, General Manager of the LNWR, had to point out (in August 1911) that all passenger trains serving the CKPR were through to or from his Company's West Cumberland District, apart from one train each way between Keswick-Penrith, and thus when the LNWR dispensed with second class carriages and bookings, it would be impracticable for the CKPR to act otherwise. The CKPR had no alternative but to give way, and from January 1 1912:

The First class single fare was reduced from 2 1/2d to 2d per mile
The First class return rate was unchanged at 3d per mile
Third class fares were broadly unchanged - and there were no second class rates.

As seen, the value of tourist travel was appreciated from the earliest days of the CKPR, but the Railway's attitude to excursion traffic, directed at 'day trippers', was ambivalent. Day return fares were featured to a greater or lesser extent through most of the Railway's life. In June 1867, the LNWR decided to increase their 'day return' rate from one and a half to one and two third times single fare - but the CKPR Board elected not to follow suit, indeed, they determined to promote excursion traffic and make through bookings to Ullswater, with the hotel proprietors providing transport from Troutbeck station, a journey (from Troutbeck to Patterdale) of about eight hilly but highly scenic miles, over which connecting coaches were advertised at many periods in CKPR history.

In 1870-71, the CKPR Board had doubts about the wisdom of running excursion trains, as such. Because of the perceived risk, the Directors decided not to provide such trains late in the evening. Clearly, their concern was not aroused by the tourists on their select day outings from Keswick to Ullswater; probably the problems arose from drunkenness after 'closing time.' Again, in May 1872, the proposition was to run excursion trains only on special occasions, when the ordinary trains 'would not suit the public'.

Keswick became a favourite destination for long day excursions from the NER, starting very early in the morning from Newcastle upon Tyne, Sunderland, Durham, Teesside, Hull or Leeds and setting off back in the early evening. This traffic was probably at its height in the period from the mid-1880s until about 1914; it contributed to the need and justification for doubling of strategic sections of the route east of Keswick.

Alongside their accelerated development of through express trains to Keswick in Edwardian times, and until 1914-15, the railways were making special efforts to make known the beauties of northern Lakeland more widely. In 1903, photographs were supplied by the CKPR for display in the glazed panels in NER carriages. In 1905, the CKPR contributed to the cost of a large poster featuring coloured scenic views, commissioned by the Keswick Urban District Council. The same year, the Company's summer timetable introduced pictures of the scenery; McCorquodale & Company of Newton-le-Willows were the printers. This prompted Mrs Edith Rawnsley to paint views of Bassenthwaite and Derwentwater which she passed to Charles Cropper, a Director of the LNWR and CKPR who

Above: Promoting tourist travel, this elaboration of plain 'Troutbeck' was adopted from July 1915. A few years earlier, on Canon Rawnsley's initiative, the style agreed (and confirmed photographically) had been:

TROUTBECK
for ULLSWATER, PATTERDALE,
GOWBARROW & AIRA FORCE

This style therefore incorporated promotion of early properties owned by the National Trust, which was founded by the Canon. *Courtesy Abbot Hall.*

had special concern for Lakeland, so that he might arrange further embellishment of the timetable bills. Mrs. Rawnsley was wife of Canon Rawnsley, of Crosthwaite Church, Keswick (Canon of Carlisle Cathedral) who was a highly respected joint founder of the National Trust (1895); his efforts secured the Trust's first properties in the Lakes. The Canon wrote the CKPR contribution to the LNWR's new illustrated and descriptive guide to the Lake District (1907).

Above: A rare and wintry scene looking westward at the Up platform at Highgate, where children from Threlkeld schools arrived on termtime afternoons (1908-28) before dispersing to their homes at scattered farmsteads. Dimly, the Up home signal is seen over the bridge and to the right is the pair of houses built for the Railway in 1898. The LNWR 0-6-2T 'Coal tank' is on ballast train duty and Jack Greenhow, ganger in charge of the length, is seen standing on the platform. *Lens of Sutton.*

The following year, at CKPR request, he wrote a paper with popular appeal describing particularly Brandelhow woods and fell (the Trust's first Lakeland property, acquired in1902) on Derwentwater's shore, and Gowbarrow Park (the second acquisition, in 1906) on the north shore of Ullswater. It is hardly surprising that the Canon's free pass on the Railway was renewed; no doubt he used it a great deal in the course of his visits to Carlisle and London on Church and Trust business. The Canon's initiative led to a decision of December 1910 to extend the nameboards of Troutbeck station to read:

TROUTBECK FOR ULLSWATER, PATTERDALE
GOWBARROW AND AIRA FORCE

It is not quite clear whether this was actually done, but, from July 3 1945, the station nameboards announced:

TROUTBECK FOR ULLSWATER

All this was notwithstanding the fact that the LNWR and LMS were disposed to refer to Penrith as 'the station for Ullswater Lake.'

The LMS too was alive, during the 1920s and 1930s, to the possibilities of long-range excursion trains to the CKPR. Favourite starting points were Blackpool and Morecambe, designed to attract holiday visitors staying in those resorts. The 'round tour' version travelled north over the former Furness Railway's coastal route, commonly with a sojourn at Ravenglass to allow 'all-in' travel by the 15in gauge railway up Eskdale and back, then through Workington to reach Keswick for a stay of a few hours, before returning via the Redhills Junction-Eamont Junction LNER curve and the main line over Shap. After the 1929 season, it is believed, these trains ceased to use the Redhills loop line and were reversed in Penrith station; this was a result of the poor condition of track on the Redhills loop. Similar round-tour day excursions operated for a time in the early 1960s, using DMU sets from as far afield as Stockport and Manchester. One notes too the opening of the CK&P line on Sundays in summer from the later 1920s until 1939, with the regular day excursions from Glasgow to Keswick and return. On summer Sundays in DMU days, from the later 1950s and even into the 1960s, a regular Newcastle-Carlisle-Penrith-Keswick day excursion train was run – heavily loaded, and sometimes calling for two large locomotives between Penrith and Keswick.

The Glasgow and other Sunday excursions of the 1930s contributed considerably to life in the town of Keswick and its lakeside, and the coaching stock was stabled as far afield as Carlisle and Whitehaven, while the long granite works siding at Threlkeld were also used for the daytime storage of up to 30 coaches, the equivalent of three substantial excursion train sets.

Period excursions developed from the close ties between folk residing in industrial Workington and its environs and North East England; passenger specials are recalled from West Cumberland to the North East and North Yorkshire at times of local holidays. The Lancashire Fusiliers had a camp near the Motherby-Greystoke road and special trains were run to bring their soldiers to Penruddock station for summer training sessions. Troutbeck was another railhead for 'Territorials' bound for camp. These military specials ran via the Redhills curve, until about 1928-29.

TRAINS FOR WORKMEN

More mundane than the outings of Lakes tourists and trippers was the daily to-and-fro of workmen. Such travel could be expected between Cockermouth and Workington and account for the longevity of a daily train from Cockermouth at around 7.20-7.40am, bound westward. Equally early in origins and long lived was a passenger train leaving Cockermouth at about 7.00am, eastbound. This would surely be used by workers bound for the pencil manufacturers and other trades in Keswick but it had also the more long-range function of providing a connection at Penrith for London and intermediate points.

During the First World War, a 'workmen's train' was put on from Workington at 8.55pm, to Cockermouth, with a return trip at 9.40pm from Cockermouth. In the same period there were also 'colliers trains' from Workington (at 5.00am and 1.05pm) to William Pit Siding, with a balancing working at 5.50am, to Workington. Presumably, the aim was to provide transport for labour from Whitehaven-Workington to supplement locally resident miners on all three shifts at William Pit, Great Clifton.

The granite quarries at Close, near Embleton, did not enjoy workmen's trains. However, those at Threlkeld not only expanded their local 'quarry village' but also attracted workers from Keswick. By 1906, workmen's trains were running at 6.55am from Keswick to Threlkeld, returning at 12.55pm (SO) and 5.35pm (SX), this service continuing until at least 1929, and probably into the early 1930s. The morning departures varied between 6.50 and 7.05am and the return run started at times which became progressively earlier over the years, to 12.50pm,12.35pm and 12.05pm, on Saturdays. The weekday return was usually timed around 5.30pm in summer but could be as early as 4.45pm on dark evenings. The train usually comprised one or two coaches and the journey time was of the order of 7-9 minutes. It was known locally as 'The Boer Train', in recognition of the Boer war names assigned to quarry workings opened out around the turn of the century. More light-heartedly, it was alternatively titled 'The Boat Train'.

The platform at Briery bobbin mill, in its secluded situation between Keswick and Threlkeld, does not figure on maps or in working timetables in the pre-Grouping era; it was however clearly installed early in LMS days and a workers' service from Keswick was provided consistently until about the time of closure of the mill (1958). Indeed, morning and evening calls at this halt (SX) still figured in the BR working timetables of winter 1958-59. The general pattern was to book a call by an Up morning passenger train, so as to enable workers to arrive by 8.00am. The folk for Briery travelled in the leading coaches in view of the short platform. Return travel was by a passenger train booked to call at lunchtime (SO), or later (SX). There were periods when calls for workers, bound home to Keswick, were made by the Keswick workmen's train from Threlkeld and it is believed that there were other periods when a shuttle was run from Keswick to Briery/Keswick, and at once back again, the locomotive propelling the carriage in one direction.

TO SCHOOL BY TRAIN

At first sight, the CKPR route east of Threlkeld station, climbing hard for all of the 4 3/4 miles to Troutbeck station, was remote from habitation. It followed the southerly slopes of the valley, which on its northern side, is dominated by the great bulk of Blencathra (known colloquially as 'Saddleback') mountain while the southerly side rises to the high fells of Matterdale Common. There were a considerable number of scattered farmsteads, both below and above the railway; several are farmhouses today, while others are now ancillary premises or purely residences and a very few are ruinous.

In 1892, local residents had asked for a station to be built near the Railway Company's Moor Cottages, a pair of small houses, now long combined into one and known as Hill Cottage. The ascending lane to Birkettfield crosses the railway route just west of the cottages, at a point between MP18 and Mosedale viaduct.

By 1900, attention had concentrated on a spot eastward of Mosedale viaduct and MP19, where a lane to upland farms crossed the double-track line by bridge No 91. The tiny signal box named Highgate was on the Down side, about 100 yards eastward of the overline bridge, and the Company was on the point of building a pair of houses on the Up side banking above the line and near the bridge; one was intended for the sole signalman and his family, the other for a section permanent way ganger and family.

Doctor Knight wrote to the Company on April 4 1900, asking for one train each way to call daily at Highgate cabin, to pick up and set down six or eight schoolchildren; the Board instructed its Secretary to reply in a typical railway vein that: "the difficulties and expense render the suggestion impracticable." The children had to walk to and from Mungrisdale school, which was across the valley and some three miles to the north of Highgate. Pressure increased, calling for a train service from Highgate to Threlkeld and back; there were indeed suitably timed trains, if only they would call. Many influential folk mustered behind the demand, including the County Council Education Committee, based in Carlisle, also the redoubtable Canon Rawnsley, of Keswick.

Towards the end of 1907, the CKPR Board decided to consult the Board of Trade, probably hoping that it would rule against proposal - but it decided in favour of the suggestion. Thus, plans were made, and estimated to cost about £170, plus the price of refinements called for by the Board of Trade. Eventually, in February 1908, an agreement was concluded; the Education Committee was to meet the costs of construction and one train each way was to call, initially for 10 years. The calls were not to be made "when the school is closed on holidays or other occasions."

Colonel Druitt of the railway department, at the Board of Trade, reported on June 18 1908 that he had "...inspected the new platforms adjoining Highgate cabin on the CKPR ...up and down platforms...150ft long, 6ft wide, 2ft 6in above rail level, approached by separate pathways from the public road adjoining... Lamps have been provided at the entrance. As the Company do not wish the general public to make any use of the platforms, no nameboards have been provided and the use of the platforms will be restricted to school children only and to one train in the morning and one in the evening. On the conditions, I can recommend sanction." Approval accompanied the report. Opening followed the summer holiday of 1908, and on Monday August 17 1908, ll children (12 on August 18) were conveyed, three joining Threlkeld Council School and nine went to the Quarry School. Highgate platforms became a happy institution in that delightful countryside for the next 20 years.

The site at Highgate is in a cutting and the platforms were staggered, bringing the western end of the Down platform close to the signalbox. This platform was reached by a fenced path, constructed along the top of the embankment at the level of its access from the road, while the children's path only came down to platform level beside the box on its east side, so that the signalman could watch over their safety. A small waiting hut is recalled, with a stove which the signalman lit on winter mornings. The blockpost was not switched in until 9.0am in the earlier days, 9.30am after about 1908, so the local signalman - the kindly Bob Tinkler, subsequently his successor Willie Nicholson - was required to put in extra duty and it is believed that the County Council provided a bonus of £5 per annum to cover the time on duty before the call and despatch of the morning 'school train', which was typically at Highgate just about 8.00am. The signalman was in any case on duty when the afternoon call was made - at about 4.00 to 4.10pm in earlier years 3.25pm from c1917.

The passenger guards also took a kindly interest in their young passengers. One Workington guard, in particular, would invite all the children into his van and make a great show of tabulating their names, then presenting each with sweets. The age range was from five to fourteen years, both boys and girls, and a maximum of more than 20 was achieved, thus -

Three from Highgate railway cottages
Five from the families in the Wallthwaite community (north west of the station)
Three from Redsike farm (north east of the station)
Two from Moorend farm (northward towards the Keswick-Penrith road)
Two from Highgate Close farm (a little above the line, to the south)
Four from Lobbs farm (higher again)
Three from High Hollows farm (farther up and over to the west of Mosedale Beck)

Attendance was divided between Threlkeld village school - a trek of three quarters of a mile across the valley from Threlkeld station, sometimes risking wet feet owing to the flooding of the road - and the school in the quarry village a much shorter and drier trip, made by a select few, among whom notably Jessie Tyson was numbered during the years 1912-19.

By the mid-1920s, the number of eligible travellers on the school journey by train, Highgate to Threlkeld, was reduced to rather over half-a-dozen and from 1926 there was potential competition from a regular bus service, between Penrith and Keswick. From 1928 (the end of Christmas term) and officially with effect from January 1 1929, the trains ceased to call at Highgate and the youngsters made their way across the fields to a black roadside hut at Red Gate, in order to catch the Cumberland Motor Services Ltd omnibus. It goes without saying that various social trips, often to Keswick, were made by the trains which called at Highgate platforms. When Jessie Tyson married Ted Titterington on May 16 1927, they had booked tickets (from Threlkeld to Penrith, and onwards) beforehand and, after a wedding breakfast at Highgate Close, they departed for honeymoon by the school train from Highgate Platform that afternoon.

There were naturally other instances of children travelling by Keswick line trains to and from their schools, indeed Troutbeck children rode to Penruddock daily and Keswick School was (and is) of such significance as to draw boys from Cockermouth; note the running, previously discussed, of the MCR train through to Keswick in the mornings.

ROEDEAN AT KESWICK, 1940-1945

The direct threat posed to the south coast of England following the German occupation of France in the summer of1940 led the governors of Roedean School to seek a new home for their prestigious public school and its girls. The elevated and prominent buildings, which face seawards at the easterly extremity of Brighton, were in demand by the army and subsequently passed to a naval shore establishment, HMS Vernon.

The school was found new quarters at Keswick, and this produced unexpected excitements and traffic for the LMS and its Keswick line, for five years. The Keswick Hotel, under the management of proprietors Mr. and Mrs. W.D. Wivell, was occupied by most of the staff and senior girls. Further accommodation was taken in smaller hotels, *Millfield* and *Shu-le-crow*, reached by the convenient footbridge over the river Greta. These provided quarters for the junior girls. With all (but one) of the pupils being resident boarders and the staff also to accommodate, it is understood that there was barely a square inch to spare.

In the main building of Keswick station, on its Down side (nearest the approach and town), the five upstairs rooms became classrooms; these included the onetime boardroom of the CKPR and one which was very small and therefore used for special tuition. A waiting room below was also used; some passengers entered and promptly withdrew, others were bolder and stayed to enjoy the welcome fire until the arrival of their trains, lessons notwithstanding! Use of a waiting room on the Up island platform was also secured in due course. Occasionally, Greek dances were staged on this island platform!

Classrooms were improvised in all three hotels. Notably, the fullest use was made of the covered way from the station's Down platform to the Keswick Hotel's side door. Double doors from the platform led into a lobby and further double doors from this to a small decoratively-glazed anteroom, which was pressed into use for teaching and known as 'the glass box'. The next glazed door led into a long lounge-conservatory, with windows along one side commanding the station square and, distantly, a view of the mountains. On its other side were the greenhouses. This main lounge was very useful and so were the greenhouses. The school installed laboratory benches, sinks and services. A huge palm tree added dignity to the lounge-conservatory but leaking glass roofs here and in the greenhouses presented a problem – each mistress and girl required an umbrella in order to cope with the oft-prevailing wet conditions indoors, which reflected the climate of Lakeland and its mountains! A further distraction was the periodic arrival of supplies by rail; the glazed doors would open and a platform trolley would be rumbled through draftily, accompanied by an aroma of kippers (or whatever!) bound for the kitchens. Accommodation was also found in the Boardroom of the nearby Fitz museum and sometimes - shared with visitors - in the adjoining Fitz art gallery. The Wesleyan chapel in Southey Street provided for morning prayers and scripture lessons and its other rooms were used too. Finally, Keswick School offered part-time use of its laboratories to Roedean's sixth form girls. The art mistress probably had the best bargain, commandeering the main garage of the Keswick Hotel and turning it into a magnificent studio and

workshop, while another garage housed the bicycles (seemingly one brought by each girl and staff member) much used for outings.

Dame Emmeline Mary Tanner (1876-1955) had been Head of Roedean since 1924 and, wishing to see the school through its wartime era and safely reinstalled at Brighton, she did not retire until Easter 1947. Nancy Banks Smith (*The Guardian*, May 17 1982), recalling her schooldays at Roedean-in-Keswick, wrote: 'Dame Emmeline's oration "On the Occasion of Two Gels being seen Eating Chips in Keswick" is still spoken of in the same breath as Cato on Catiline....'(Topic: degenerate conspiracy in the Roman Empire).

Dame Emmeline herself wrote in the school magazine: "On a perfect October day, 43 girls climbed Great Gable, 16 climbed Scafell Pike, 79 climbed Helvellyn, 16 bicycled to the Langdales (46 miles), 7 walked all round Derwentwater. I was obliged to go to London". In fact, as well as such outings on Saturdays, school holidays were sometimes given in impromptu fashion, to permit fell and mountain walking on exceptionally fine days.

The railway conveyed Roedean's furniture, equipment and books from Brighton to Keswick in July-August 1940, whilst the staff arrived during August and the girls on September 5.

Subsequently, a special train was run south at the end of each school term and north at the beginning of the next. It would be the southbound train of December 1940 - running, it has been suggested, from Keswick through to Brighton - which distinguished itself by arriving far behind booked time. This was a during a period of blackout and major air raids, not to mention heavy traffic. The tale in railway circles was that such strident protest came from influential parents, who had awaited their daughters into the cold and dark night hours, that instructions went out to railway staff to ensure that in future the girls' train should have priority over all other wartime traffic - an injunction still recalled in Cumberland in 1945.

The school train seems to have settled down to run from Euston - or a suburban station at periods when heavy air attack was threatened - at around 10.00am, due to arrive at Keswick at approximately 7.00pm. End of term departures from Keswick were booked at 5.25am or 5.30am. This was regarded as the Keswick line's heaviest working in the years 1940-45, one of the few to call for double-heading or even require a 'Black 5' 4-6-0 or other big engine. On one occasion, the end of term empty stock, due at Keswick at 5.00am, eventually arrived at 9.00am. In consequence, all the connections at Crewe for south-westerly destinations were missed; much telephoning and many telegrams ensued. Miss Barbara Patterson, teacher of classics and a house-mistress in those days, along with a colleague, took a party from Crewe to Shrewsbury that evening,where they found cramped accommodation for the night. Next day they journeyed on to Exeter, reached about 6.00pm (leaving several girls on the darkened station in the hope that they would be met) and on to Teignmouth. One mistress took the remaining pupil home for the night and saw her off next day for Plymouth and her holidays.

A snowy January resulted in an arrival of the 'school train' from London at about 7.00am at Keswick, 12 hours late; there had not been much heating, nor food (except as provided by individuals) and not even corridor stock. Several girls from other parts of Britain reached Penrith very late on that occasion and were provided with accommodation in the vicinity by the ever-caring stationmaster.

Notable indeed was the universal friendly help of folk in Keswick, starting with Mr. & Mrs. Wivell, and Dixon the Keswick Hotel porter, who was always ready with weather forecasts and advice about the Lake District. Police Inspector Bell and his colleagues let the school staff know when Derwentwater was safe for skating, which was enjoyed in three winters out of five, with skating by moonlight permitted to the older girls on one superb night. The boatmen readily made their launches available for outings to the further shores, en route for walks or climbs. Keswick stationmaster Pickthall and every one of his staff showed cheerful patience and helpfulness through the five years of 'occupation' of their station by the girls and their mistresses.

The final departure from Keswick was late in 1945. While most of the school staff stayed behind to pack and despatch Roedean's possessions, the girls and a few staff members left on the special 'school train' at 5.25am on November 29 1945, for a long Christmas holiday, the previous summer holiday having been curtailed to permit this. Everyone was out on the platform in good time, including the Wivells, Dixon, Inspector Bell, many other Keswick friends and especially Mr. Pickthall and his staff. Mr. Denwood provided music from his loudspeaker van. An informal dance was staged on the platform, and 'John Peel' (a traditional Lakeland song) and 'Auld Lang Syne' were sung. Then, the train left on time, accompanied by a fusillade of detonations from the battery of fog signals placed on the outgoing track.

THE KESWICK CONVENTION

This week-long annual conference of evangelical Christians - of all denominations and attracted from all over the world - remains a feature of summer life in Keswick. It was first held in in 1875, its establishment credited to Canon Battersby, Vicar of St John's, Keswick, who died in 1883. The gathering, based in a huge central tent and with overflow to halls in the town, was held in the fourth week of July in the earlier years and into the 20th century but by the 1930s it was staged during the third week in the month, and subsequently - with some breaks in wartime. The atmosphere of 1900 is recalled by reference to the presence in goodly numbers of 'Missionaries to the Heathen'.

The strongest support has come from and via the south of England, with a demand for travel which was first met by the enterprising J.T. Budd, of (significantly) 'Ambleside', New Barnet, Hertfordshire. Commencing in 1899, he advertised "special train arrangements from London and the South of England to Keswick, on Friday July 21 with return." The gathering that year was from Monday 24 to Saturday July 29 and the general pattern was to arrange addresses on Monday evening and at intervals during from Tuesday to Friday. 'The Budd' was sometimes running in two and three portions during the 1920s and 1930s, on a fast daytime schedule from Euston to Penrith, then (reversing direction) assisted in the rear to Blencow or Penruddock, en route to Keswick.

After the 1939-45 war, one train sufficed, but this was usually well-loaded and double headed between Penrith and Keswick. It returned a week later and in this period, through to 1969, Saturday running in each direction was favoured. The traditional steam working continued until 1967. After that, only a shuttle service between Penrith and Keswick was possible, but the charter train was worked, as shown on this page, by large diesel locomotives at each end

Above: 'Budd's Special' between London and Keswick for the July interdenominational gathering was always a heavy train. Returning from Keswick on Saturday 21 July 1962, 12 vehicles are here headed by Fowler 2-6-4T No. 42357 and Stanier 'Black 5' 4-6-0 No.

45190. From November 23 1964, this direct outlet to the Down main line at Penrith No.1 signalbox was not available, and all traffic from Keswick had to run thereafter into the CKPR back platform. *Derek Cross.*

Above:On July 22 1967, a return Convention special train is seen climbing out of Keswick, hauled by English Electric Type 4 (later Class 40) No. D313 and Ivatt Class 4MT 2-6-0 No. 43139. The diesel-electric locomotive ran round the stock at Penrith and worked the train south, bound for Euston. *A.C. Gilbert.*

Left: A very rare view of a Class 50 diesel electric locomotive at work on the Keswick road. Following the downgrading of the truncated Penrith-Keswick section for one-engine working, with all run-round facilities withdrawn, Convention specials were worked on a push-pull basis, with a locomotive at each end of the formation. In July 1969, D417 rounds the curve into Threlkeld at the head of the empty stock of a Down Convention special. An EE Type 4 is visible at the Keswick end of the train. The carriages were being worked empty to Carlisle. D417 later became 50017 *Royal Oak* and in Spring 1989 was based at Plymouth Laira. D313 subsequently became 40113 and was withdrawn in November 1981. *Peter W. Robinson.*

of the train, to permit the prompt return of the empty stock.

In CKPR days, these special workings to the Keswick Convention, together with others originating in North East England and Scotland, provided a valuable boost in revenue for the Cockermouth Keswick & Penrith Railway Company, but by the 1930s it was the LMS at Euston which gained the financial credit for the induced charter travel to Lakeland's northern railway.

Chapter 5

BRIDGES

A SHORT LINE WITH MANY RIVER CROSSINGS: COCKERMOUTH-WORKINGTON

The route of the Cockermouth & Workington Railway was some nine miles in length, in which it crossed a major river (the Derwent) six times. Subsidiary channels and tributaries were also crossed, Leaving aside the Derwent viaduct at Workington (used by CWR trains but owned by the Whitehaven Junction Railway) the CWR had to commission 11 bridges of nominal lengths of between 50ft and 300ft. The single track railway was built in 15 months, between February 1846 and April 1847. John Dixon (1796-1865) of Darlington was the Consulting Engineer; he was a respected figure, with experience under George Stephenson on the construction of the Stockton & Darlington and Liverpool & Manchester Railways.

The CWR had been built cheaply. Thus, not only were the intermediate stations of primarily timber construction, but so were the 11 bridges mentioned. John Dixon, Engineer, referred to: "the best timber.....of large dimensions" in a progress report of July 1846. By the mid-1850s, the vibration of bridges under passing trains was causing concern and in April 1856 William Brown was asked to examine the bridges, in company with J.W. Fletcher, chairman of the CWR, and fellow directors Thomas Westray and George Cape, the last mentioned probably being a builder by trade.

The resulting report was by William and James Brown, of Whitehaven, and dated May 27 1856. It stated that most of the CWR's river bridges required only minor attention, such as realignment of approaching tracks, relaying or reballasting of track on the bridge and the application of a protective finish to the timbers. However, Ribton High bridge (alternatively described as Upper bridge) was found unsafe, calling for the replacement of washed-away piles and other work. In June 1856, tenders for tension rods for this bridge were considered. They were submitted by: Piele, Tulk & Ley, Cowan & Sheldon and G.D. Richardson. The Richardson tender was accepted. Bowling or Low Moor iron was to be used and by August 12 1856 the ironwork had been forged at Carlisle and delivery to site was imminent.

Towards the end of the same year, 1856, the CWR Board took further advice, asking James Dees of the MCR and WJR (presumably being the James Dees who joined the CWR Board in 1863) to inspect the permanent way and state of the line generally. He was also to cosnider a possible very local doubling between Harrygill and Lowther pit connections, west of Marron, and on Merchants' Quay at Workington. The report by Mr. Dees was submitted to the proprietors at their half-yearly meeting on January 3l 1857; it stated that the various timber bridges were standing well and had in many instances been much strengthened and recently improved. However, probably resulting from this review, and also a derailment in March 1857, severe speed limits were imposed over the bridges (from April 7 1857): 10mph for passenger trains and 8mph for coal trains. During that year, William & James Brown were entrusted with more trussing (with iron rods) at Stainburn and Salmon Hall bridges, along with selected water channelling works. Browns did further work in 1858; the two 42ft spans at Middle Tail Race bridge and the two 34ft spans at Tail Race bridge were noted for trussing and two piles were to be fixed each side of the trusses on Beer Pot Tail Race bridge.

Below: Ribton Hall No.2, subsequently retitled Ribton Bridge, No.22, was rebuilt in 1862 with six spans (carried by stone abutments and piers) varying between 32ft and 38ft, and with an overall length of 300ft. It was the longest of the CWR's succession of bridges over the River Derwent, seen here probably in the 1930s. *Richard L. Pattinson/CRA.*

MAJOR BRIDGES ON THE CWR ROUTE AND THEIR REBUILDING IN 1860-1863

THOMAS DRANE'S LIST OF DECEMBER 3 1859 (from east to west)

1859 TITLE	LMS TITLE (1940)	DRANE'S QUOTED BRIDGE LENGTH	REBUILDING PROGRESS REPORT (from minutes of 1860-63)
Marron	River Marron (one span)	70ft	Old bridge temporarily strengthened with timber, in 1860. AT August 1861, to proceed with rebuilding using 'stone piers and iron girders'. Opened January 1862, completed by autumn 1862. *See footnote.*
Ribton Hall	Ribton High (two spans)	180ft	At January 22 1862: both abutments built, a pier still to be constructed. July 29 1862: traffic was passing over new bridge
Ribton Hall No.2	Ribton (six spans)	300ft	At 1859: 'recently strengthened with iron trussing rods'. January 31 1861: rebuilding authorised. At April 9 1861: tenders accepted - W. Hodgson for masonry, Gilkes, Wilson & Co. for iron girders. At June 11 1861: stone piers in hand. At January 22 1862: rails to be laid this week. At July 29 1862: No. 2 coffer dam commenced.
Camerton	Camerton (three spans)	270ft	At 1859: 'recently strengthened with iron trussing rods'. At January 22 1862: one abutment complete, one abutment and three piers to build. *(I would only expect two piers - Author).* At July 29 1862: track being laid.
Table top	Stainburn (two spans)	165ft	At April 9 1861: tenders accepted (as for Ribton) At January 22 1862: abutments complete, centre pier to build. At July 7 1862: track being laid
Salmon Hall	Salmon Hall No.1 (three spans)	165ft	At 1859:' recently strengthened with iron trussing rods'. At January 22 1862: abutments in progress, one pier to build (implying one built - HDB). At July 29 1862: traffic passing over new bridge.
Salmon Hall No.2	Salmon Hall No.2 (two spans)	120ft	At January 22 1862: masonry complete, girders to fix. At July 29 1862: traffic passing.
Salmon Hall Byefall	Byefalls (two spans)	90ft	At June 11 1861: work in hand, a stone pier in mid stream. At January 22 1862: 'completed'. At July 29 1862: traffic passing.
Canal	Mill Race (one span)	60ft	At January 31 1861: decided to rebuild Mill Race bridge. At January 22 1862: abutments completed and girders to fix for 'Mill Race' *(presumed to refer to this bridge - Author.)* At July 29 1862: traffic passing over 'Mill Race.'
Canal No. 2	Canal (one span)	60ft	At January 31 1861: decided to rebuild 'Boat bridge. At January 22 1862: 'completed.' At July 29 1862: traffic crossing.
Beerpot (stated to cross tail race for Beerpot Ironworks)	Beerpot Mill Race (one span)	50ft	At July 15 1862: decided on permanent rebuilding (over tail race at Beerpot). At January 1863: rebuilding in hand, last bridge in programme. July 4 1863: opened.

NOTES:
Mr Harrison Hodgson, of Durham, undertook the contracts for masonry for Marron, Ribton Hall, Ribton Hall No. 2, Camerton, Table Top, Salmon Hall No. 1 and Salmon Hall No. 2 - in April 1861 and July 1861. It is not clear whether he also carried out the masonry work for the four more westerly bridges. The wrought iron girders for all the bridges were provided by Gilkes Wilson & Company, who would be of Middlesbrough, under orders of April and June 1861 One notes that the rails were laid and traffic commenced to pass over some of the new bridges before the final completion of intermediate river piers.

The 1861 reference to Marron Bridge may well refer to stone abutments and iron girders *(Author)*

The railway's mineral traffic was gradually increasing, with promise of continued development, and it was realised that the timber structures of 1846-47 must be coming to the end of their useful lives. Accordingly, a major report was commissioned. It was dated 3 December 1859, at Cockermouth, by Thomas Drane, CE, who was by then Engineer of the CWR.

All the indications are that each of the original timber bridges was supported on numerous timber piles, on piled foundations in the riverbed, the spans between them being comparatively short. Mr Drane's report of 1859 listed 11 timber bridges and recommended their rebuilding, using wrought iron girders for the superstructure, with spans of typically 50-60ft, in order to minimise the number of piers obstructing the river. In general, the girders would be supported by masonry abutments, supplemented by masonry piers in the stream, as required. The piers were to be erected in water conditions of 'low summer'. Ribton Hall bridge (which would be the one known also from time to time as Ribton Upper or Ribton High) would need iron piling for the piers, in view of the depth of water. All abutments and piers would be of adequate width for double track but only one pair of girders, for single track, would be installed for each span at this time. The Engineer's estimate for the full scheme, to be spread over several summers, was £6,500, which was very different from the individual expenditures of £11-£113 for the repair work previously carried out by Browns on the timber structures. Nevertheless, the Board accepted Mr Drane's recommendations and the first work was put in hand in spring 1860. The bridge over the Marron and those over the Derwent were all completed by autumn 1862. The new Beerpot bridge was opened to traffic on July 4 1863 and this was stated to eliminate all timber bridges on the CWR - although a small timber bridge near Broughton Cross station was seemingly not rebuilt with iron girders until 1865.

Doubling of the Cockermouth & Workington route - and its bridges

The Whitehaven Junction Railway provided double track between Workington joint station and Derwent Junction (the divergence of the CWR's own route) but the first serious reference to prospective double line between Derwent Junction and Cockermouth appears to have been in December 1856, when local doubling was considered, in the vicinity of the colliery branches near Marron. Doubling from Workington (meaning Derwent Junction) to the River Marron was contemplated by the estimate of £14,500 put to a special meeting on October 28 1862; this meeting authorised the seeking of parliamentary powers for various works, and an Act was secured on June 30 1863. However, the first ordnance survey of the route, in 1864, found not even the 1856 project executed. There was simply a double line, or crossing loop, of just about one quarter-mile in length, between the junctions for Harrygill colliery and for Linefitts Colliery, inclusive. This took in, intermediately, Marronbridge Junction (the later Marron Junction, West) and the station site. There could also be limited stowage of mineral trains on the southerly branch line from Marron (west) or the several industrial connections, of which the one at Melgramfitz colliery (operational from November 1863) was double-ended.

Following an estimate of £2,500 (provided for on 23 February 1864), on April 5 1864 a tender was seemingly accepted for doubling 'from the east end of Ribton High bridge to Melgram Fitz Colliery', about one mile, and including the already existing quarter-mile of double road. The only major bridge involved was at Marron, and Gilkes provided a girder for its widening, also under order of April 1864. It is believed that the work was done that year.

Doubling from Workington Bridge station to Derwent Junction had been mooted for some time and was doubtless carried out in the first half of 1865, as a relevant addition to capital was made at a general meeting of July 29 1865.

Widening between Lowther pit and Workington Bridge - involving extra girders over all the other recently-built major bridges - was held over (decision of May 9 1865) and Melgram Fitz to Cockermouth Junction was not seriously considered at the time. This was the position when the LNWR took over, midway through 1866. In fact, the LNWR was quick to widen the remaining bridges and the CWR main line, to achieve double track throughout. The demands of MCR traffic between Brigham and Cockermouth Junction led to this portion being given priority and opened to traffic even before its inspection for the Board of Trade. The section from Brigham westward to Melgramfitz was ready on that date and clearly opened as double line soon afterwards. The length from the vicinity of Lowther pit to the approaches to Workington Bridge station (including the remaining major underline bridges) was opened as double track very soon after inspection of October 5 1868.

Improvement to stations in the CWR era, to 1865

Work on the CWR's Cockermouth station was under way in September 1856, when George Cape (a Director, presumed to be a builder) undertook to see to the foundations, for which the bricks were already on site. Workington Bridge and Camerton stations were provided with platforms, in front of the old buildings, around autumn 1860.

New and worthy buildings for Broughton Cross and Brigham stations were erected between March and autumn 1863, by H.Hodgson, whose tender for the work had been £738. Both were in neo-Elizabethan style, built in stone with steep-pitched gables and heavy roofing; the Broughton Cross building can still be seen today, beside the A66 road. Camerton, remote from habitation, was also to have a 'permanent' new station building (1863) but this was held over in 1863-65 and the eventual building was very different from those of 1863.

Marron Junction platform and shed were built in 1866 at the CWR's cost, but the WCER had to make annual contributions. Workington Bridge station did not benefit from new buildings until 1881, a modest rebuilding in wood by the LNWR.

The bridges from Cockermouth to Workington, 1866-1966

The principal bridges of 1847 to 1859 have been tabulated (see page 125) and their rebuilding during 1860-1863 has also been discussed, as has the doubling of the line in 1864-65 and 1867-68.

The bridges, as they stood during most of the century of successively LNWR, LMS and BR control are listed clearly in the LMS register compiled in the 1940s and much of this is reproduced below. Most are underline bridges, the few overline being distinguished. Stone abutments and stone piers are universal except in a few instances noted in the table below, for example, CWR No. 43 (a footbridge) and various Whitehaven Junction Railway structures. Underline cattle-creeps and culverts and the occasional accommodation or public way - mainly under 10ft span, - are omitted from the table; most of them comprised stone abutments and stone arches but a few had stone abutments with cast iron girders and infill planking. As viewed by the engineers of LMS days and after, the Derwent bridges of the CWR line were unduly light in superstructure. The wrought iron cross girders under the double track road deflected significantly under the load of a train, causing the longitudinal wrought iron girders to lift at their ends, where supported by abutments or piers at the end of each span. The prospective cost of replacing these superstructures in steel was an ever-looming factor - and perhaps not justified in the 1960s.

BRIDGES: COCKERMOUTH-WORKINGTON, 1866-1966

No.	BETWEEN STATIONS	MPs	TITLE	SPANS BETWEEN ABUTMENTS/PIERS No./LENGTH (SKEW)	REMARKS
7	Cockermouth Jn-Brigham	1.25/1.5	Thompson's Arch (underline)	1/12ft	
10	Brigham-Broughton Cross	2.25/2.5	Stoney Beck Broughton Road	1/17ft 4in (20ft 9in) (over stream) 1/25ft 7in (30ft 6in) (over public way) 1/17ft 1in (20ft 10in) (over occ. way)	WI girders and planking CI face girders to Up line. Stone arches under Down line. *Lost in A66 redevelopment.*
12	Bro'ton Cross-Marron Junction.	2.75-3	Paisley's Arch (underline occupation)	1/12ft	*Lost in A66*
13	Bro'ton Cross-Marron Junction	2.75-3	Cattle creep	1/13ft (14ft)	*Lost in A66*
16	Bro'ton Cross-Marron Junction	3.75-4	RIVER MARRON	1/ 53ft 6in	WI main and cross girders and planking. *Span survives 1984.*
20	Marron Junction-Camerton	4.25-4.50	RIBTON HIGH (over Derwent)	1/ 66ft (72ft 4in) 1/ 63ft (73ft)	WI main and cross girders and planking. *Spans removed.*
22	Marron Junction-Camerton	4.50-4.75	RIBTON (over Derwent)	1/ 38ft (46ft) 1/ 34ft (42ft) 1/ 36ft 4in (44ft 6in) 1/ 32ft 6in (44ft 3in) 1/32ft (40ft 3in) 1/ 34ft (42ft 6in) with wrought iron main and cross girders and planking. *All spans removed since 1966 closure.*	Occupation. river. island. river. river. river.
25	Marron Junction-Camerton	5-5.25	CAMERTON (over Derwent)	1/ 50ft 8in (62ft 8in) 1/ 56ft 6in (70ft 2in) 1/ 50ft (63ft 4in) *All spans removed since 1966 closure.*	Construction as Ribton. West abut. partly reb. in concrete in 1948.
26	South of Camerton Station (which closed March 3 1952)	5-5.25	Footbridge over Derwent (giving access from south to station)	1/ 40ft 2in 1/ 40ft 5in 1/ 39ft 10in 1/ 39ft 4in	Bridge was of timber but *sold June 1 1959 to Cumberland County and since replaced.*
28	Camerton-Workington Br.	5.50-5.75	Miser (overline, by-road to St. Peter's Church	1/ 30ft 1/ 16ft 1/ 16ft	Construction of stone Broad arch over double track, flanked by arches set into sides of cutting.
30	CamertonWorkington Br.	at 5.75	STAINBURN (over Derwent)	2/ 66ft (71ft 9in) *Spans removed since 1966 closure*	WI main and cross girders and planking Timber decking (up side renewed 1964)
31	Camerton-Workington Br	5.75-6	William Pit (overline)	1/ 29ft (occ'n) 1/ 17ft (Allerdale Coal Company)	WI lattice girders and plates for occn span. Coal Company's span had steel beams, concrete floor, corr. iron parapets, stone and brick abuts.
	Table continues overleaf......			*The whole structure sold in 1979 : since demolished*	

No.	BETWEEN STATIONS	MPs	TITLE	SPANS No./LENGTH (SKEW)	REMARKS
33	Camerton-Workington Br	6-6.25	SALMON HALL No.1 (over Derwent)	1/ 41ft 8in (52ft) 1/ 38ft 6in (49ft 6in) 1/ 44ft 8in (53ft) *All spans removed since 1966 closure. The two river piers demolished c1983.*	WI main and cross girders and planking.
34	Camerton-Workington Br	6.6.25	SALMON HALL No.2 (over a Derwent channel)	1/ 44ft 3in (50ft) 1/ 34ft 4in (38ft) *Both spans removed since 1966 closure.*	Construction as for Salmon Hall No. 1
36	Camerton-Workington Br	6.25-6.50	BYEFALLS (over a Derwent channel)	1/ 25ft 6in (40ft 4in) 1/ 29ft (39ft 2in) *Both spans removed since 1966 closure.*	Construction as for Salmon Hall bridges.
37	Camerton-Workington Br	6.25-6.50	MILL RACE (over canal from Derwent to Seaton-Mill and Beerpot Works)	1/ 41ft (57ft 6in) *Span removed since 1966 closure. Seaton corn mill was just south of line and became a farm by circa 1930.*	Construction as for Salmon Hall bridges.
39	Camerton-Workington Br	6.50-6.75	CANAL (being above canal but downstream of mill race.) (served Beerpot Works)	1/ 34ft (59ft 4in) *Water piped and site largely filled in*	Constructions as for Salmon Hall, etc; very much on skew.
41	Camerton-Workington Br	6.75-7	BEERPOT (over former mill race, old Beerpot Works to Derwent)	1/ 16ft (29ft)	A very skew bridge, steel beams and floor plates; with concrete jackarches as reconstructed in 1896. *Survives 1984.*
42	At Workington Bridge Station	7.25-7.50	CALVA (overline carrying public road)	1/ 26ft (28ft)	Steel girders and brick jack-arches. Recon. significantly in 1960.
43	At Workington Bridge station	7.25-7.50	Passenger footbridge (over-line)	1/ 39ft	WI lattice girders and planking. *station closed January 1 1951 and bridge subsequently removed.*
44	Workington Br-Derwent Jn.	7.25-7.50	'LMSR' but generally known as 'navvies bridge' (carrying CWJR over LNWR)	1/ 49ft (57ft)	WI girders and planking Bridge No.49 in CWJR line schedule. *Maintenance transferred to Workington Corporation after closure*
45A	Workington Br.-Derwent Jn.	7.75-8	Highway viaduct (B5298 over line)	1/ 53ft 7in	Steel main and cross girders and plates. *It was maintained by Workington Corporation.*

THE SECTION OF ROUTE OVER THE WHITEHAVEN JUNCTION LINE, DERWENT JUNCTION TO WORKINGTON MAIN STATION:

No.	BETWEEN STATIONS	MPs	TITLE	SPANS No./LENGTH (SKEW)	REMARKS
37	Derwent Jn-Workington	7-7.25	DERWENT VIADUCT (over the tidal mouth of Derwent)	8 spans:- No.1 43ft (45ft 9in) 2-4 35ft (44ft) each 5-7 44ft 9in (56ft) each 8 43ft 9in (55ft)	Stone abutments; piers of WI cylinders each 6ft 1in dia and filled with brick in cement; steel main girders; footway on up (west) side - *reconstructed.*
36	Derwent Jn-Workington (at Jn. of Merchants Quay branch)	7-7.25	Public footbridge over line	1/ 42ft 3in	Stone piers, WI lattice girders and timber decking; timber steps renewed in concrete in 1960s.

No.	BETWEEN STATIONS	MPs	TITLE	SPANS No./LENGTH (SKEW)	REMARKS
35	Derwent Jn.-Workington	6.75-7	Harbour (Brewery Beck) (over tidal water)	1/ 32ft (32ft 5in)	Brick abutments, steel longitudal girders, brick jackarches and concrete floor.
33	Derwent Jn-Workington	6.75-7	South Quay (public road over line)	Two spans:- No.1 over main line 26ft 5in: S. end 35ft 9in: N. end No.2 over goods lines: 25ft	Stone abutments, stone piers, WI girders and floor plates. *This bridge was maintained by Corpn.*
32	At Workington Main Station	6.75-7	Passenger footbridge (overline)	Three spans:- 1 of 60ft 11in 2 of 10ft 1.50in (over platform)	Cast iron columns WI lattice girders, timber floor.

NOTES:

W.Jn. Railway Nos 37-32 are on open line today, unlike the structures which survive on the route of the CWR or the CWJR route.

Note that the river bridges on the C&W route all appear to reconcile with those rebuilt 1860-63, as widened subsequent to original construction in order to accommodate a double line of way.

Bridges on the C&W route have been presented in order of the Railway's numbering, east to west (Cockermouth Jn to Derwent Jn), whereas those on the CKPR will be taken west to east, in up direction, in line with their numbering and the mileposts on the route.

BRIDGES ON THE COCKERMOUTH, KESWICK & PENRITH LINE

Just as the nine-miles CWR route was notable for the number and dimensions of its bridges, so the 31 miles of the CKPR could claim similar distinction and it also displays a number of highly individual designs. These were mostly evolved by its Engineer, Thomas (later Sir Thomas) Bouch during building of the line in the years1862-64. The route was in a superb setting and involved negotiation of mountain streams, fast-rising and swift-flowing rivers and often-flooded pastures. Thomas Bouch had only recently completed the Stainmore route, designed to carry Durham coke to Furness and Cumberland and including among its works the lofty, spidery and quite spectacular iron viaducts at both Belah and Deepdale. It is interesting that nowhere on the CKPR route did the obstacles take the form of the deep ravines found on the Stainmore crossing of the Pennines. Had it been so, the appropriate drawings might have been taken out in Edinburgh, dusted and adapted. However, Bouch adopted various standard designs for his CKPR structures but the designs were of quite different standards, to suit widely differing locations on the route. The following may be distinguished:

1. Underline bridges with wrought iron trough girder spans of up to 20ft between their stone abutments, the transverse joists being also of wrought iron. One 25ft span is noted but that incorporated concrete jack arches and would probably date from works of 1901-02. Bridge No. 134 (over the NER double track near Redhills) was of 36ft 6in span, employing wrought iron main girders and cross girders but this may have been of NER design and construction.

2. Overline bridges having wrought iron girder spans on stone abutments, with jack arches and tie rods beneath the carriageway in the original design and finished off by the insertion of delightful cast iron railings in the parapet walls beside the road.

3. Handsomely-proportioned stone arched bridges, with stone abutments and sometimes with wing walls, for both overline and underline spans of up to about 20ft.

4. Comparable stone arched underline bridges of rather greater span.

5. Underline viaducts with several arches (for example, 12 arches over Mosedale) of around 22-30ft individual arch-span, the structures being in masonry but with the actual arches sometimes in brick. I have not established whether the brick arches were original or introduced during the reconstruction works of the 1890s.

6. The screw-piled underline bridges. These were commonly (but not invariably) employed in crossing low-lying lands subject to flooding and seen between Braithwaite and Keswick, also at bridge 78, Screw Ghyll. over the Glenderamachin river. Cast iron piles, threaded at the foot, were screwed into the ground using a suspended augur or 'whim' type of tool and then built-up by superimposing and bolting cast iron tubular columns to achieve the desired height. Each pier was formed of a pair of these columns, of 12in diameter, inserted and set up transversely to the line of the route and connected by light diagonal stays. The span between the piers was typically of 23-24ft, having cast iron side girders and timber transverse joists, timber longitudinals and timber decking, the whole stiffened by 1 1/4in diameter iron tie rods in the timber floor. The width across each twin pier and the superstructure was adequate for a single line of railway, never double track in the CKPR examples of this construction. Stone abutments were located at the ends of these multiple-span bridges.

7. Bowstring girder underline bridges of wrought iron construction, on land-based stone abutments, each bridge a single span of 64-119ft and with no intermediate piers. The 64ft (upright) span was in bridge No. 47 over the Derwent.

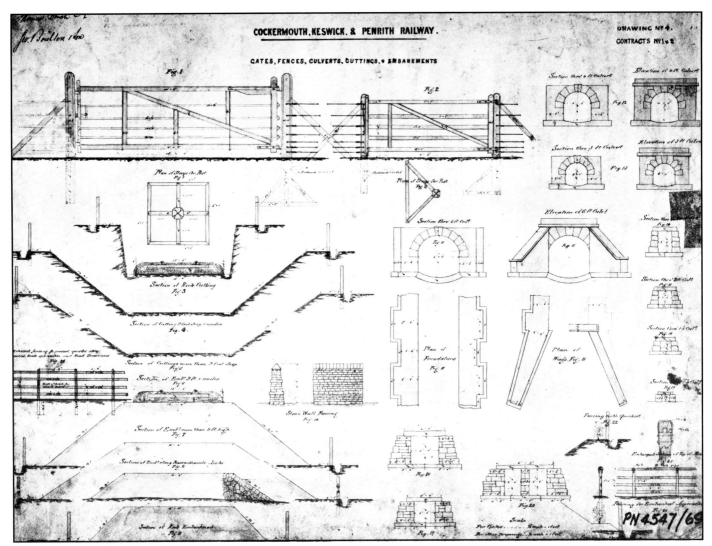

Above: A selection of culverts, smaller bridges, fences, gates, embankments and cuttings - drawn and signed by 'Thomas Bouch, CE' and his contractors 'Geo Boulton & Son'.
Courtesy Chief Civil Engineer LMR/BR.

Right: A contemporary Teesside name of the1860s - seen embellishing an underline accommodation bridge near Embleton.
Richard L. Pattinson/CRA,

Spans of 80-119ft were employed for the river bridges in the Greta gorge between Keswick and the Glenderamachin. Of these, three have upright bowstring side girders (the curved boom being above rail level) and four employ inverted 'bowstrings' (with the curved boom below rail level). The range of span is much the same for each type. It is suggested that Bouch preferred the inverted arrangement but clearance above the river bed and high water was not in all cases adequate to permit this arrangement

8. Single-span overline bridges of substantial length, for example, 60ft, with slightly-arched lattice side girders and (originally) timber transverse joists and timber decking, the bridges springing from stone abutments set in the upper part of the sides of cuttings. These structures (seemingly eight in number) were primarily intended for 'accommodation' use between farmers' fields and suitable only for restricted loads. That giving access to Threlkeld quarry was

the one most severely treated and it still carries some road traffic today; steel transverse joists were substituted at some date in its history. These are bridges of graceful, almost airy, appearance and have been informally styled 'birdcage bridges' or 'fly bridges'.

It is believed that all these designs date from Bouch's work as Engineer and that of Boulton as the original contractor to the CKPR - although original drawings have not been found in all cases.

The widening of the line to double track between
Continued on page 133

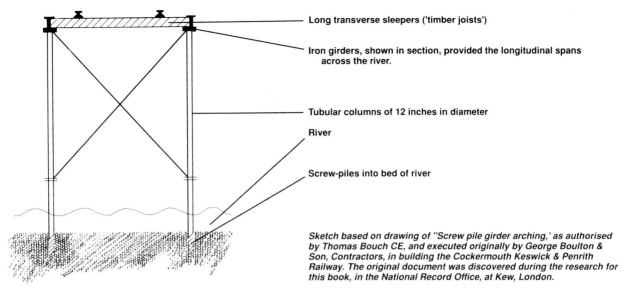

Long transverse sleepers ('timber joists')

Iron girders, shown in section, provided the longitudinal spans across the river.

Tubular columns of 12 inches in diameter

River

Screw-piles into bed of river

Sketch based on drawing of "Screw pile girder arching,' as authorised by Thomas Bouch CE, and executed originally by George Boulton & Son, Contractors, in building the Cockermouth Keswick & Penrith Railway. The original document was discovered during the research for this book, in the National Record Office, at Kew, London.

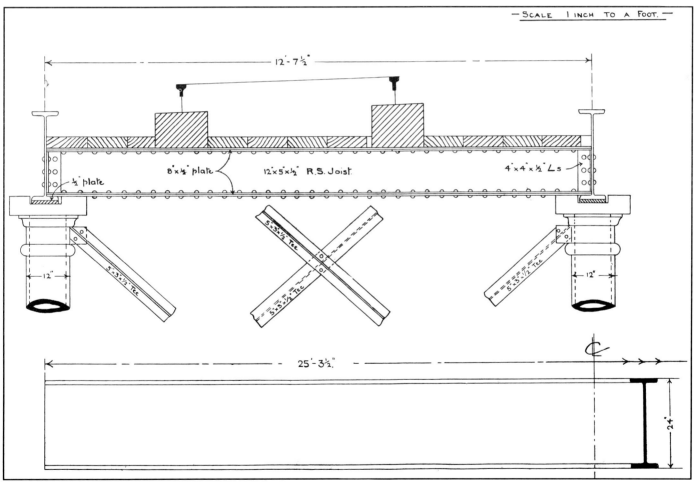

— SCALE 1 INCH TO A FOOT. —

12'-7½"

8"x½" plate

½ plate

12x5x½" R.S. Joist.

4"x4"x½" Ls

5x3x½ Tee

12"

12"

25'-3½."

24"

Above: The troublesome multi-span bridges, carried on cast iron columns and screw piles figured mainly between Braithwaite and Crosthwaite, their numbers within the range 39-51. This LMS drawing (undated, but probably of 1936) shows the upper portion of a pair of original 12in diameter cast iron columns of 1863-64, still in use and tied together by original diagonal iron stays, of which the dimensions and form are apparent. It is bridge No. 41 (Newlands Beck) and the steel girder span (shown) was installed in 1914 (or slightly later) to replace the original transverse timber joists which had been supported by cast iron side girders and strengthened by 1.25in diameter iron tie rods in the timber floor. The columns were still based on screw piles in the 1930s.
J.M. Hammond collection/Carlisle Record Office.

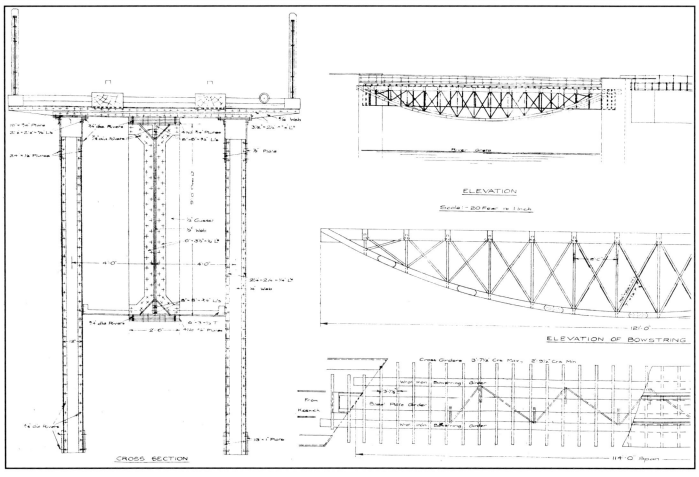

Threlkeld and Troutbeck in 1893-94 involved the rebuilding of several overline road bridges. An interesting standard was adopted for this work, employing deep, cast iron outer girders to a curved profile and four intermediate straight webbed girders, on stone abutments. Brick jackarches, each of 4ft or so span and five in number typically complete the deck, which supported the foundation 'puddle' for a carriageway, which was about 20ft wide between parapets. It was a late date for the use of cast iron in new bridgeworks, albeit these were not underline bridges; steam road vehicles could well be required to cross them. The only *underline* bridge not of masonry/brick arch construction on the section doubled in 1893-94 was No. 86 (Guard House) of nearly 20ft span, and here steel girders were employed. By the time the doubling was extended from Troutbeck to Penruddock (1900-01) the CKPR's Engineer was employing steel girders and *concrete* jackarches for underline bridges crossing roads.

In LMS and BR days, reinforced concrete was prominent in new bridgeworks on the route, particularly in construction of bridge decks.

Facing page, upper: Between Keswick and Threlkeld could be found a series of mostly bowstring girder spans in wrought iron, within the Greta gorge. This is Stank Dub, bridge No. 59, at Keswick, viewed upstream into the gorge. The bridge is formed of a pair of inverted bowstrings, of 113ft 6in span. strengthened in 1933 with a massive steel centreplate girder. *Harold D . Bowtell.*

Facing page, lower: Part of the LMS drawing prepared for the strengthening of bridge 59 in 1933. The upper right portion of the drawing shows how the longitudinal girder lay between the bowstrings, whilst on the left is a vertical cross-section of the structure as modified. *J. M. Hammond Collection/Carlisle Record Office.*

Below: Bridge No. 59, illustrated in detail on April 4 1984 and clearly showing the strengthening girder. *Harold D. Bowtell.*

The CKPR line was thus notable for the aesthetic and technical interest of its bridges – but it was also notorious for the amount of trouble and anxiety which many of them caused throughout the 101 years of its existence as a through route, from 1865 to 1966. The accompanying study of timetables and train working shows that this was never a heavily used route for minerals, goods or passengers, nor did speeds range high.

In December 1885, the Board of Trade asked for a report on iron underline bridges but the Company's Board, realising their weakness, resolved (January 1886) on a non-committal reply, and they were not pressed by the Board of Trade. Their Permanent Way Committee was at this time already expressing its concern about the screw-pile bridges. John Wood had been resident engineer under Bouch during the CKPR's construction and had been Company Engineer from the opening of the line. He was authorised by the Board (in February 1886) to substitute wrought iron cross girders for the wood beams in one span of the screw-pile bridges. One wonders whether this decision is correctly recorded. Should it not point to putting *one* wrought iron cross girder in *each* span of the relevant bridges?

The near-flimsy construction of the CKPR's screw-pile bridges, the relatively light dimensions of the long-span bowstring girder bridges and developing defects in the arched viaducts were not major problems until the new century, as meanwhile the LNWR 'Special DX' and NER '1001' 0-6-0 locomotives had jogged contentedly to and fro, with a maximum of no more than 35 tons or so spread over three coupled axles. However, in 1901 the NER built its first eight-coupled mineral locomotive, the 'T' class, with more than 58 tons carried by four coupled axles, and in February 1904, NER Locomotive Superintendent Wilson Worsdell wrote to suggest running these engines through to Cockermouth with the coke trains. John Wood joined Peter

Thompson, CKPR Secretary and General Manager, in meeting Vincent Raven, Assistant to Mr Worsdell, to discuss this proposition. Prompted by his board, Mr Thompson then wrote to enquire whether the NER would help with the cost of necessary bridgeworks. This brought a response from NER General Manager George S. Gibb, who replied sternly, indeed with asperity, suggesting that it was the responsibility of the CKPR as a revenue-earning concern to renew its own bridges!

In 1906, the issue was still live, with the NER wishing to run the 'T' locomotives through and also now asking for the 'C' and 'C1' class 0-6-0 engines to run over the line, probably on excursions from the NE to Keswick. A meeting was held at Penrith with Messrs Thompson, Wood (by now engineering consultant) and A.M.Bristow (the newly-appointed Engineer) representing the CKPR whilst Messrs Smeddle (District Locomotive Superintendent, Darlington) and Bengough were the NER representatives. The proposition was to run the 'C' engines for a few months and monitor the effect on rails and bridges. In July 1906, the CKPR agreed to spend £60 on work necessary to allow the 'C' engines but in August, following costings by Mr Wood, the Board decided not to undertake strengthening of bridges for the much heavier 'T' class 0-8-0s. Consequently, the NER settled down to running 'P' or 'P1' 0-6-0s, little heavier than the old '1001', on its mineral trains over the CKPR. Presumably, the

Above: White Moss bridge, No.69, is an upright bowstring, with 80ft skew span, seen here looking west. No spectacular strengthening is reported but four supplementary transverse understruts extend as outriggers and carry stays to stiffen the main bowstrings.

Right: Brundholme, bridge No.71, an upright bowstring of 100ft skew span, looking broadly east. Much strengthening is apparent in the sides, *and beneath*, whilst longitudinals are also riveted on top of the curved upper beams of the bowstrings.
Both: Harold D. Bowtell.

larger-wheeled 'C' class mixed-traffic type came in on special passenger trains. Meanwhile, the LNWR was content to run 'Special DX' and '18in Goods' (alias 'Cauliflowers') – both lighter locomotives than their NER contemporaries – on passenger and goods trains.

Around 1912, some work (not radical) was done on screw-pile bridges. Subsequently, with the permission of the LNWR's General Manager, the District Engineer for the Company's Northern District, Mr Thurstan, based at

Continued on page 138....

Top: Rowsome, bridge No.73 (an inverted bowstring of 80ft span) clearly showing the massive strengthening of 1926; a very deep central longitudinal, in steel, is inserted beneath, with stays beneath to the bowstring girders (earlier, in 1905, additional cross girders had been installed) *Harold D. Bowtell.*

Above: This is Crozier Holme (No. 75, 101ft skew) seen looking westward with an Up train approaching. This view shows features of the strengthening of 1931: transverse under-girders with outrigger extensions and stays. Note the superelevation of the curved road, and the longitudinal baulks beneath the rails. *Richard L. Pattinson/CRA.*

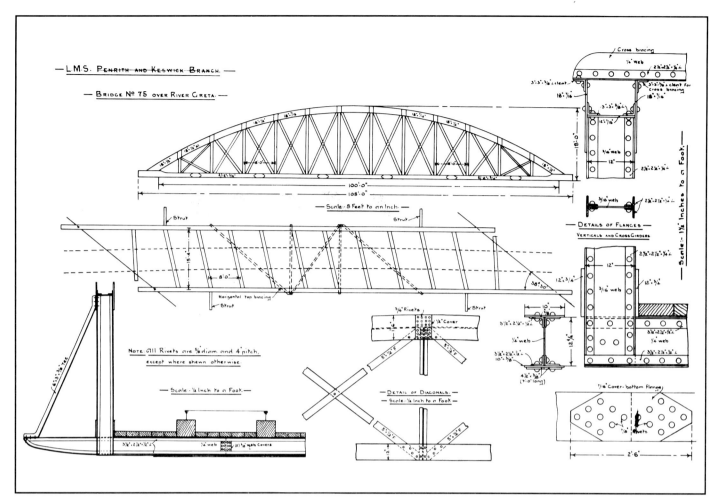

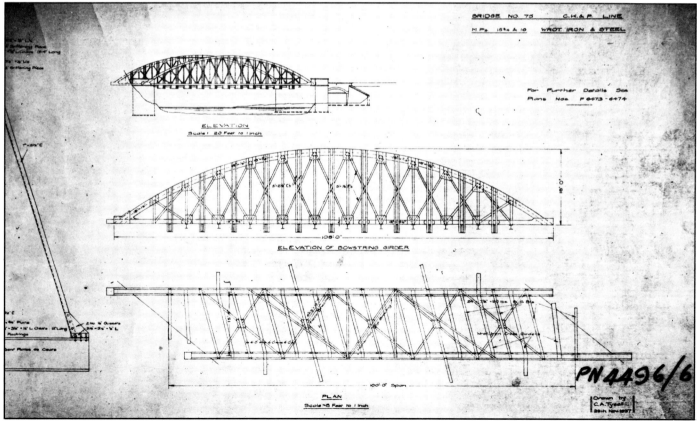

Facing page: These Manchester (Hunts Bank) drawings of bridge No. 75 show the structure in its original form, and as strengthened by the LMS. The later drawing (lower) is shown as 'drawn by C.A. Tysall, 29th Nov. 1937', but the main work was done in 1931. The older drawing (upper) is believed to have been done by Jimmy Alexander, who had been third man at Barrow, Furness Railway, under Rutherford, the chief engineer (civil and mechanical) and Tom Mason, the second in command there. Mr Alexander went on to be District Engineer, Low Moor, after earlier promotion in Manchester. *Courtesy Chief Civil Engineer/LMR/BR.*

Above: Out of the Greta gorge at last; this is Screw Ghyll (alternatively Glenderamachin or Glenderamackin) bridge No.78 had cast iron columns on screw piles and six spans but was rebuilt as seen in 1936. This featured a single 77ft steel span of riveted construction between abutments of concrete, with stone facings; it has a floor of rolled steel joists and concrete and is seen from the southerly side. Threlkeld station is not far to the right. *Harold D. Bowtell.*

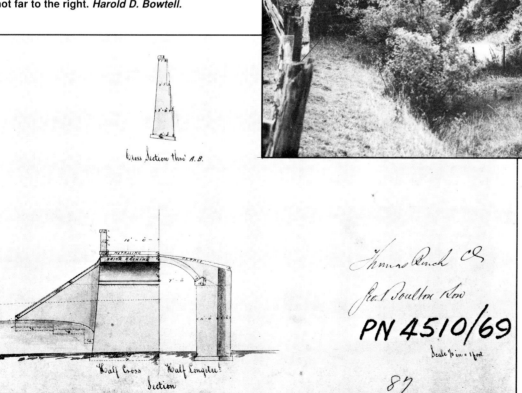

Above: Bridge No. 87 at Hill Cottage, looking east, is seen as rebuilt for doubling of the line, with cast iron side members which carry the raised inscription: PRATCHITT BROTHERS CARLISLE 1893. The abutments and parapet walls are in masonry with brick barrel (or 'jack') arches, the ridges of which are faintly visible between the cast side members. *Harold D. Bowtell.*

Left: This is part of an original drawing for bridge No. 87, then for single line, by Bouch and Boulton. *Courtesy Chief Civil Engineer/LMR/BR.*

A general view of Mosedale viaduct, bridge No. 89: it had masonry abutments and 12 brick arches, each of 29ft 4in span, of which the left (easterly) one is almost hidden.
Harold D. Bowtell.

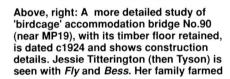

Above, left: Looking past the catchpoints, westwards down the bank between Troutbeck and Threlkeld, accommodation bridge No. 90 is seen spanning the running lines, doubled after 1890.
Richard L. Pattinson/CRA.

Above, right: A more detailed study of 'birdcage' accommodation bridge No.90 (near MP19), with its timber floor retained, is dated c1924 and shows construction details. Jessie Titterington (then Tyson) is seen with *Fly* and *Bess*. Her family farmed

(and still do, at the time of going to press) at Highgate, close by. The question arises as to whether this bridge was reconstructed or renewed for the doubling of this section of line in the 1890s.
Jessie Titterington Collection

Lancaster, was invited to report on civil engineering aspects of the CKPR. This was in May 1913 and his reports were forthcoming between July and September 1913. Mr Thurstan recommended infilling the screw pile bridges between Braithwaite and Keswick so far as practicable and strengthening those spans retained to cope with streams or flood waters. Meanwhile, in November 1913, a speed limit of 45mph was imposed over the whole length of the CKPR. This probably caused no inconvenience for the slow mineral and goods trains but it could cramp the downhill style of the sprightly 2-4-0- 'Jumbo' passenger engines, which were then coming into use on the line. In January 1914, the CKPR Engineer issued a list of screw- pile bridges for partial filling and strengthening: Nos. 41, 48-51 and 78 (Screw Ghyll/Glenderamachin). No.41 was tackled at once. The committee on bridges walked the line from Braithwaite to Keswick in April 1914 and their recommended list for attention on this section embraced Nos. 39, 40, 42-45 and

48-50. The committee at this time had an eye to heavier locomotives and the tendency for subsidence of screw-piled columns under railway loadings - as distinct from those of, for example, seaside piers, which were built in similar style. They suggested that extra intermediate columns set on concrete bases be provided - but in fact this course was never adopted by the CKPR.

Work proceeded during the years1914-19 on the above-mentioned bridges and is detailed in the ensuing schedule. In 1918, the Railway received vociferous complaints from landowners concerning flooding attributed to infilling at bridge No. 43 (Watery Lane, near MP11, north of Braithwaite); an additional element of flood relief was then introduced. Filling of screw pile bridges was resumed after nearly 10 years interval, in 1928 and 1930 - and total reconstruction took place in 1935, 1936 and 1938, No. 78. (Screw Ghyll) was replaced by a single-span steel bridge, while the others in this period were rebuilt in steel or reinforced con-

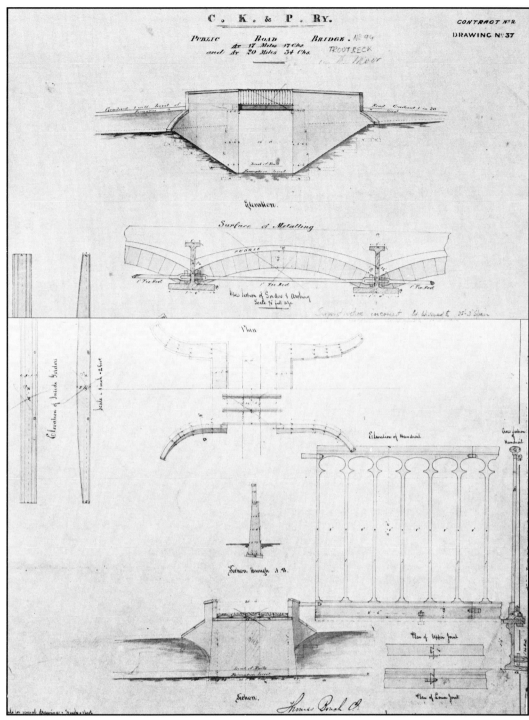

C. K. & P. RY.

PUBLIC ROAD BRIDGE. No.94
At 17 Miles 17 Chs
and At 20 Miles 34 Chs

CONTRACT No.2
DRAWING No.37

Left: It is good to see these original Bouch/Boulton drawings of Gibson bridge (No.94) located east of MP20, between Highgate and Troutbeck. Observe the delicate cast iron handrails, inset in the parapet wall, also the jackarches below the carriageway. *Courtesy Chief Civil Engineer/LMR/BR.*

crete. Finally, there was work in 1950 and 1955, also recorded in the schedule. In filling, the usual practice, was to remove the old superstructure and tip 'fill' material, burying the piers in the resulting embankment, commonly with one modern bridge span or just a penetrating culvert (for flood relief) retained. In retrospect, how much easier it would have been to adopt the 'embankment with culverts' approach of 1862-64.

The lofty multiple-arched viaducts also caused anxiety and the resultant work was primarily seen at Penruddock, Mosedale and Cockermouth. At Penruddock, after urgent inspection by Mr Thurstan of the LNWR at Lancaster, five arches were filled, in the 1918-20 period. At Mosedale

viaduct, buttressing of arches, particularly in 1943-44, was carried out and is self-evident today. Inadequate thickness and strength in the spandrel walls above the arches prompted the insertion of transverse tie rods in many arches, notably at Mosedale. The Cocker arched viaduct was converted during 1944-45 to a three-span bridge of reinforced concrete beams. Leonard Fairclough, a Lancashire contractor experienced in concrete work, were enlisted for this job. The casting and curing of pre-cast concrete beams was done on an adjacent site, and the LMS brought large cranes from Crewe and Horwich. It will be observed that crises tended to develop inconveniently during the difficult days of both world wars of the 20th century.

Right: Penruddock viaduct, (bridge No.105) east of the station of that name. As seen, this featured four arches of 25ft 3in apiece, but it had been built with nine arches; Nos. 1-5 (nominally) were filled in the period 1918-20. This structure was never widened. The view is from the south east.
Harold D. Bowtell.

There is a hint on record that work was in hand on bowstring girder bridges in the Greta gorge in 1897 and No.73 (Rowsome) was fitted with additional cross girders in 1905. The problem with the CKPR bridges of this type was simply that they were not of sufficiently robust design for the locomotives which the LMS of the 1920s and 1930s wished to run over the route from Penrith to Keswick and beyond. The NER/LNER coke traffic had declined to virtually nothing by 1925, but the LMS was then looking at tourist potential for the route and it was probably around this time that the Chief (Civil) Engineer promised the Chief General Superintendent (the senior commercial and operating officer) that he would reconstruct, strengthen or eliminate at least one weak bridge each year on the CKPR/CWR route, with priority for the Penrith-Keswick section. The bowstring bridges were consequently dealt with in 1925 (No.73), 1928 (No.74),1929 (Nos. 67 and 71), 1931 (Nos.66 and 75) and 1933 (No.59). No.69 required no substantial works.

Each reconstruction was a major operation, typically involving a long weekend line possession, the new components being prepared and brought to site in advance, so far as space permitted, while two or three cranes were in attendance for the selected weekend.

In the upright bowstring girders, the curved upper flange is the compression flange or boom and an inherent weakness in the original design was the inadequate bracing of these flanges. Transverse stays could be installed between the pair of curved upper flanges if the depth was sufficient to do this, while clearing the loading gauge for passage of trains below the stays - and in any case these stays could only be placed towards the centre of the span. This practice was adopted by LMS engineers but its limitations explain why the universal method followed was to install transverse cross girders below the bowstrings and under the bridge deck, with these girders extending as 'outriggers' from which rigid stays (superficially reminiscent of the much-less rigid stay wires to a tall signal post) were erected to give strength to the bowstrings.

Various extra vertical stays were also bolted onto the sides of the bowstring girders to improve rigidity. There was less interruption of railway traffic during this work than in carrying out the operation required for the inverted bowstring girder bridges.

These structures called for different treatment, as the lower curved flange was overstressed in *tension* and the strength of the whole superstructure had to be increased. This was accomplished by installing a deep steel plate-web girder longitudinally beneath the centre of the bridge, the abutments being cut away to receive its ends. On completion, the new substantial under-girder carried a substantial share of the load of the bridge. Total occupation of the line and site was necessary during the crucial stages of the work on this type of bridge. An example readily viewed today is bridge No. 59 at Stank Dub, Keswick.

The conversion to single track of the section between Blencow (exclusive) and Redhills Junction in mid-1938 enabled the stronger side of the underline bridges (none of which were major structures) to be retained and this was generally the Up (original) side. This work completed the programme to give access as far as Keswick to locomotives such as Class 5MT and 5X 4-6-0s although, until the new 60ft turntable at was commissioned at Keswick in the summer of 1939, it was not helpful to run these engines.

Some of the nominally lesser bridgeworks could have their problems. Roy Hughes has recalled from his early days as a bridge engineer, based at Hunt's Bank, Manchester, the replacement of Thornthwaite aqueduct, which carried the waters of a beck *over* the railway (a most unusual situation) to flow towards the Bassenthwaite lake shore. There were two 'accommodation' farm lanes on the same bridge, above the water channel. The superstructure of the new bridge comprised a welded tank, fabricated in position on top of the old bridge, its weight being transferred to trestles from which it was lowered after the old bridge had been dismantled; the farm ways were replaced by a joint road on top of the covered aqueduct. During the operations, the beck was diverted beside the railway into a large storage pond. At this critical stage, torrential rain over-filled the stream and the railway became a river!

In this vicinity, sadly, the A66 road obliterates the course of the railway today together with part of the neighbouring meadows. However, a new bridge maintains the earlier tradition by carrying the aqueduct channel and providing access between the farms and their fields.

The tragedy at Brigham, December 16 1936

With one exception, the long-span bowstring girder bridges of the CKPR have been left standing since the closure of the line and can still be studied today.

Another bridge of comparable design for long existed in the district of the CWR line and its construction was roughly contemporary with that of the CKPR's bridges. It was an upright bowstring girder structure, in wrought iron, crossing the river Derwent diagonally and carrying the single track of the MCR Derwent branch, from Bullgill to Brigham, opened in 1867 and giving M&C trains access to Brigham, and thence to Cockermouth and Keswick. The span of 130ft was greater than any of the CKPR line's bowstring girder bridges. The LMS closed the Derwent branch wef 29 April 1935 and towards the end of 1936 it put in hand the demolition of its most notable engineering feature, the bridge at Brigham.

The civil engineer in charge of the work was Richard Gauld, 40 years of age and highly regarded for his varied practical experience and professional knowledge. He was noted for his judgment and care, especially his concern for men working with him. Mr Gauld had for several years been the LMS resident engineer, bridge gangs, in the northern division, based at the divisional headquarters, Hunt's Bank, Manchester; there were four gangs in the division. From August 1935, he held the appointment of resident engineer in charge of all LMS bridge gangs in England and Wales and was responsible to the Chief Engineer of the LMS.

Richard Gauld planned the method of dismantlement and entrusted it to his bridge gang based at Barrow. Work proceeded for some five weeks, with seven or eight men employed. On Wednesday December 16 1936, the job was approaching a critical stage and Mr Gauld travelled from his home in Cheshire to take charge, arriving on site at 11.00 am. The prevailing weather was typical of December in Cumberland, with the Derwent in spate and swift-flowing, but wind conditions did not call for postponement of the work. The deck of the bridge had been dismantled and steel cables had been secured and stretched across the river immediately beneath the bridge. This was in order to provide tension members when the oxy-acetylene cutting down of the bowstring side girders eliminated its upper curved boom (normally the compression member of the bridge) and converted the horizontal booms to compression members.

While the cutting operation was under way, there was suddenly a jerk, when the crucial reversal of stress probably occurred (as visualised in advance) but the cables failed to play their part; one parted, and four men were hurled into the surging river below, clinging to scaffold planks. They were: Richard Gauld, the engineer in charge; Alexander ('Sandy') Riddett, foreman of the Barrow bridge gang; Robert Mitchell, chargehand plater and second man of the gang, and workman T. Davies. The alarm was conveyed by railway telephones from Brigham, westward to stations and signal boxes on the Workington line, which crossed and recrossed the Derwent in the next few miles. All within range of the emergency calls rushed to access points on the riverbanks, while at Camerton a barrier of wires and ropes was rigged across the river, secured to the structure of the footbridge which crossed the stream to reach the station.

Below: The LMS (originally MCR) bridge (No. 166) over the River Derwent at Brigham was dismantled during November-December 1936 and this shows the structure, looking north to the MCR line, following closure. A telegraph pole at extreme right marks the CWR route from Brigham station, heading for Cockermouth. One may recall the early view in the MCR platform of Brigham station. This photograph was taken by Richard Gauld, the engineer, probably in summer 1936. *Albert Timms Collection.*

Davies was soon swirled into flooded fields on the left bank and was saved, although unconscious, by A. Birkett, Stationmaster at Broughton Cross. Robert Mitchell, a young man, succeeded in steering his plank towards the same bank and was successfully grabbed by Porter Weightman, also of Broughton Cross. Mitchell had been carried by the current, estimated at 15mph, close to Richard Gauld and almost propelled the latter's plank into arresting bushes on the bank. He thought he had achieved this but unhappily the engineer was carried on. Both Gauld and Riddett were seen, still clinging to their planks, further downstream but the water was bitterly cold and both lost their lives.

A squall of wind may have contributed to the collapse but the occurrence and its fatal outcome pointed, with hindsight, to the wisdom of a different or modified technique or equipment. More to the point, the job should perhaps have been postponed until a more favourable time of year. At least one friend and colleague of Richard Gauld held that the underlying cause was prevailing pressure on him to complete a heavy programme of work, of which this task was just one part, if a hazardous one. Another life could have been lost, but Mr Gauld had earlier noticed that his Inspector, Robert Hogg, was ill and had sent him home. Robert Mitchell reported that the engineer's last words, in the rushing stream, were of concern for Riddett, the Barrow Foreman.

Subsequently, 22 colleagues contributed to a book entitled 'Richard Douglas Gauld, Civil Engineer: In Memoriam.', in tribute to his kindness to his staff and friends. He was well known on the CKPR line and often motored out from Disley to be on site cheerfully through a wet Lakeland Sunday, to see a bridge job through to completion. On a lighter note, he was the engineer who, in charge of the reconstruction of bridge No. 60 over Penrith Road, Keswick, in 1933, had problems because the steam crane was necessarily on the Penrith side of the bridge when its water ran low. It could not cross the gap to reach the water column - the 'elephant' - at Keswick station, so he organised the spectators into a human chain, from river to crane, passing buckets of water from one to another. Readers may recall a similar occurrence in the 1950s Ealing Comedy, *The Titfield Thunderbolt!* It perhaps illustrates the point that there can be a prototype for most things in the railway film and model world!

The reason for the reconstruction of bridge No. 60 was to enable it to carry the 36-tons stream crane which would uphold the last end of the new plate-web girder to be added to the adjacent bridge No. 59

Above: The MCR bridge at Brigham in early December 1936, again recorded by Richard Gauld. The bridge has been prepared for demolition and partly dismantled. The temporary staying, in preparation for further weakening, is seen. Alexander Riddett (foreman) and Robert Hogg (inspector) are on the right.

Right: The same scene on December 18 1936, following the disaster of December 16, when Alexander Riddett and Richard Gauld had been swept away to their deaths, when the bridge collapsed into the swollen river. *R.L. Brydon.*

Chapter 6

THE PERMANENT WAY

Above: A vintage view of a group of permanent way staff are seen by their cabin, in a westward view towards Bassenthwaite Lake Station. *Richard L. Pattinson/CRA.*

The Cockermouth and Workington Railway's permanent way

In the period 1856-60 (at least), sleepers were being ordered from Mr McGlasson; the price in 1860 was 3/8d each for sleepers 10in wide, 5in deep and 9ft long. This Railway's independent existence was during the time of iron rails and ,ten years after its opening, the CWR was still ordering rails of the early 'bridge' section, which had a broad base, or legs, bolted down to sleepers, and a narrower head or running surface. These rails weighed 72lbs per yard and were punched ready to take the holding-down bolts, they were invoiced at £8.15.0. per ton, at Gateshead. After mid-1866, the CWR was integrated with the LNWR and the practices of that Company's Lancaster & Carlisle section prevailed, as explained later.

Permanent way of the Cockermouth, Keswick & Penrith Railway

This company too employed iron rails in its early years. Its first orders were placed in the years 1861-62, in anticipation of the contractor's progress with the works; the Aberdare Company were to supply the rails, Cowan & Sheldon of Carlisle the chairs and Hopkins & Company of Middlesbrough the fishplates, bolts and nuts. Thus, chaired rail was preferred to the earlier pattern bridge rail. When

the track was mostly laid and opening of the line in prospect, the Board of Trade required (July 1864) that all the chairs adjoining rail joints should be replaced by heavier items, around a month's work. By the end of September 1864, the BOT was content with the track, although fringe problems remained.

Replacement with steel rails commenced early in 1871, after some six years of operating on the iron road, and the main programme of renewals was completed during the years 1871-75, when 2,700 tons of new steel rails of (mostly) 76lbs per yard section were acquired - from Barrow Hematite Steel Company in 1871-72 but from West Cumberland Iron & Steel Company, of Workington, in 1874-75. The price paid was £11 per ton in March 1871, rising steeply to £15 per ton in August 1872, then falling back to £10 per ton in October 1874 and progressively to £9.1/3d per ton (for a substantial order of 1000 tons) by December 1875. Some iron rails remained in use, but doubtless in sidings, until a special effort was made to clear them, in 1879-82. A scrap sale price of £3.0.0d to £3.10.0d per ton was the general order and a dealer in Middlesbrough who quoted £6.6.0d per ton in February 1880 not surprisingly found that he had overreached himself and cancelled his order in May 1880.

Also in 1880, it was reported by CKPR Engineer John Wood that the Company had until then used larch sleepers, with chairs of 20lbs weight, and heavier chairs of 30lbs weight adjoining rail joints, this feature no doubt deriving from the BOT's stipulation of 1864. He further reported that no accidents had resulted in course of 15 years running, but it was noted that the LNWR (L&C section) had latterly substituted chairs of 46lbs in its road. It was therefore agreed to use heavier chairs and imported (and creosoted) sleepers in future for progressive replacements.

The price of steel rails fell remarkably after the boom of the earlier 1880s. Supplies in 1885 came from West Cumberland Iron & Steel Co. Ltd at £5.0.0. per ton and in 1888 from Charles Cammell & Company (the most recently established of West Cumberland steelmasters) at only £3.19.0. per ton, delivered from Workington to Cockermouth; this was the cheapest of three competitive quotations. Rails of 1892, ordered for doubling a section of the CKPR route, cost about £4.10.0d per ton.

Rail sections were reviewed by the CKPR towards the end of 1897, it being noted that the Caledonian Railway had adopted 90 lbs per yard for when relaying its main lines, while the NBR employed 92 lbs per yard; be it noted, this was a time when much heavier locomotives were coming into service on the northern lines. The CKPR adopted 84 lbs per yard and abandoned the use of a double-headed (reversible) section. Both Cammells, of Derwent Works, and Moss Bay Iron & Steel Company, of Moss Bay Works, quoted £4.12.6. per ton for 84 lbs per yard rails in February 1898; in the event Cammells' quotation was accepted. Rails for widening works were supplied in 1900 by both Cammells and Moss Bay at £7.7.6. to £7.12.6. per ton, but delivered to Troutbeck and Blencow. Similar rails were being acquired in 1909 at £5.18.6. (after some haggling and reduction in price) from Moss Bay Hematite Iron & Steel Co. Ltd. The amalgamated Workington Iron & Steel Co. Ltd (James V. Ellis, Commercial and General Manager) quoted in January 1912 for steel rails "to Mr. Sandberg's latest specification for silicon steel," at 85 lbs per yard, to British

Above: At the east end of Keswick station, Jack Tyson (left) is ganger in charge of the Keswick 'length'; Jack Mills (centre) and Jack Ward are members, in LMS days. *Jack Tyson Collection.*

Standard (BS) section; and an order for 260 tons was placed in August 1913, at £6.1.3. per ton, for delivery over a period. Following the review of line and structures by Mr. Thurstan of the LNWR in 1913, significant relaying was required and the cost was kept down by purchase of enough second-hand materials from the LNWR's 'Marron line' (the 'Joint line', presumably) to relay four miles of CKPR track with 27-30ft rail lengths at 80 lbs and upward per yard. Wartime supplies were not always available and by February 1916, 85 lbs per yard BS rails were quoted at £10.17.6. per ton. The state of the main line and passing places in June 1916 was recorded as follows:

Total Mileage .... 41 miles 30 chains

Comprising 84lb rails of 1898 onward.... ....17mls 60 chains
    "   85lb rails of 1913 and 1916........... 3mls 2 chains
    "   80lb rails of 1914 and 1916.......... 4mls 44 chains
    "   76lb rails of 1888-95................. ......9mls 40 chains
    "   76lb rails of 1872-76......................6mls 44 chains

Right: LNWR 'Special DX' 0-6-0 No.1424 is in charge of the ballast train, at Keswick sometime between 1890 and 1910, and before the background trees grew up. *Stanley J. Rhodes Collection.*

DOUBLING OF THE LINE ON THE CKPR

The provision of a second track between Derwent Junction (Workington) and Cockermouth Junction was achieved piecemeal between about 1857 and completion in 1868. It has already been recorded, following study of the bridgeworks on the CWR section.

The CKPR was built as a single track route throughout, apart from provision to cross trains at (initially) four of the intermediate stations. The need for double track became apparent as traffic developed in the 1880s and 1890s, especially over the steep gradients between Keswick and Penrith, notably between Threlkeld and Troutbeck. In December 1892, the Permanent Way Committee reviewed the situation and recorded that Threlkeld to Troutbeck was a section of 4 mls 59 chains and had always been difficult to work, as the line climbed eastward from Threlkeld station for about three-quarters of a mile at 1 in 68 and then at 1 in 62 for the whole distance beyond. The times usually taken by trains to traverse the section were:

	Passenger	General Goods	Minerals
Down (westbound):	10min	13min	15min
Up (eastbound):	14min	18-20min	20min

However, due to weather and other factors, the eastbound times ranged to 30min, and even 40min when normal loads were exceeded. The *normal* service of the previous summer had reached 16 trains daily in each direction, comprising eight passenger, four mineral, three goods services and one ballast train. To these were added on most days relief or special excursion passenger trains and some additional goods trains, the additions sometimes numbering six or eight in the day, with the heavy long-distance excursions arriving, westbound to Keswick, during the morning and leaving, eastbound up the gradient, towards evening. These heavy excursions sometimes had to be shunted from one line to the other at Troutbeck (or elsewhere) to permit other traffic to overtake. As long as the Up traffic was worked under 'permissive block', three or four trains had been allowed to follow one another on the 4 3/4 miles of ascent. However, by recent Board of Trade order an intermediate blockpost had been built at High Gate and not more than two trains could now be accommodated at one time between Threlkeld and Troutbeck. As land for doubling had nearly all been purchased under Board authority

of December 1891, the committee recommended execution of the work of doubling this section of line.

R.H. Hodgson secured the contract fort the formation work, presumed to include bridges (there were two under-line viaducts to widen) while the supply and laying of track was undertaken by the Railway Company. Work was in hand from around July 1893 and was generally complete, with provisional approval granted by the Board of Trade, in August 1894, formal approval being secured in December 1894. The Company obtained an Act of June 1 1894 in order to regularise the financing of the widening works.

The next step was the doubling east of Troutbeck. No attempt was made to widen between Penruddock and Blencow, a section with an underline viaduct and heavy earthworks, including a rock cutting. Neither was widening contemplated between Redhills Junction and Penrith No.1 signalbox, a portion of the route not traversed by the majority of mineral trains or of long-distance passenger excursion trains. However, in March 1900 contracts were placed with W. Grisenthwaite of Penrith, for the formation on:

Section 1: Redhills Junction-Blencow - tender price £4,820.11.3d

Section 2: Troutbeck-Penruddock   -   "   " £5203.19.6d

Mr. Grisenthwaite had optimistically undertaken to complete his work by September 16 1900 – a mere six months – and the Company was displeased when their inspections between October 1900 and January 1901 revealed that progress was well behind target. The double line from Troutbeck to Penruddock was eventually brought into use on June 1 1901, with Board of Trade authority and subject to the recommendations of Colonel Yorke being complied with. By August 8 1901, the Board of Trade had provided a copy of Major Druitt's report on both newly-doubled sections of line sand it is believed that both were in use.

Reconversion of sections to single track is covered in the chapters dealing with stations and signalling of the route in LMS and BR days.

Chapter 7

SIGNALLING & GAS LIGHTING

Various signal boxes figure in the 'landscape' views already presented, so in this chapter interiors and unusual aspects are covered in greater detail

Above: A general view of the neat LMS signalbox at Brigham, built in 1936. *Peter W. Robinson.*

Right: An interior view at Brigham. The LNWR normally placed signalbox lever frames so that the signalman faced the line whilst operating his points and signals and could keep a continuous watch on trains and other movements. This interior at Brigham illustrated the LMS Company's adoption of frames based on Midland Railway practice and installed 'back to front'. Joseph Watson is working the level crossing gates. The loading bank and limestone sidings can be seen to the west, over the crossing. *Phoebe Wallace*

Signalling on the Cockermouth & Workington Railway

The term 'signalling' must have had a very limited meaning for the CWR's nine miles of route. After 10 years existence, in March 1857, the Company agreed to contribute to the Whitehaven Junction Railway's expenditure on installation of semaphore signals in the areas of Workington joint station yard and Derwent Junction. In April 1861, the CWR itself instructed the Electric Telegraph Company to install a single telegraph line between Workington and Cockermouth, with three single-needle transmitting instruments, at a rental of £55 a year.

In May 1865, nearing the end of its days, the CWR became concerned at the total absence of distant (warning) signals for its 'roadside stations', so Saxby & Farmer were commissioned to supply and erect semaphore signals at all the roadside stations, at a cost of £506.15.6. A year or so later, the Railway was part of the LNWR and its more critical approach and practices towards signalling began to take effect.

Signalling on the Cockermouth Keswick & Penrith Railway

The CKPR itself was little more than 30 miles in length but it came on the scene at a time when Railway Companies throughout Britain, and the Board of Trade as their 'Keeper', were beginning to evolve and encourage more sophisticated systems for safer operation. This called for: better communications, the provision of semaphore signals and associated equipment and buildings - and more men.

The Board of the CKPR Company turned down an early suggestion from the LNWR that it might at the start secure adequate land to permit later doubling of its line. All bridge-works and other structures, with formation and main running lines, were thus designed for a single track, with loops to permit 'crossing' of Up and Down trains initially at Cockermouth (passenger station), Bassenthwaite Lake, Keswick and Penruddock stations. Troutbeck, between Keswick and Penruddock, was provided with a crossing loop in 1874, nine years after the general opening to traffic.

The suggestion that electric telegraph communication would in the assist safer despatch of traffic on the railway came in October 1862 from contractors George Boulton & Sons, who were by then at work on construction. The telegraph was installed between Penrith and Keswick - and subsequently also between Keswick and Cockermouth. In due course, the LNWR's well-tried telegraph regulations provided a model for the CKPR. A few years after the opening of the line, it was noted that Stationmasters on the CKPR must be able to read and use telegraph communication - "on pain of dismissal." The Telegraph Acts of 1868 and 1869 nationalised the services in Britain and the Telegraph Company handed over the Penrith-Cockermouth installation to the Postmaster General, who paid the CKPR £1,300; the Railway Company thenceforward provided and operated the relevant lines with, in general, priority for their needs over the PMG's public messages. Progressively, telegraph messages lost their relevance for safe working of a railway but they long retained importance for the railway's commercial communications, even into the 1950s and early 1960s.

The 'train staff' method of working the CKPR was in force from the start of public operation in January 1865, and the Board of Trade had been appraised of the details. A substantial wooden 'staff' was allocated to the section between each pair of 'staff stations' and represented the authority for a locomotive driver to travel over the route between the

Left: Mr Tyer, pioneer signal engineer, put in for the CKPR his successive designs of train tablet instruments, for working single lines and the last variant was the 'Tyers No.6'. This example is illustrated in workshops but for many years the type was found in CKPR signal boxes and station offices. On authorisation electrically from the box in advance, the signalman can pull out the drawer at the bottom of the case and remove a circular brass tablet as authority for the engine driver to proceed through the section. This tablet has engraved upon it the name of the relevant track section and it is the driver's duty to check that he has received the correct tablet. He gives it up on reaching the next box. *Harold D. Bowtell/Courtesy Gordon Nichol.*

Above: Cockermouth station signalbox started life as a Saxby & Farmer installation of 1875, part of the CKPR's first 'modern' signalling to meet Board of Trade demands. It is seen after the LMS had installed a replacement MR-stylelever frame, facing south, away from the main running lines, which are in the foreground. *Roy Anderson Collection.*

Right: The LMS quickly replaced all Tyers tablet instruments on the CKPR with Tyers 'key token' equipment. This pair are illustrated in the station office at Embleton; one is concerned with working to/from Cockermouth and the other is for the opposite direction, to/from Bassenthwaite Lake; in the latter section, the 'key' was used to release the ground frame for access to Close Quarry sidings. *Phoebe Wallace, courtesy Thompson Collection* .

Below: A group of Tyers' key tokens used in the instruments at Embleton and neighbouring cabins. They are inscribed (L-R): Braithwaite-Bassenthwaite Lake; Bassenthwaite Lake-Embleton; Embleton-Cockermouth Station; Brigham-Cockermouth. *Harold D. Bowtell/ Courtesy Gordon Nichol.*

specified pair of stations. He was forbidden to run over the section concerned without the staff in his possession.

Block telegraph working, with its purposely-designed and distinctive instruments, is something which one has come to relate to double track railways rather than single lines, but in 1869 the Board of Trade (in accordance with its contemporary views) recommended it to the CKPR. The Keswick Board, not enamoured of the complication and expense envisaged, instructed its Secretary to reply, detailing reasons for *not* adopting it on the Lakeland line. By November 1874, following a fatal collision between passenger trains near Norwich, the Board of Trade pressed the matter and this time the Keswick Company acted promptly and installed the block telegraph. It was used solely to control the passage of trains and provided a means of securing authority to pass a train from one station or other 'block-

post' to the next; even so, the appropriate staff was still handed out to the driver as tangible evidence of his authority to enter a single line section. It is interesting that in the LNWR's record of single lines and train staff sections throughout its widely dispersed spheres of operation, in 1885, only one section of one route had the benefit of a train tablet system, or equivalent, and that appears below:

From L&NWR Appendix, April 1885
Single Lines and Train Staff Sections, West Cumberland Division, CK&P Line Section: Train Staffs:

Cockermouth Junc and Cockermouth............*(See footnote)*
Cockermouth and Bassenthwaite Lake...........Round Yellow*
Bassenthwaite Lake and Keswick..................Round Red
Keswick and Troutbeck.................................Round Blue
Troutbeck and Penruddock............................Round Yellow

*Tyer's Train Tablet System in operation between
Cockermouth Jct and Cockermouth station.
Block telegraph also operational in addition throughout.*

It may be noted that Embleton, Braithwaite, Threlkeld
and Blencow had not achieved the status of train staff stations at the time of this LNWR Appendix and that only one
focal point for train staffs at Keswick is implied; this may
have been either the old westerly signal box or the
Stationmaster's office. Staff working was supplemented at
discretion by 'staff and ticket' working, reinforced by the
block system, and successive trains could be despatched
from one blockpost to another by giving each driver a
ticket (of authority), while also showing him the relevant
staff, until arrival of the last driver of the sequence, who
would be given the staff to carry through the section.

Reverting to the 1870s, CKPR Engineer John Wood
reported in October 1873 from his formal professional
address at the time, at 8 Victoria Chambers, Westminster, on
the current disposition of points and signals on the railway.
As was common among railways of the period, the basic
signalling at a typical crossing station consisted of a platform signal, sited near the Stationmaster's office (which
contained the Post Office telegraph instruments and
housed a train staff for each section, when the staff was not
out in use). A semaphore arm for each direction of travel
was displayed on the post of the platform signal and a
distant signal for each direction of travel was sited some
distance out. Most of the main line facing points were bolt

Above: The ground frame at Limestone Sidings, Brigham, was
released by an Annetts key, normally held in the signal box and
here seen with its lettering 'Brigham'.
Harold D. Bowtell/Courtesy Gordon Nivchol.

Above: Aproaching Bassenthwaite Lake station, eastbound, a two
car 'Derby lightweight' DMU is nearing the Up platform. The CKPR
made a pretty job architecturally when replacing the Saxby cabin
here with this example of its own design, placed marginally closer
to the level crossing, in 1911. A rather crude little subsidiary cabin
containing a ground frame was sited at the opposite end of the
station and was for working the points at the far end of the lengthy
crossing loop. *National Railway Museum.*

locked with the distant signals, but not at Cockermouth, where both Up and Down trains used the platform nearest the town. Mr. Wood was thereupon authorised to remodel the signalling at Cockermouth, Bassenthwaite Lake, Keswick, Troutbeck and Penruddock stations at a cost quoted by the chosen signalling contractors, Saxby & Farmer, of about £3,500. Signals would be erected to meet the Board of Trade's standards: basically comprising distant, home and starting signals for each direction for a simple crossing station on the single line. All facing points would have facing point locks, which, along with other points on main running lines and the semaphore signals, would be

worked from a signal box, housing a fully interlocked lever frame, under the direct control of a signalman. The work was completed progressively by December 1875; in the process, Cockermouth was provided with independent Up and Down platform lines for through passenger trains and Troutbeck became a crossing station, with both Up and Down platforms.

Another unique feature of the table of staff sections in 1885 was the reference to the Tyer's train tablet system, in force between Cockermouth Junction and Cockermouth station. It put the CKPR well ahead of its time. Mr. Tyer had recently inaugurated his invention on the Callander & Oban

Right, upper: The lever frame in Bassenthwaite Lake signal-box of 1911 was by Tweedy of Carlisle. Edwin Thompson is seen as signalman, c1964. *Phoebe Wallace, courtesy Thompson Collection.*

Right, lower: The approach to Keswick from the west: the LNWR bracket signal, which-presumably replaced a CKPR signal in LMS days, is well loaded with balance weights, and 'slotted', to permit shared operation with No. 2 box (glimpsed over ballast wagon) and the quite distant No.1 box. *Richard L. Pattinson/CRA.*

Above: Keswick No. 2 box ('Box A' until 1924) originally contained a Saxby & Farmer lever frame of 1874 and the structure was also of their architecture. The building suffered modification in time and during the 1930s a LNWR frame was installed, facing (unusually) towards the rear of the cabin. The range of workshops behind the cabin also dated from CKPR times. *Roy Anderson Collection.*

line, operated by the Caledonian Railway, when early in 1883 he wrote to further prospective clients, including the CKPR. The neighbouring MCR showed a cheeky initiative in writing to Keswick to request that the Tyer's tablet system be introduced on the single track from the Junction to passenger station at Cockermouth "to obviate the repeated delays" - presumably referring to delays to the MCR's modest local passenger trains from Bullgill (on its Carlisle line) via Linefoot and Brigham, to Cockermouth. The CKPR was interested in this proposal and by August 1883, approval by the Board of Trade and the LNWR was obtained and a year's trial was authorised. The equipment was installed and had operated successfully for nearly five years when a review was undertaken. As a result, Mr Tyer's improved (No. 2 or 2A) type of electric tablet instruments were installed during 1889 at Cockermouth station (one instrument - presumably supplementing the existing installation), Bassenthwaite Lake (two) and Keswick (one) followed in circa 1891 by comparable instruments at Keswick (one – additional to the1889 installation), Troutbeck (two), Penruddock (two), Redhills (two) and Penrith (one) - while leaving existing block instruments in the 'intermediate or non-passing stations'.

There remained one creaking skeleton in the CKPR's signalling cupboard. When the Secretary and the Engineer of the Company met General Hutchinson of the Board of Trade on June 18 1892, to consider primarily the relatively innocuous topic of signal arrangements at the small or non-passing stations, the General's attention became sharply focussed on the revelation that permissive block working (trains following one another at sight or time interval) was operated between Threlkeld and Troutbeck in the Up (eastbound) direction, for some 4 3/4 miles, mostly ascending at the tough inclination of 1 in 62. An ultimatum was delivered: three months were allowed to bring in absolute block working on this portion of line. The problem had come about through pressure of traffic, especially slow-moving empty coke trains from the West Cumberland furnaces to Durham collieries, and the succession of return excursion trains running from Keswick to mainly NER destinations. The CKPR management had already been aware of its predicament, and had been buying land for widening the line and making the necessary plans, so they brought forward the establishment of a small intermediate blockpost (signalbox) at Highgate and thereafter the doubling of the whole section from a rebuilt station at Threlkeld, to Troutbeck, and eventually also from Troutbeck to Penruddock and between Blencow and Redhills Junction.

The CKPR engineer was responsible, in the 1865-1922 period, for signalling as well as civil engineering, permanent way and buildings. Whilst his main needs (including the earliest signalboxes) were designed and usually supplied by signalling contractors, notably Saxby & Farmer and Tyer, he later built boxes of distinctive designs, also making and modifying equipment and semaphore signals. The workshop accommodation for his fitters at Keswick was very restricted. The Company's blacksmith had other work to do and it is recalled that local smiths were called on from time to time to work on signal locking frames, and probably also in making rods, cranks and other components.

Signal boxes and junctions on the route

The following summary sets out the signal boxes on the route of the line from Derwent Junction (Workington) to Cockermouth Junction (opened in 1847 but only tabulated in its double track form) and on the CKPR from Cockermouth Junction to Penrith No.1 signalbox (opened to passengers in 1865). It touches on the main changes which affected signalling at each site, through both expansion and subsequent decline and closure of the route, ending effectively with the introduction of electric working on the West Coast Main Line between Preston to Glasgow, when BR's newly-electrified Anglo-Scottish expresses swept for the first time past the site of Penrith No. 1 box and the obliterated junction with the CKPR, in May 1974.

SIGNALBOXES (& SUBSIDIARY SIGNALLING FRAMES DERWENT JUNCTION (WORKINGTON) - PENRITH (No. 1)

MILES/YARDS	NAME/TYPE/DATE	HISTORY/REMARKS	CLOSURE DATE
-	**DERWENT JUNCTION** Saxby/prob c1870	Replaced a pointsman's cabin of 1847. Box had over sight of ground frame (GF) for Merchants Quay branch divergence. LNWR locking frame installed in 1888. Box replaced in 1955 by BR box with 1943-type frame of 40 levers.	The 1955 box remained open until repl. by GF on Nov. 12/13 1988
/1436	**WORKINGTON BRIDGE JN** LNWR type/1885	There was a hint in 1877 of the building (impending?) of this box.	c1950
/568	**DERWENT TIN PLATE WORKS** SIDINGS/1872	Beer Pot Siding and Bear Pot Gate dated from 1847. Box ceased to be a blockpost c1910; shown on plan, 1915. Barepot level crossing just to the east survived	Box prob demolished in the period 1916-22 April 18 1966
-	**SEATON MILL LC** 1847	Never a blockpost and was for many years under oversight of William Pit box	April 18 1966
1/ 37	**WILLIAM PIT COLLIERY** (becoming William Pit Sidings) LNWR type, 1881	contained LNWR frame of 14(later 18) levers	on January 27 1965
/1248	**CAMERTON** Probably 1870s.	Replaced a pointsman of 1847, Open only as required by 1906. Ceased to be a blockpost by 1916. Repl. from June 20 1935 by open GF (2 levers), entitled 'Camerton Station Level Crossing' but sited at colliery junction east of old box.	Box and its frame survived to 1935 January 27 1965
1/ 499	**MARRON JUNCTION** LNWR type, 1902	Replaced West and East boxes of c1871 (Nos. 1&2?) which had themselves repl. pointsman's cabins. Box repl. by GF (2 levers), November 7 1960 - In 1847 a pointsman was required at Broughton Cross but there was never a signal box or blockpost at that station.	prob. January 26 1965 GF
1/1704	**BRIGHAM No.2** LNWR type, 1883	The site enjoyed some supervision 1847-1966 on account of the LC here at west end of stn. Another signal box is shown to westward, on down side, on map of 1898, at jn. for branch to the quarries, but by 1905 ref is to a GF (although 'signal box' survived here on diagram of 1915). In 1950s a GF of one lever remained.	See below.
/ 196	**BRIGHAM No.1** LNWR type, 1877	Control in some form at this site would date from 1867, when MCR branch to Bullgill opened.	See below
	BRIGHAM LMS, Circa 1933	Replaced Nos 2 and 1 boxes. It was at west end of stn but east of the L.C. It contained LMS reversed frame of 29 (later 30) levers. Operation eastward became single May 16 1960.	April 18 1966
1/1430	**COCKERMOUTH JUNCTION** (responsibility of CKPR 1864-1922) Boxes built 1864 and 1873-76. LNWR type, 1886. GF installed 1960. Cockermouth Gas Works GF of L&NWR type, 1920s	Running Junction opened from CWR (soon to be LNWR) to the newly-built CKPR, in late 1864. on down side. First true signalbox built on Down side at this period. Electric tablet working to station from 1883. New box on Up side repl. the above in 1886; LNWR frame of 27 (later 36) levers Demise of GF Never a blockpost. The GF had 2 levers, released by key token for section	May 16 1960 (Box) Sept. 29 1965 (GF) 1963
/ 924	**COCKERMOUTH STATION** Saxby, 1875	with Saxby frame of 40 levers. Box structure modified over the years. A replacement LMS 45-levers frame of 1941 (or 1935?) was installed, reversed to face south (as was the earliest one?)	April 18 1966

MILES/YARDS	NAME/TYPE/DATE	HISTORY/REMARKS	CLOSURE DATE
2/1364	EMBLETON (never a box here)	Open GFs installed for yard and by LC. Block instruments were in station, repl. c1893 by electric tablet instruments.	April 18 1966
-	RAKEFOOT LC (no box) 1864	Never a blockpost. Acquired LNWR GF but later the signals were connected by wire to the gates.	April 18 1966
-	CLOSE GRANITE QUARRY SIDINGS (no box) 1912	Never a blockpost. LNWR type GF dated 1912 was put in by CKPR - released by tablet for section	1953 or 1954
2/550	BASSENTHWAITE LAKE Saxby, 1874	Repl. by CKPR box in 1911, with Tweedy frame. Electric tablet working in each direction from 1889. Additionally, a crude small box with 2 levers was put in by CK&PR, 1902, at east end, and lasted until...............................	April 18 1966 April 18 1966
4/1694	BRAITHWAITE (never a box here)	Open GFs installed for yard and by LC. Block instruments were placed in station office, and repl. c1893 by electric tablet instruments (akin to Embleton)	April 18 1966
2/792	KESWICK BOX 'A' (Keswick No.2 from c1924) Saxby, 1874	With originally a Saxby frame A repl. frame, LNWR type with 24(later 25) levers, was placed in the existing box, c1931, located (reversed) in back of box, unusual practice a LNWR frame. Ceased to be a blockpost wef April18 1966.	Line westward closed wef April 18 1966 December 4 1967
-	KESWICK BOX 'B' (Keswick No.1 from c1924) CKPRprob. 1889	Located on down platform, to south end. Replaced by LMS box reversed LMS frame of 24 levers, in 1932.	December 4 1967
-	BRIERY SIDING GF (no box) 1892	Never a blockpost. An open Tweedy GF (2 levers), released by the tablet for the section. It would not be used commercially after 1958.	Removed c 1962
3/836	THRELKELD CKPR 1893	With Tweedy frame of 18 levers, retained through-out. Electric tablet working with Keswick and with Troutbeck introduced prob. 1892, ie before the box was commissioned. Authority to cross trains given by BOT' recently (as at October 4 1893) and authy. for double line working eastward given August 1894.	December 4 1967
2/880	HIGHGATE CKPR, 1892	With Tweedy frame of 4 levers (but this internal frame was not installed and in use until cAug-Oct 1894). Initially, from November 9 1892, it was a blockpost on single line; from August 1894, double line.	May 1931
2/418	TROUTBECK Saxby, 1874	With Saxby frame. Troutbeck became a blockpost and crossing place on the single line from the date of the box. Electric tablet working with Threlkeld introduced prob. 1892 (but note that Highgate was opened late 1892) and with Penruddock likewise. From August 1894, double line block working with Highgate and from June 1901 (or July 1901) double line block with Penruddock. At unknown date, seemingly after 1901, a replacement frame of 16 levers, by Tweedy, was installed.	In later years the box could switch out. November 21 1966 or December 5 1966?
2/462	PENRUDDOCK Saxby, 1874	With Saxby frame. Located at down end of up plat. Penruddock was a crossing place from the start in 1865, with train staff. From 1874, staff working was with Troutbeck and with Redhills Jn. From prob. 1892, electric tablet wor-king operated with both those boxes. Double line block was worked with Troutbeck from June 1901 (or July 1901) - but working eastward was always on single line (tablet to Blencow from 1901). A replacement box (at up end of up plat.) by CKPR, dated from 1896, with Tweedy frame of 18 levers. A small supplementary box at west end of layout existed only from 1896 until 1901 (until doubling). The instruments were removed from Penruddock box to the station office in LMS days (or a little later).	December 4 1967
-	HARRISON'S LIME WORKS SIDING (Flusco) (no box) 1916	Never a blockpost. Original GF prob. by Tweedy. Repl. 1938 by a Tweedy frame (2 levers), released by key token for section	June 19 1972

MILES/YARDS	NAME/TYPE/DATE	HISTORY/REMARKS	CLOSURE DATE
-	FLUSCO QUARRY SIDING (No box) 1892	Never a blockpost. GF released by tablet for section	c1922
4/22	BLENCOW CKPR, 1901	With Tweedy frame of 22 levers; replaced 1938 by LMS frame of 35 levers, (reversed) in back of box. Electric token (Tyer's tablets in CK&PR days, as elsewhere) working with Penruddock from opening of Blencow box in 1901. Note that Blencow station had not been a crossing place prior to coming of the box and double line block working with Redhills Junction box, which applied from June 1901 until June 17 1938, after which single line electric token working (with key tokens, LMS practice) applied between Blencow box and Penrith No.1 box. A GF was in use for the Blencowe Quarry connection at Blencow station from December 4 1967 until final closure of the line wef June 19 1972.	December 4 1967
2/ 110	REDHILLS JUNCTION believed NER, 1866	Replaced by CKPR brick box of c 1890, with Tweedy frame the box having the air of a Saxby structure of earlier times Note single line electric tablet working with Penruddock from prob. 1892 and likewise with Penrith No.1 from that time. But the NER/LNER link with Eamont Junction box (originally an L&NWR box, 1866) was always double track. On CK&P, double line block with Blencow came in June1901, when that box opened along with the section of double track.	June 17 1938
1/ 418	PENRITH No1. (Keswick Junction) L&NWR type, 1879-80	This main line box replaced earlier cabins (see itinerary text in referance to Penrith). Note that the Keswick line's final portion, Flusco-Blencow-Penrith, closed wef June 19 1972	March 5 1973

The foregoing table shows in heavy type the blockposts and milages recorded by the L&NWR in 1906. As was commonplace in L&NWR/LMS practice, mileages shown between boxes varied a little over the years, even when the structures remained firmly unmoved!

Note that Brigham LMS box (blockpost) replaced Nos 2 and 1 signal boxes in 1936.

Right: On the main Down platform at Keswick, the unusual construction of CKPR signal-box 'B' is apparent - and we also have a glimpse of the signalman and his lever frame. The LMS renamed this box 'Keswick No. 1' and replaced it in 1932. (See picture, opposite page) *J.W. Brownrigg Collection.*

Above: A sunny day at Keswick during the later 1950s finds another 'Derby lightweight' DMU coasting into the main Down platform at Keswick, bound for Workington. The driver is holding out the leather covered hoop and pouch, for collection by the No. 1 box signalman. The pouch contains the token which had authorised the driver to work over the single line section from Threlkeld. *Ivor Nicholas.*

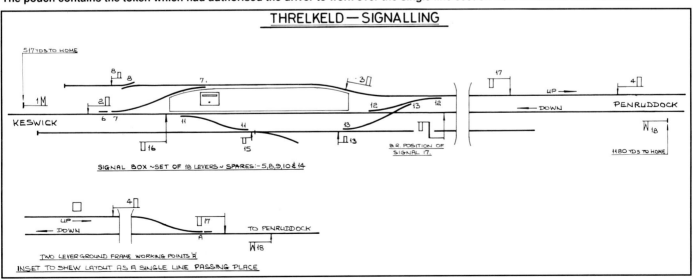

Above: The signalling arrangements at Threlkeld from 1893-94, as drawn by LNWR signalling chronicler and historian Richard Foster.

Below: The approach to Keswick station from the east also featured an LNWR home signal, slotted for shared operation, but its configuration as seen is unusual. The road is set for a Down train to enter the outer face of the Up island platform. The signal box on the down platform was built by the LMS in c1932. *Richard L. Pattinson/CRA.*

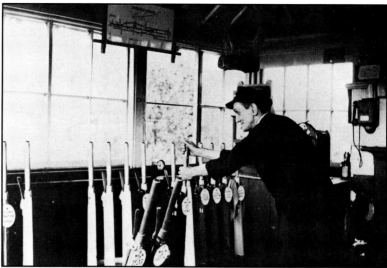

Right, upper: Threlkeld box always housed a Tweedy frame of 18 levers, of 1893. The layout diagram is seen and Bob Wren is 'pulling off' for the Up road, probably c1966. *Phoebe Wallace/Courtesy Jack Tyson Collection.*

Right, lower: The unique little signal cabin of 1892 at Highgate was, from 1894, upgraded as a blockpost on the double line and thereafter housed a Tweedy frame of four levers. This view is westward, in May 1983; the 'hump' beyond the box is the remains of the down platform used by schoolchildren from 1908 to 1928. *Harold D. Bowtell.*

Right: This 'snapshot' of May 1931, records the end of Willie Nicholson's service as signalman at Highgate, in the month when the blockpost was abandoned as an LMS economy and Mr Nicholson and family had to move away to, eventually, Carnforth. *Elizabeth Cook/ Courtesy Mrs Elizabeth Cook.*

Top: Penruddock signalbox was of CKPR design and construction, in 1896, with a Tweedy frame. It replaced a Saxby installation of 1874. A special train for Keswick Convention is seen on July 15 1967. *Derek Cross*

Above: Redhills Junction signalboxbox, and signalman. Note that the name-board is akin to that on the 'snap' of Highgate, on page 155. *Richard L. Pattinson/CRA.*

Left: Contrasting with the LNWR bracket signal at Keswick, this is the Up home marking the end of the single line approaching Blencow. This is a CKPR signal and box. Observe the alternative route by the Up goods loop, left. *Richard L. Pattinson/CRA.*

LIGHTING BY ACETYLENE GAS

The CKPR used town's gas for lighting Cockermouth Joint station, probably from its opening, and there was a public electricity supply to Keswick station and yard, from 1899-1900 onwards. Most railways used paraffin oil lamps at lesser stations, as also for signal lamps. Remarkably, the wayside stations on the CKPR acquired individual gas generators, which have been described as looking like an old-fashioned washing boiler in a wash house, which was in fact the 'gas house'. Water was fed by gravity to acetylene (housed in a container which was recharged daily) and the reaction produced gas, which was then piped to the various lamps. These embraced external lights on platforms, yards and approach, as well as in rooms, also in various neighbouring signals.

The following dates are those of authorisation, which was followed by an order to the manufacturers of the equipment. Penruddock came first (November 1898), and a larger capacity plant was soon substituted (August 1899). Then came Blencow, which received Penruddock's original plant (in August 1899) but which was subsequently fitted with a larger replacement plant (in August 1901). There followed Braithwaite (in April 1902) and Threlkeld (April 1902), but the Threlkeld plant was a large one, providing for 50 lamps, and its replacement (in August 1916) was for

40 lamps. At Troutbeck (December 1903) the plant went back to a standard capacity, like the replacement installations at Penruddock and Blencow but was probably enlarged in 1910. Bassenthwaite Lake was authorised in June 1907. Finally, Embleton (December 1909) was to have a plant with the modest capacity of 20 lamps; this equipment, including lamps, piping and installation, also its shed, cost £49.10.0. from John Lee & Company, of Hull. A replacement gas house was proposed at Embleton in 1949 and certainly a plant operated here until after closure of the station to public use, and into the early 1960s.

From a date in the 1950s or early 1960s, as the gas equipment became worn out, replacement paraffin oil lamps were installed, sometimes preceded by a temporary interlude with Tilley pressure lamps. Some stations still had gas lamps until closure in 1966 (west of Keswick) or the loss their staff in 1968 (east of Keswick)

An amusing characteristic of the acetylene equipment was the fading of the lights on frosty nights. When this occurred, the stationmaster had to hasten out from his cosy house, bearing a kettle of boiling water, with which to thaw the freezing water in the supply tank, within the gas house. An engineer familiar with the line explains that spent carbide is slaked lime and, if retained, it came in useful at the time of annual whitewashing of station premises.

Left: Here is a gas generating plant, disused but virtually complete, seen in 1985 in the 'gas house' at Threlkeld station. The two horizontal lower circular chambers held the charges of carbide. Water could be admitted via one or other downpipe, to the selected charge. Gas was then generated until exhaustion of the carbide, when the top cock could be switched over to divert the water to the unused charge. The duty porter would recharge the plant as required. As gas was produced it would rise into the cylindrical vertical holder (of which the upper section. seen to left, fitted tight on top). The gas filter is to the right, on the piping to the station lamps, and those in the railway houses.
Harold D. Bowtell.

Right: The gas house is visible in this view of Threlkeld: it is the building on the banking between the Up line and the stationmaster's house, beyond the signal. The fireman of the 'Mickey Mouse' 2-6-0 is enjoying the ride downgrade as his train rolls into the station, westbound. The distinctive signalbox is glimpsed at the far end of the island platform buildings.
Preston Whiteley.

OPERATIONAL ASPECTS

ACCIDENTS AND INCIDENTS ON THE COCKERMOUTH & WORKINGTON RAILWAY

Operation was delightfully casual on the nine miles of the CWR, as seen during its last 10 years of independence, from 1856 to 1865.

Driver James Shippen worked coal trains and was said to make a practice of having his engine on the main line when the passenger train was due, with collision only narrowly averted in one or two instances. He was reprimanded in September 1856, but a year later his pay was nevertheless increased to £1.10.0. per week, albeit mainly to recognise the long hours he worked. William White, also an engine driver, and Hugh Dodd, his fireman, seem to have indulged in fisticuffs on the footplate (December 1857), the blame being placed on Dodd, who was reprimanded. Dodd had earlier been blamed for neglecting his engine on Sunday March 8 1857, when the CWR passenger train missed the 6.24pm from Workington to Carlisle, leaving mail bags and several passengers stranded. His downfall followed in March 1858 when, for the second time, he was found very drunk in charge of a passenger train, and was dismissed. His pay was 18/- weekly. The other passenger fireman, William Christian, was severely reprimanded when the poor performance of his engine led to the Sunday evening connection for Carlisle and the south being missed on June 21

1857. This time, a gentleman from London lodged a claim but the CWR Board maintained that: "he could have posted from Workington to Carlisle." Christian again came to notice when, in June 1860, he fell from his engine, owing to being drunk on duty.

The pointsmen were few in number and easy going by nature. J. Anderson was dismissed for failure to secure the points properly at Marron Siding, on August 30 1856; the engine of a passenger train from Workington was derailed, along with a wagon. In September 1858, Anderson's successor also was dismissed for allowing the horse-drawn coal wagons of Fletchers, the coal owners, onto the main line. In the same vicinity, two or three coal wagons, probably of chaldron type, were wrecked when, on January 25 1859, they were blown out of Lowther sidings into the path of the 9.00pm Workington-Cockermouth passenger train. Again, late on December 18 1862, a Whitehaven Junction Railway locomotive collided with a CWR wagon which had blown out of the Merchants Quay branch onto the main line; the locomotive and the Derwent viaduct were damaged, and the wagon. Pointsman Wildman lost his job.

Finally, two successive Stationmasters at Broughton Cross were dismissed (November and December 1862), the first for intemperate habits and the second for being very drunk on duty.

Above: An 'M&C' wagon is included in this pile-up of 'empties,' seen just westward of Bassenthwaite Lake station and level crossing - the date is stated to be 1899. *Richard L. Pattinson/CRA.*

Above: An eastward view at Cockermouth passenger station, from the road bridge. This view shows the scene just after closure in 1966, with the latter day layout visrtually intact. Note the water tower amidst the trees on the right. *Harold D. Bowtell.*

CONFUSION AT THE CROSSROADS: COCKERMOUTH JUNCTION

One has long sympathised with railway signalmen in traditional cabins, when exposed to the problems of conflicting movements at times of heavy traffic. Probably, until recent years, the classic example was at Borough Market Junction, the dividing of the ways for Cannon Street and Charing Cross. But spare a thought also for the man in the much smaller signalbox at Cockermouth Junction, a few years after the CWR had become LNWR property and with the CKPR was still only eight years old. Traffic had expanded far beyond CWR experience. The signal box was now described as a raised cabin, with steps, adequate signals and interlocking of points and signals, so it was presumably the new box of 1873.

On April 14 1873, a MCR passenger train from Cockermouth to the Brigham-Bullgill line ran past the box at 3.28pm. The driver helpfully signalled to the man in the box, by a display of fingers, that the LNWR passenger train from Penrith to Whitehaven, which should already have passed, was reported 18 minutes late from Penrith. The MCR train was promptly followed down the 1 in 70 single-track bank from Cockermouth passenger station by a Down-bound light NER engine and then an NER Down mineral train, comprising engine, 30 wagons of coke and a brake van. These were disposed of, apart from the mineral brake van, which was left for a time on the Down running line.

Meanwhile, *two* Up trains arrived on the double track route from Workington direction, each with a LNWR engine and conveying, respectively, 29 and 18 mineral 'empties', bound from the West Cumberland ironworks to County Durham. These trains were well behind time, as they had to be formed to provide a train for the two NER locomotives to take eastward, and by rights that would have been away at 3.5pm. Complicated shunting movements followed and they were overtaken by the appearance of the LNWR passenger train from Penrith at about 3.50pm. It was descending the bank faster than seemed prudent to eyewitnesses - the road being blocked by empty mineral wagons and the signals being at danger. The driver ran through the adverse signals at 15-18mph and collided with the wagons. Eight were damaged, of which three were derailed, while the engine's buffer beam was broken; 11 passengers were cut and bruised and 12 shaken. The passenger guard was hurt and so was the driver, who jumped from his engine. His train had been delayed at Penrith awaiting late-running main line trains - *plus ca change*. The driver, Shippen, was stated to have worked on the line for 26 years and had been in LNWR service since 1866. He had thus joined the CWR in its first year of operation, 1847; indeed, we first met James Shippen in 1856 (see previous page). Lieut. Col. C.S. Hutchinson, RE, inspecting officer for the Board of Trade, placed the blame on Driver Shippen (primarily), the signalman next (with some sympathy expressed), the lack of block working (note earlier references under Signalling) and on the inadequate braking of the passenger train, comprised of 10 vehicles, of which two were brake vans, but with only one guard conveyed.

TRAGEDY AND COMEDY ON THE CKPR ROUTE

The CKPR does not appear to have had any accidents to trains in which a passenger was killed, and few in which passengers suffered injury. Workers on the Railway were, in relation to their numbers, far less fortunate. In the first year of operations (1865) platelayers James Thompson and John Pattinson were killed, in separate incidents; each widow received a gratuity of £5 - and Mrs. Pattinson was left with five children. In 1910, platelayer Thomas Gibson was killed. In 1906, Joseph Whitham, a porter signalman, lost his life at Troutbeck, run down by a light engine, his widow receiving 'the full compensation' of £156 under the Employers' Liability Act, by then effective. Porter Joseph Wilson was badly injured that year at Cockermouth station and, after investigating the circumstances, the Board of Trade pressed for a reduction of daily working hours to a maximum of twelve. Locomotive firemen died: at Troutbeck on April 9

1873 NER footplateman Isaac Snowden fell from the *front* of his engine while running through on a mineral train; T. Dalton, LNWR, was killed at Cockermouth Junction on December 14 1885; and, at Bassenthwaite Lake station on November 14 1898, LNWR fireman Gilbert Howard of Workington fell from the engine of a passing empty stock train after exchanging the tablet.

Conditions of the day - and of long after - at level crossings emerge from the death of Sarah Johnstone, killed on January 17 1867 at Rakefoot, when helping her husband David, the official gatekeeper, by handling the gates. The rule was that the gates must be kept closed to the highway except when road vehicles required to cross and the keeper had to be on call 24 hours daily, but the Company would employ only one person. Crossings at Bassenthwaite Lake (twice) and Embleton (on three occasions) figured in accidents.

Left: A westward view at Troutbeck, looking down the bank towards Threlkeld (a double track section) with the signalbox behind the camera (See below). The bridge was demolished in 1984 and the road now crosses the formation at former rail level. This picture was taken on October 9 1966. *Harold D. Bowtell.*

Above: An interesting view at Troutbeck in BR days, which highlights both the bleak and rugged nature of the surrounding landscape, and also some unusual motive power. Fowler Class 4F 0-6-0 No. 44081 is seen just east of the platforms, shunting an Up goods, under the control of the 1874 Saxby & Farmer signalbox. At the time of going to press (spring 1989) this signalbox was still standing, albeit in very decrepit condition, and was clearly visible from the A66, which passes nearby. *Ainley Collection/CRA.*

Mechanical Failures

Broken axles and other defects in wagons caused derailments but on May 22 1899, a LNWR passenger train engine broke its crank axle, in Wythop cutting. On August 22 1910, derailment whilst running followed failure of a spring of the leading pair of tender wheels on LNWR locomotive No.3069, an 0-6-0 (Special DX), working the 9.38am up passenger from Keswick.

Collisions and the human element

Collisions and 'near misses' occurred chiefly in the earlier days, from 1868 to 1896, and were usually due to the failure of pointsmen and others to set turnouts correctly.

On October 23 1868, the passenger train due into Penrith at 5.0pm ran onto the turntable instead of into the station. An incident at Bassenthwaite Lake on January 10 1889 led to the fixing - at this early period - of an *electrical detector* for the east-facing points, which were remote from the signal box, and similar protection was to be installed at Penruddock and Troutbeck.

Another weakness was revealed at Bassenthwaite Lake on August 5 1901, when the driver of the 6.5pm Up passenger service from Cockermouth ran into the station against

Above: Making a smoky departure from Bassenthwaite Lake station in BR days, with a standard 20-ton brake van attached, is Ivatt Class 2MT 'Mickey Mouse' 2-6-0 No. 46456, allocated to Workington shed, (Code 11B). Taken during the late 1950s, this interesting view from the signalbox shows the neat station building on the Down platform, also the immaculately manicured topiary on the Up platform. The goods yard (see picture, opposite) is to the left. *Ivor Nicholas.*

signals. As a Down train was approaching from the east and 'had the road' into the station, the west-facing points took the erring driver into the Down platform - and the path of the oncoming locomotive. The trains were , fortunately, halted about 150 yards apart. Resulting refinements permitted entry of a Down train without the west facing points being set for the Down line.

There was also an incident at Keswick on January 16 1896 when an early morning Down NER mineral train with SDR '1001' Class 0-6-0 No.1184 in charge, ran past the unlit signals (doubtless at danger) into the Up platform road, as an LNWR eastbound passenger train approached. Collision was only narrowly avoided, but No. 1184 was derailed.

Above: A familiar feature at 'Bass Lake' station for many post-war years was this pair of green and cream liveried camping coaches, stabled in a disconnected siding in the goods yard. Each winter, the adjacent siding was slewed to enable the vehicles to be taken to works, for refurbishing.

Interesting detail includes the white-painted dustbin, the 'chocks' placed beneath the wheels to stop the carriages rolling and the admirable neat and tidy condition of the site. A bottle of gas (for cookers, lights and, probably, heaters,) can be seen in a special cage between the frames of the nearer vehicle, whose sole bar carries a bold painted warning for railwaymen: 'No Brakes.' *Ivor Nicholas.*

A military occasion with a disastrous outcome

By far the most serious collision occurred at Penruddock on Friday September 2 1870. This was a gala day in Penrith, the racecourse being the scene of a review of four troops of the Yeomanry Cavalry. They were headed by Colonel Edward Hasell (1796-1872), of Dalemain, who had been Chairman of the Lancaster & Carlisle Railway at its opening, in 1846. Four special trains had brought folk from West Cumberland and three trains returned from Penrith shortly after 7.0pm, at short intervals. The first of these comprised an engine and tender and about 15 carriages and was correctly held at Penruddock to cross the Up Cockermouth-Penrith passenger, due there at 7.55 pm. The second train was allowed to draw up close behind; an engine and tender and 39 carriages, plus brakevan, a horsebox containing three horses, and a second engine and tender attached in rear. The third train, with T. Smith driving and about 20 vehicles behind the engine, passed Penruddock's distant signal at danger (this being subsequently established, although Smith continued to deny it) and collided in the

centre of the single line viaduct with the double train (the second train, with an engine in rear). The most serious damage was the near destruction of the last passenger carriage in the second train, but by great good fortune it had been standing outside the covered station at Penrith, in heavy rain, and was empty. Three doctors on the train gave prompt assistance. More than £4,000 was paid in settling claims from injured passengers and, as is still the case today, arbitration was necessary to allocate liability between the CKPR and LNWR.

Runaways

The CKPR distinguished itself by a number of spectacular runaways. Dramatic episodes in BR days down the bank from Flusco and Blencow to Penrith have been described but there was also a westward runaway from Troutbeck, in the 1940s. In CKPR days (Pre-Grouping) there had been six incidents, two of them westward from Troutbeck.

On Monday February 13 1871, an Up goods train reached Troutbeck, where the engine was detached, and about five minutes later its train started to run back down the long and steep incline to Threlkeld and away through the gorge, speeding by Keswick and over the lowlands, to come to rest beyond Braithwaite – a distance of well over 10 miles - and without harm.

The CKPR's second 'runaway spectacular' occurred on Tuesday April 18 1882, when an NER Down mineral train No. 6 left Keswick westward that morning, with two tender engines, 28 loaded coke wagons and two brake vans. As the train ran along the shore Bassenthwaite Lake, the 'ticket' of authority for the section was duly carried. However, both guards were (irregularly) riding in the rear van and, when this became detached, they were thus left to coast to a stand, while the train proceeded, with a single unattended brake van at the rear, past Bassenthwaite Lake station. Here, the leading driver collected the train staff for the next section. He soon noted the absence of one brake van but proceeded to Embleton, whence the second engine took the train forward to Cockermouth. He held the staff for the section between Embleton and Bassenthwaite Lake, so went back and joined the head guard, who came up on foot, and the Stationmaster. The latter knew that another train was en route from Braithwaite, yet set off with the driver, fireman and guard to find and retrieve the missing van. After about a mile, on a curve by the lake, the van was seen approaching, propelled by the the the No. 7 Down NER mineral train, which was duly carrying the train staff for the section. The light engine driver reversed, the other three leaped clear of the footplate and the driver jumped (or was knocked off) when the propelled van struck his engine.

This locomotive had been reversed and steam applied before impact and it now ran away at speeds estimated at 40-60mph, passing Bassenthwaite Lake, Rakefoot and Embleton before running downhill to crash into the MCR's 1.25pm passenger train, which had been ready to leave Cockermouth for Brigham and Bullgill. It comprised an MCR tender engine and four vehicles. The last two carriages were reduced to matchwood but, happily, a telegraphed warning from Porter Robinson at Bassenthwaite Lake to Clerk Patterson at Cockermouth had been received and acted upon with alacrity; this enabled the railway staff to get all the passengers clear just in time. The MCR locomotive became detached but a porter dashed after it, climbed into the cab and brought it to a stand before it accelerated down the very steep bank to the Junction, thereby averting yet greater tragedy.

Further runaways occurred during the years of the First World War. Trap points just east of Blencow on the bank down to Penrith, saved the situation on October 16 1916. A heavy down mineral train with two engines ran back when the drawbar of the leading (NER) wagon broke at Blencow. Had the trap points not been installed there would have been a fearful incident at the main line junction. In the earlier days of single track working east of Blencow there were no catch points and on December 26 1889 the 6.0am double headed Down goods from Penrith stopped at Blencow to shunt. While the engines were detached most of the train ran back all the way downgrade to Penrith station, happily with few ill effects.

A far more spectacular runaway followed on Saturday October 28 1916, at about 8.0pm. The No. 30 Up goods was heavily loaded and hauled by two engines ascending the bank to Troutbeck, when the rear coupling parted on an LNWR wagon - the second vehicle in the train. The brake-van at the rear could not hold the train, which ran away 'wrong line' down the bank. Guard Kirk, of Tebay, jumped for his life at Highgate Platform. The train, including 14 wagons loaded with steel shell cases from Workington, destined to be filled with explosives at the huge Ministry of Munitions factory at Gretna, derailed at the catchpoints in the cutting west of Highgate and an almighty pile-up resulted, partly on the lands of Highgate Farm. Mr Tyson, the farmer, ministered to the shocked guard with tea and his schoolgirl daughter Jessie clearly remembers the dramatic scene of the crash. It occurred close by the distinctive 'la'al pikey hut' - a superb Cumbrian description of the lineside cabin, which resembled a sentry box.

Just over a year later, on December 13 1917, another runaway occurred. Fred Slee was conducting shunting movements at Troutbeck when, owing to a defective brake, Caledonian Railway gunpowder van No.20 (containing powder for use at Greenside lead mines) ran away down the bank, presumably 'right line' as it was not derailed by the Highgate catch points. The Highgate signalman warned Threlkeld, where the Stationmaster and his porter signalman placed sleepers across the line just beyond (west of) the station; the van approached, running at about 30mph, and pushed the sleepers ahead of it for a distance before stopping short of the overline bridge carrying the Penrith-Keswick road.

Hazard by fire

There was a fire in the screw pile bridge at the Glenderamachin river, west of Threlkeld, on the night of

Right: In LMS days, an Up goods is climbing the long bank of almost 1 in 62, near Troutbeck, between Hill Cottages and Mosedale viaduct. This bank caused concern for the CKPR and LMS both in terms of maintaining traffic flow towards Penrith at busy periods, and it was also the scene of several 'runaways.'
Richard L. Pattinson/CRA.

Above: A major problem with snow in St Andrews cutting, some half-mile west of Blencow station and between MPs 26 and 27, with the locomotive facing Penrith and showing Low Fluskew Wood, in February 1932. The personalities (L-R) are: William Storey, George Watson, the Keswick inspector (possibly Mr Dickinson), Bob Bainbridge and Anthony Horsley. In the tragedy of January 1940, at almost this point, in snow, three lives were lost. (See text) *John Jameson/Courtesy Abbot Hall.*

August 1-2 1917. Pending the eventual arrival of the Keswick Fire Brigade, good work was done by the Stationmaster and signalman, along with the porter and his wife, platelayer W.Lamb and Miss Julia Lamb, also Police Constable McMeithan.

Two gas tank wagons and an LNWR four-wheeled vehicle, all attached in rear of the 2.5pm Workington-Penrith passenger train of November 22 1921, were derailed short of Blencow station and finally left the rails completely as they approached the platform. A fire followed, but Porter Bewley uncoupled the main portion of the train, which was thus drawn safely into the station. A joint enquiry by the CKPR and LNWR blamed the driver for allegedly running at excessive speed.

THE SNOW FIEND

Snow blocked this rugged railway route from time to time. This was chiefly at Gibson and Gillhead cuttings (west of Troutbeck) also at a point immediately west of Penruddock station and at three places between Penruddock viaduct and the western entry to Blencow

station. Following the blockages of January 28-31 1910, the CKPR wrote seeking advice from the Caledonian and Highland Railways and members of the Board called on Sir Vincent Raven and his assistant at Darlington, viewing with them the NER's wooden snowploughs of 26 tons weight, also a new 27-tons steel plough.

However, the CKPR's response was limited to the construction of additional stone walls and sleeper snow fencing, which was extended in 1917. The lengthiest and most notable blockage involved the Keswick-Penrith section, which was impassable from Friday January 26 1940, as already explained. This led to a tragic mishap on Wednesday January 31 1940, in St Andrews rock cutting, between Flusco and Blencow. A stranded engine with snowplough and another assisting engine had been dug out after which the blocked cutting at St Andrews overline bridge was tackled by railway staff and some 80 soldiers. They were protected by detonators to eastward but, when empty wagons were propelled into the cutting, the detonators were either already buried in packed snow, or slid ahead of the wagons on the icy rails. There was no warning from these 'shots' and three men were killed outright when the wagons ran into the team of diggers. They were: goods guards Bob Watson of Penrith, and Joseph Hugill of Yanwath, and John Jardine White, a young soldier from Workington. Seven other people were slightly injured and many others barely escaped.

The exceptional snowfalls of 1947 caused blockage between Keswick and Penrith on February 26 and again on March 13-14.

RAILWAY LINKS THAT MIGHT HAVE BEEN

1846-1864

The Cockermouth & Workington Extension Railway project of 1846 has been touched on in the section detailing the building of the CWR itself. Had it come to fruition, it might have carried that line to Keswick, even Windermere.

Around 1860, the MCR had ideas of a route by way of Caldbeck to Penrith but it was overtaken in 1861 by the CKPR's Act, followed closely by the building of the CKPR in the years 1862-64. Meanwhile, the CKPR in June 1864, had thought of connecting its line, in the Cockermouth-Embleton vicinity, with Ullock and the contemporary developments from Cleator way; this thinking was not pursued and, as we know, the WCER made its own way north to Marron Junctions in course of another couple of years.

Attraction of the Midland Railway, 1867-1876

Encouraged by the MR Act of 16 July 1866 for the Settle & Carlisle main line, the CKPR proposed in February 1867 to survey a route from Penrith to (provisionally) Langwathby; this would transverse about five miles of easy country, but with a crossing of the River Eden. When the Midland failed to secure parliamentary approval to the abandonment of its Pennine main line project, interest was revived in Penrith in the idea of a locally-promoted link line. A committee was set up in April 1873, with the CKPR represented by directors Dover and Spedding, of Keswick. The committee's deliberations dragged on and eventually, in July 1876, the CKPR decided against giving support. By then, the Settle & Carlisle line was open to traffic. Right from the start, the Midland intended to have, and indeed made, a physical link at Appleby with the NER Eden Valley line; this was, however, not exploited as a through route from the MR system (and Keswick) until the 20th century.

The Mid Cumberland Railway, 1881-1914

In 1881-82, an initiative came from London promoters, under this title, designed to conjure up a picture of minerals being exploited in amazing variety. After launch in the villages, Joseph Wilson, as Secretary of the promoters, addressed a letter to the CKPR. The miracle was to be achieved through the medium of a railway between Blencow (CKPR) and Mealsgate (MCR), via Hesket Newmarket and Caldbeck. The CKPR compared notes with the MCR; by October, they decided that any line should be from Troutbeck station to Hesket Newmarket and points beyond but they referred the proposal to a special meeting of shareholders - which was held at Keswick on November 4 1882, when a decision against further consideration at that time was recorded

A fresh initiative came in May 1897, from L.R. Wilson, of Manchester. This suggested a link between Troutbeck (CKPR) and Wigton station, on the MCR - with the title Mid Cumberland Light Railway - and for a couple of years exchanges continued. In November 1898, attention was concentrated on a shorter (branch) light railway, still under the same name, to extend from Troutbeck (or Penruddock) station to Hesket Newmarket and possibly onwards to Caldbeck. A cautious financial contribution by the CKPR was proposed by Directors James Cropper and Sir Henry Vane, the latter having an estate at Hutton-in-the-Forest near the route. However, the matter did not proceed beyond the early months of 1899. The Light Railways Act had been effective since 1 January 1897, and had probably inspired the scheme, but no Order for the line was secured under the Act.

Note also the plans of 1904, and traffics through later years, for the Carrock Mines (J. Wright Wilson, of Penrith, promoter), mentioned in the 'itinerary' in reference to Troutbeck station. In January-April 1900, a proposed quarry branch from Troutbeck to near Carrick Fell (meaning Carrock Fell?) was also raised with the Railway Company by a widely-based deputation, but it did not gain CKPR support. Surprisingly, in November 1914, a letter from Mr A.E. Beck to the Company mentioned a proposed line from 'Carrick End', but this was not elaborated or developed.

The Braithwaite and Buttermere Railway, 1880-1883

The Buttermere Green Slate Company have for long quarried attractive and high quality Lake District slate, near Honister Pass, between Buttermere and Borrowdale. In 1880, the Company was looking for expansion. A governing factor was the cost of transporting their output by horse-drawn two-wheeled carts, to Keswick station. If cheaper transport could be arranged, the Company believed it could find a market for lower quality slate and boost its current output of 50-100 tons weekly to around 400 tons. This would be achieved, they reasoned, by a railway between the Honister quarries and Braithwaite station. The proposition was put to the CKPR in June of 1880. The slate folk hinted at the 'competitive' options of an extension of the Rowrah & Kelton Fell Railway or a line up Ennerdale, each of these reaching Honister from the west, but they were hardly realistic alternatives and the CKPR was not inspired to offer encouragement.

Undeterred, the Slate Company proceeded to 'sound' the LNWR and, in November-December 1881, came back with a proposal. CKPR Chairman Spedding, of Keswick, and his colleague Captain Henry Gandy, of Penrith, met at Carnforth on 7 November 1881 with five Directors of the Slate Company - Messrs Poole (solicitor), Massicks, Cook, Swan and Storey. Edward Waugh MP was a member of the Slate Board and, after years as solicitor to the Railway, was by this time listed in their Board too. He was later revealed to be in favour of the scheme but very correctly did not attend the meeting. A railway of about 2ft gauge and some eight miles in length was proposed, to pass along the slopes of Cat Bells, above the western shore of Derwentwater. The Railway's response was still very cautious. The Quarry Company promoted a Bill but it was withdrawn in April 1883, following four months of attacks, progressively fiercer and better organised, as the Reverend H.D. Rawnsley, at that time still Vicar of Wray, on Windermere, led the campaign on behalf of the 'environmentalists' of the day. No more was heard of the intriguing narrow gauge steam line from Braithwaite to Honister; Buttermere was always a misnomer.

An initiative from the Solway Junction Railway: Brayton Junction-Bassenthwaite Lake, 1882-83

Contemporary with the Honister scheme was a plan for a railway from the north. The Solway Junction Railway, with its long, lightly-used and flimsy viaduct over the Solway estuary undergoing three years repairs after damage by ice, sought in November 1882-January 1883 to interest the CKPR

Left: An ex-works five-plank private owner wagon, of 10 tons capacity, of the Cumberland Granite Company, of Bassenthwaite Lake. The vehicle is marked with the inscription: 'When empty to Quarry Sidings, Embleton, CK&P Rly.' *Peter W. Robinson Collection.*

in a joint scheme. This was for the promotion of a Bill to permit construction of a line to reach Bassenthwaite Lake station. Potential traffic from Scotland to the Lake District was mentioned encouragingly, but the CKPR did not approve of the proposed layout at Bassenthwaite Lake and liked still less the suggestion in the draft Bill (of January 1883) for running powers over its line. They probably had doubts too as to whether the Solway Junction Company seriously intended to press on as far south as Bassenthwaite Lake. The scheme came to naught.

Below: The locomotive *Cocker* is here depicted around 1890-93, having since 1874 been owned by contractor Joseph Firbank - recalled to me affectionately as 'old father Firbank' from the days of his building the Appleby section of the MR's main line from Settle to Carlisle. This inspection train has halted between Cowburn Tunnel East and Edale, on the Dore & Chinley Railway (MR), this part of which was being built by Firbank. 'T.O' on the wagons indicates Thomas Oliver, who was building the portion from Hathersage to Dore. This interesting engine's origins with the Cockermouth & Workington Railway, in 1846, are discussed in the following pages. Quite early in its career, on March 31 1857, it figured in a dramatic mishap. In the run-up to a parliamentary election at Cockermouth, the CWR ran special trains. *Cocker*, originally an 0-4-2 type, had recently been modified to 0-4-0 arrangement, with lengthened wheelbase, and was hauling a 'special' of 11 carriages and a van, carrying about 300 passengers. The train was returning from Cockermouth to Whitehaven and was seemingly just clear of the viaducts in the Salmon Hall vicinity (below Seaton) when the engine 'split the road' and rolled over the right-hand bank, coming to rest facing east. The fireman was injured and the Company Secretary John Mayson was severely injured, but passengers in the carriages appear to have escaped. Captain H.W.Tyler RE, of the Board of Trade inspectorate, was scathing in his comments on the design of the engine, the condition of the viaduct and of the permanent way. Note (next chapter) that the locomotive was promptly rebuilt again. *MR/Courtesy J.B.Radford.*

Chapter 9

THE LOCOMOTIVE STORY

Locomotives of the Cockermouth & Workington Railway

During its independent working career, from 1847 to 1866, the CWR owned six locomotives: two at its opening in April 1847; three by the autumn of that year (reduced to two by a sale in 1853), again increased to three in 1854, then four by mid-1856 and a maximum of five from 1864. These five were taken into the LNWR 'capital list' in December 1866 and allotted LNWR numbers, although the first LNWR numbers(12/1866) were never carried, representing a proper transaction only. Incidentally, numbers between 1 and 5 have been quoted for the engines in CWR stock but that Company always referred to them by names; the numbers may have been introduced by LNWR locomotive historian S.S. Scott.

The following list derives from my own reading and interpretation of the CWR's surviving minutes and the broadly parallel (and earlier) findings of Mr E.Craven from that source, along with information from LNWR sources.

DERWENT: An 0-4-2 with 4ft 9in diameter coupled wheels, cylinders (probably inside) of 14in x 21in - with tender; built by Tulk & Ley, of Lowca. It was ordered in January 1846 and received by CWR in October 1846, the makers' eighth locomotive. *Derwent* was found too heavy and disposal was in mind by 1850; it was eventually sold in 1853, possibly to the Whitehaven & Furness Junction Railway? This possibility is derived from a suggestion in the records of LNWR locomotive historian S.S. Scott.

Above: The last of the six locomotives built for the Cockermouth & Workington Railway was *Eller*, of 1864, built by Hudswell Clarke of Leeds and seen at this company's works as a new engine.
R.N. Redman Collection.

COCKER: An 0-4-2 with 4ft 9in diameter coupled wheels and inside cylinders of 13in x 18in - with tender. The locomotive was built by Alfred Kitching of Darlington, quoted as their No.15. ordered on March 2 1846 and delivered either in December1846 or January 1847 and promptly loaned to J. & W. Ritson, the CWR's contractors, to supplement their own locomotive during the completion and ballasting of the line.

On May 14 1847, the CWR was complaining to the makers that this locomotive could not perform its work satisfactorily, alleging a defect in the pumps - presumably referring to a boiler feed pump. A valve gear with expansion links, such as Stephenson's gear was probably fitted in 1852. The locomotive was rebuilt early in 1857, as an 0-4-0, with a lengthened coupled wheelbase, lengthened firebox and new cylinders (13in x 22in). However, it was derailed whilst working a passenger train on March 31 1857, and was therefore modified as an 0-4-2. More misfortune followed; *Cocker* broke its crank axle on November 231858, with delay to traffic (the report suggests that it was hauling a passenger train at the time). The axle was presumably renewed. The locomotive was again rebuilt, in March1866 (this time by the LNWR at Crewe) when it acquired new (lengthened) inside frames, the cylinders being enlarged to 13in x 22in and the boiler replaced.LNWR numbering: 1550 in

December 1866; 1577 in April1867; 1259 in July 1867 and 1821 in November1871; *Cocker* was sold by the LNWR (possibly through the agency of Fletcher Jennings) in March 1874 to well-known railway contractor Joseph Firbank, initially (it would seem) at Camden. The engine was resold to J.P. Edwards and rebuilt for him at Crewe in January 1886. The tender was removed and a saddletank substituted. The wheel arrangement was 0-4-2, with inside cylinders. It worked on construction of the Brighton and the Dyke Railway, 1886-87, being in Brighton Works of the LBSCR in March and April 1887 for repairs and the fitting of a wooden cab and windows to the contractor's order. The cylinders are recorded as 15in x 24in by this time - it is not known whether or not this is accurate. The locomotive was with Edwards during building of the Nottingham Suburban Railway (GNR), 1886-89; and with him during construction of the Dore & Chinley Railway (MR), probably during the years 1890-93. It was photographed there towards the end of that time, when outside frames were noted, also the wooden cab, hauling an inspection train. After this 'Cocker' disappears from the records; its ultimate fate unknown.

MARRON: An 0-4-2 tender engine with 4ft 9in diameter coupled wheels and 13in x 18in inside cylinders. *Marron* was built by Alfred Kitching, of Darlington, believed to be works No.16 and delivered in 1847, probably during August. In March 1847, when this locomotive was on order, the CWR Board suggested to John Dixon that 14in diameter cylinders might produce a more powerful engine, but Mr Dixon considered this an affront to his technical judgment and threatened to resign forthwith; the Board hastily withdrew the proposal. This was regarded as a mineral locomotive.

In 1852, the coupled wheels were re-tyred and link motion was probably fitted. The engine became very run down in 1856; a broken crank axle was replaced towards the end of 1856 and major repairs were done in 1857-58, also a 'rebuilding' in 1861. The cylinders were bored to a larger diameter in March 1867, at Crewe, although the 0-4-2 wheel arrangement was retained and presumably the tender.

LNWR numbering: 1549 in December 1866; 1576 in April 1867; 1147 in July 1867 and 1822 in November 1871. Between July 1867 and at least July 1871, No.1147 (quoted as 0-4-2 tank) worked on the High Peak line. No. 1822 was sold by the LNWR in February 1874 to William Horsley Jnr., of Newcastle upon Tyne, who had his business at Whitehill Point. He may well have bought the locomotive on behalf of the owners of the Brunton & Shields wagonway, which in 1886 became the Seaton Burn Coal Company's wagonway for bringing coals from their collieries in Northumberland, down to the north bank of the Tyne for shipment.

DERWENT: (The second locomotive of this name on the CWR): A 4ft 9in 2-4-0T, with outside cylinders (12in x 18in) and built by Neilson, of Glasgow, Works No. 75 of 1854 - delivered new to the CWR and known as 'the small tank engine', probably used as for passenger duties. LNWR numbering: 1548 in December 1866; 1575 in April 1867 and 1192 in July 1867. Broken up by the LNWR June 18 1868, this being some 18 months after takeover, with "boiler very bad, frame patched, etc."

SOLWAY: A 5ft 0in 0-4-0ST, with outside cylinders (14in x 20in), built by Neilson as Works No. 324 of 1856 - delivered new to the CWR. It was intended as a mineral engine but at once proceeded to do the line and its weak bridges little good, whilst fracturing its own frames. Neilson declined to accept responsibility for its shortcomings, attributing these to the specification of John Dodds, who tendered his resignation as Secretary, Manager and Engineer of the CWR in May 1856, effective August 12 1856. The following report states: "She was a tank engine of great overhanging weight, the framing was too light and of poor workmanship, and soon fractured." One may surmise that Dodds and Neilson 'boosted' the size of wheels and cylinders, and saddle tank, to convert Neilson's contemporary design of 'pug engine' from an industrial yard shunter into a mineral engine for main line trip working.

Rebuilding was by R. & W. Hawthorn, of Newcastle upon Tyne, with a shorter coupled wheelbase and a pair of 3ft 3in carrying wheels, together with a tender supplied by Sharp Stewart, of Manchester, around the end of 1856. The locomotive later appeared in Crewe records as a 2-4-0-tender engine. LNWR numbering; 1547 in December1866; 1574 in April 1867 and 1183 in July 1867. *Solway* was broken up by the LNWR on June 18 1868 (the boiler having been scrapped in November 1867 - an even shorter survival after takeover than that of *Derwent* (No. 2). This was the most obscure locomotive owned by the CWR.

ELLER: A 4ft 9in 0-6-0 tender engine with inside cylinders (15in x 24in), built by Hudswell & Clarke, of Leeds, Works No. 28 of 1864 (its tender being HC No.29), despatched August 27 1864 from the works to the CWR and carrying *Eller* nameplates on the boiler cladding. This was the only six-coupled loco of the CWR and of more sturdy dimensions and weight than its predecessors; Mr Tosh, as engineer, would be influenced by increasing mineral loads and the rebuilding of the river bridges.

The cylinders were 15 3/8in diameter by 1871. LNWR numbering: 1546 in December 1866; 1573 in April 1867; 1185 in December 1867 and 1823 in November 1871.

Eller was scrapped by the LNWR on May 71881, having survived nearly 15 years in LNWR stock.

During October-December 1858, coal-firing was substituted for coke in all four locomotives of the time and Mr Tosh reported a saving of £248.17.9 in fuel costs during the following half-year: a saving of more than 60% on previously recorded expenditure. Coal was always cheaper than coal, but the railways had previously opted for coke because of pressure to minimise the smoke nuisance.

Passenger Carriages:
The CWR had four passenger carriages built for its opening, in 1847, by Atkinson & Phillipson. These comprised: two first class vehicles, one second class coach and a composite. In 1856 and after there were eight carriages: two first, two second and four third class vehicles. Two more carriages were added to the stocklist in 1864-65. The June 1856 inventory also showed 14 merchandise trucks (increased to 20 a year later), 302 coal and lime chaldron wagons, six stone wagons, a travelling crane with 'fly bogies', two horses, three carts and a road wagon.

The arrival of LNWR engines and men

From the start of regular passenger and goods traffic over the new CKPR, in January 1865, The LNWR provided engines and footplate crews, which involved operation from Penrith to Cockermouth and back. With the LNWR takeover of the West Cumberland lines from mid-1866 it soon became necessary for LNWR locomotives to work between Penrith, Cockermouth, Workington and Whitehaven - effectively from about the beginning of 1867.

LNWR locomotives would be based at Penrith, presumably stabling in the open until the engine shed was built. From 1867, they would have had the use of the former Whitehaven Junction Railway's restricted facilities at Whitehaven (Bransty) for stabling and servicing engines. There was said in 1855 to be a turntable, south of the station at Workington, but it is not apparent on the map of 1864. The first known shed available to LNWR engines in Workington was a six-roads structure built in 1876. It acquired LNWR number 32 in September 1877 and was doubled in size, to 12 roads, under authority of 1890 - continuing in use for steam power until closure wef 1 January 1968. Some stabling at Cockermouth is implied by the passenger train service of the 1860s; CKPR services in 1865 would require as a minimum one Penrith-based engine making two return trips daily to Cockermouth and one engine based at Cockermouth to make a return trip to Penrith. Goods would presumably be worked from Penrith. The integrated CKPR-LNWR passenger service of 1867 embraced six or seven trains each way on the CWR section and three each way on the CKPR, including two Up and three Down through trains. In general, services operated to and from Whitehaven. Even so, Cockermouth would have

to provide power for the early 6.35am to Penrith and the 7.50am to West Cumberland; in later years, a Workington engine ran out 'light' to take this morning 'commuter' train.

Once Workington shed was open (from 1876-77) it undertook the lion's share of locomotive duties on the Workington-Penrith route. By the 20th century, there was a consistent allocation of around 20 locomotives at Workington for Keswick line work (and others reserved for coastal line and local work). Penrith shed provided between five and seven engines for the Keswick line. Workington's contribution declined in 1948 to about 15 and during the years 1950-54 it fell further to eight, an allocation curtailed even further as DMU trains took over most passenger work, commencing in January 1955 under a scheme fully effective by 1956. Penrith shed closed entirely wef 18 June 1962, by which time the diesel sets were mostly running through between Workington and Carlisle, via Penrith.

The identity of the LNWR locomotives working the Cockermouth and Keswick route between the mid-1860s and the 1880s is lost in the mists of time. However, it seems reasonable to suppose that the early engines would be of the 'Crewe Goods' 5ft 2-4-0 tender type (first built at Crewe in 1846), with outside cylinders (15in x 20in) within their distinctive wrapper; also the 'Crewe Goods Side Tank', a

Below: The LNWR 'Special DX' 0-6-0s provided the prime passenger and goods motive power for the CKPR and CWR section lines through most of their history prior to LMS days (1923) and indeed ran for a little longer. This example, No. 3331, was built as LNWR No. 358 *Falstaff*, third of a huge class in 1858. It ran as No. 3331 from 1900 and was finally withdrawn as LMS No. 3000 in January 1928. The engine is seen at Penrith engine shed, pleasantly posed. *James L. Slater Collection.*

Right: It is good to see a tank engine on CKPR passenger duties in the last century: this is an LNWR 4ft 6in 2-4-2T, in charge of a train of early LNWR stock. As seen here, these engines were built with horizontally-hinged smokebox door (an inconvenient arrangement for the engine-men and shed staff) c1879-83 and the train is entering Troutbeck through the single track arch of Matterdale Road bridge, before the doubling of 1893-94. This may well be a scene before electric tablet working. One cannot see the type of 'staff' or 'tablet' which is about to be handed out.
Courtesy Abbot Hall.

Left: An LNWR-design 2-4-0, running in post-Grouping condition as LMS No. 25001 *Snowdon* is also seen at Troutbeck on September 10 1934. This locomotive is remembered with affection as it was the last 'Jumbo' in passenger service anywhere on the LMS system; it was based at Penrith shed and worked the Keswick road until withdrawal in October 1934.
A. St G. Walsh Collection.

somewhat rudimentary 2-4-0 side tank conversion of 1856 onwards. Based on the 2-4-0 'Crewe Goods' design were 20 5ft engines with 17in x 20in cylinders, by Rothwell, and seven with 17in x 24in cylinders, by Fairbairn, all built for the Lancaster & Carlisle Railway in 1856-59. Some of these engines could well have worked on the Keswick road in the period from 1865 to about 1880.

Established locomotive types on the route

Obvious candidates for the route, likewise suitable for passenger or goods traffic in the days before the continuous train brake, were the substantial 0-6-0 tender engines of the 'DX' type, with 5ft wheels and 17in x 24in cylinders. They were built in huge numbers for the LNWR between 1858 and 1872 and were favoured by the Northern and North Eastern Divisions. A sloped-back smokebox with a horizontally hinged door, ornamental chimney and the absence of a cab were characteristic features of the class, although a hint of sophistication was present in the later examples

built. Cabs were fitted during the 1870s and this was doubtless appreciated in Cumberland. As rebuilt from 1881, the 'DX' became 'Special DX'; in this form, Webb boilers were fitted, with 150 pounds per square inch boiler pressure, and there were also cabs. The fitting of the automatic vacuum brake was the most vital improvement, from about 1887 onwards. The last non-vacuum example was eliminated from LNWR stock in 1902. The 'Special DX' was the class of locomotive remembered far back on the Keswick route and illustrated in the years before 1910 working both passenger and goods over the line. An observer in August 1920 recorded five of these locomotives between Penrith and Keswick - all examples which he noted being later withdrawn by the LMS between 1921 and 1926. Two are known to have been allocated to Workington in 1912 and five in 1917, while indications are that about five continued to share the line's work (from Penrith and Workington sheds) until early LMS days, about 1925.

The 'DX' and 'Special DX' were supported by the 4ft 6in 2-4-2 side tanks, (cylinders 17in x 20in) which were built by Crewe in this form from 1879, and we have photographic evidence of one at work on CKPR passenger duties before 1893 , so some of these may well have arrived new in the 1880s to work the passenger trains. Cecil J. Allen was told when visiting in 1921 that the line "used to employ 2-4-2 tanks."

Another class of tank engine had a long career on the line. This was the eminently suitable 4ft 3in 'Side Tank Coal' of 0-6-2 design with inside cylinders (17in x 24in) built by the LNWR in goodly numbers from 1881 onwards and employed in West Cumberland and on the Keswick road certainly by the 1890s, and probably during the previous

Right: The LNWR '18in Goods' 0-6-0, or 'Cauliflower' more familiarly, was the type which, after the 'Special DX', became most associated with the Keswick line. Many have been illustrated and here is an excellent view of No. 8526 at Keswick, with an Up passenger train. *L&GRP.*

Below: Two successive generations of Keswick road staple motive power are illustrated here. 'Cauliflower' No. 28417 is keeping company with a very new arrival, Ivatt 2MT 2-6-0 No. 46455, at Penrith engine shed on August 13 1950. Penrith Beacon is on the skyline, seen to the left of the shed roof. *Neville Fields.*

decade too. They were included for many years in Penrith's modest allocation but their stronghold was at Workington: 14 examples there in the 1912 list, 16 in 1917, probably much the same in 1919-20, still eight in 1933 and four in 1934. They were useful for 'trip' duties within reach of Workington, as well as for goods as far afield as Cockermouth and Keswick. The 5ft 6in 2-4-2 tanks (with 17in x 24in cylinders) do not appear to have come to Workington in their earlier years - they were built between 1890 and 1897. They came, it is believed, in the years 1919-20, and worked the occasional through passenger journey to Penrith. Workington had three examples in the 1930s and two in 1945-46. The engines ended their days on light van trains, but they were previously found on the Bullgill-

Above: This is the LNWR steam shed at Workington, in LMS times, on August 3 1946, when little had changed structurally. The 'north light' roof covers all 12 roads. The varied locomotives outside (L-R) are: an LMS standard 4F 0-6-0, a Midland Railway 0-6-0 (tender seen), an LNWR '18in goods' 0-6-0, a Lancashire & Yorkshire Railway 0-6-0 and an LMS Fowler 2-6-2T. *Harold D. Bowtell.*

Brigham-Cockermouth (and sometimes Keswick) passenger services, which connected with the MCR Carlisle trains at Bullgill and which conveyed a carriage for Carlisle. The MCR's sole 0-4-4 well tank loco, No.26, is understood to have worked to Cockermouth from Bullgill; it was built in 1897 and withdrawn by the LMS in 1925.

This brings us to the engines which will be associated with the Keswick road as long as it is remembered : the 'Cauliflowers', strictly '18 inch Goods' of 0-6-0 tender type, with 5ft diameter coupled wheels and 18in x 24in inside cylinders. They were notable for pioneering the use of David Joy's inside valvegear when F.W. Webb (at Crewe) introduced the design in 1880; the gear was retained throughout their long lives. For Keswick line duties, they were based at Penrith but were allocated in far greater numbers at Workington, taking over progressively from the 'Special DX', with which design they shared 5ft wheels. They were established by the time of the First World War, with six examples allocated at Workington in 1912 and seven in 1917, rising to 19 at the shed through most of the years 1930-47, falling back into 14 in 1948, four in 1950 and none in 1954. Concurrently, Penrith commonly had six or seven, the last two examples here being replaced late in 1954. Until then, one of these engines was likely to appear on the Penrith-Keswick goods turn. For years, Workington contrived to reserve a 'Cauliflower', fresh from Crewe Works in the spring, to work 'The Lakes Express' during the following summer.

It was the limitations of many bridges - discussed elsewhere in this work - that restricted the axle loading permitted on the line and thus the locomotive types employed. This was why the only express passenger locomotives employed. in LNWR days were the 2-4-0 tender engines so

well-known as 'Jumbos' and affectionately remembered by older enginemen for their lively and economical performance.

It is probable that the first examples were based at Workington from about the time when 'Jumbos' were demoted from express duties to main line assisting locomotives and secondary lines services, around 1900, perhaps a little later. There were none at Workington in 1896 but Nos. 793 *Martin* and 1166 *Wyre* were based at the shed on November 9 1912; as were Nos. 124 *Marquis Douro* and 739 *Ostrich* in October 1917. *Ostrich* was observed to be active on the route in August 1920. *Sister Dora* went ex-works from Crewe to Workington, still as LNWR No. 2158, in December 1924 and probably stayed until withdrawal from service in September 1927. LNWR No. 424 *Sirius* (allotted LMS No. 5107, but broken up in July 1927) had a spell at Workington shed and ran on the Keswick road.

The pattern of allocating a couple of the 6ft coupled wheels variant to Workington was probably constant until LMS Nos. 5102 *Cuckoo* and 5104 *Woodlark* were withdrawn from that shed in 1931. It was a delight when, for my first journey from Penrith to Keswick, in June 1930, *Woodlark* figured at the head of five varied bogie carriages and made a faultless run into the evening sun. The 6ft 6in-wheeled variant appeared from Penrith shed and on through workings at busy times from Carlisle; for example No.1675 *Vimiera* is illustrated in June 1919, captured by Ken Nunn, and W.E. Boyd found 2193 *Salopian* regularly at work in August 1920. Penrith, formerly a sub-depot of Workington, was controlled by Carlisle (Upperby) from 1923, using shed number 29 (like Upperby) for some years, indeed nominally 29P. Around 1930, the line was favoured by 'Jumbos', which were perhaps numerically in the ascendant, but not for long. In 1932, Nos. 5001 *Snowdon* and 5050 *Merrie Carlisle* were based at Penrith for a time, No. 5050 being withdrawn in 1933 (from Carlisle) while *Snowdon* remained at Penrith and was in regular use on Keswick line passenger trains until close on withdrawal in October 1934. By that time, the engine was numbered 25001 and was often prominent as seen from passing expresses.

Midland and LMS/BR locomotives

The LMS brought in a few of the former MR 2-4-0 express locomotives; No.185 came to Penrith shed in 1933 and No. 87 joined it in 1934. In the autumn of 1935, Nos. 185 and 20087 (which derived from 87) were also present. They were permitted over the bridges throughout from Penrith to Keswick and Workington but were employed mainly on stopping passenger trains from Penrith to Carlisle, or double heading with a 'Cauliflower' between Carlisle and Keswick.

From 1946, the LMS and BR-built light 2-6-0 locomotives (classed 2F, later 2MT) with 5ft diameter coupled wheels and outside cylinders (16in x 24in), Walschaerts valvegear, rocking grate and hopper ashpan and a superheated boiler; the maximum axle load was about 13 1/2 tons. They arrived on the Keswick road from late 1950 and in due course four examples at Penrith whilst eight examples at Workington virtually monopolised the route. After the introduction of DMUs in 1955-56 their numbers were reduced and thereafter they chiefly worked 'The Lakes Express' and goods duties.

This class was popularly given the nickname 'Mickey Mouse', doubtless because of their perky appearance and performance. At Upperby, a shed which worked 'Pacifics', they were known as 'Penrith Lizzies'. Their maximum load was usually six bogies of 57ft stock; my train of five more variable-length stock with *Woodlark* will be recalled for comparison.

Some locomotive and train workings, daily and occasional

While the daily passenger duties for engines and men were usually end-to-end between Penrith and Workington

Above: One of the MR 2-4-0 locos which infiltrated Carlisle-Penrith-Keswick workings. This is believed to be No. 20185, which came to the district in 1933 as No.185. The train is coming off the Cockermouth line at Derwent Junction, Workington. A MR 2-4-0 would not be common at the western end of the route. The overline bridge No. 45A of about 1904 is in rear of the train and the long terrace of ironworks cottages still appear to the left at the time of taking. Richard L. Pattinson/CRA.

and vice versa, the goods train duties were normally booked as detailed here:

Workington - Cockermouth and return
Workington - Keswick and return
- *both worked by Workington men.*

Penrith - Cockermouth and return
Penrith - Keswick and return
- *both worked by Penrith men.*

In 1906, the locomotive on 'duty 24' to Cockermouth was employed from 12 noon until 1.45pm for shunting the coal depots and warehouse sidings. If the mid-day 'fast goods' from Workington to Penrith required assistance, the duty 24 engine would interrupt its shunting to 'bank' the train from Cockermouth Junction to Embleton, then returning light engine to the Junction and yard. In LMS days, 'the Keswick goods' duty for Workington men was quite a tough assignment owing to the number of shunting calls, typically at: William Pit sidings, Camerton Brickworks, Brigham, Cockermouth Yard, Cockermouth Gas Works siding, Cockermouth Cattle Sidings and Oil Tank Siding, Embleton (as required), Close Quarry siding, Bassenthwaite Lake, Braithwaite and Keswick, where it met the Penrith-Keswick goods for exchange of traffic. If the return goods to Penrith produced an overload, the Workington locomotive banked it all the way to Penruddock, then returned to Keswick, turned, and collected its homeward traffic.

From Penrith, a change in locomotive duties is found between 1906 and 1921, owing to the coming of the eight-hour working day. The engine of the 'traditional' mid-morning goods from Penrith to Keswick (then 11.10am) was booked in 1906 to leave Keswick again at 5.55pm, light engine for Threlkeld, and to bring the 6.20pm Threlkeld-Penrith goods home, due at 7.45pm. In 1921, a return into Penrith at 5.55pm (booked) was specified. In latter days of the CKPR, circa 1918-22, the mid-afternoon goods from Penrith to Keswick, was commonly worked by Penrith men with an 0-6-2 'Coal' tank, returning in the early evening from Keswick. In late LMS days, the very early morning goods from Penrith, successor to the 'mixed train' of old, was worked through to Cockermouth by Penrith men, who came back with the morning goods of the time from Cockermouth Yard to Penrith. They were supposed to conclude with out and back 'trip' workings to Clifton Moor and then Southwaite to shunt the respective station yards, but this proved to make an excessively long day. It may be noted that Penrith men normally came off Down goods trains at Cockermouth passenger station, in order to turn their engine, before continuing with the train to the Junction and Cockermouth (lower) Yard.

An interesting sidelight on the working of passenger trains is provided in the LNWR 'Appendix'. In April 1916, under 'Passenger trains; CK&P Railway', it is stated:

	Small Tank Engines	Goods Engines, 18in Tanks Side Tank Coal	Max permitted four or six-wheeled pass. vehicles
Workington to Cockermouth:	160 tons	200 tons	16
Cockermouth to Keswick:	160 tons	200 tons	11 *
Keswick to Troutbeck:	135 tons	170 tons	9*
Troutbeck to Penrith:	160 tons	200 tons	16 *
Penrith to Troutbeck:	135 tons	170 tons	9 *
Troutbeck to Workington:	160 tons	200 tons	16 *

* Without bank engine.

The omission from this chart of 6ft and 6ft 6in 'Jumbo'

2-4-0 locomotives may indicate that they were not usually working over the line in that year, although this does seem surprising. An excursion train from Edinburgh Waverley by the LNER Waverley Route was reported on May 18 1936, arriving at Carlisle behind NBR 'Atlantic' No. 9906 *Teribus*. The train ran forward to Keswick hauled by Midland class 2 (Belpaire) 0-6-0 No.3655 (acquired by Upperby from the recently -closed Durran Hill shed) as pilot to 'Cauliflower' No. 8415. One evening in August 1938 (or possibly 1939) a return excursion came off the Keswick line at Penrith with a 'Cauliflower' and 2-4-0 No.185; the train ran to Carlisle behind No.185 unaided, 'out of section' being received in about seven minutes.

Circa 1928, John Roberts fired on a 'Cauliflower' which took over its special passenger train at Springs Branch, south of Wigan, bound for the Keswick Convention. The load was about six bogies and the route was via the LNER link line between Eamont Junction and Redhills Junction. A conductor joined the train at Eamont box and the water picked up from the troughs at Dillicar (before Tebay) lasted to Keswick. An amusing 'Cauliflower' working from the western end of the line, in the 1930s, concerned an excursion run via the Furness coastal route to the 'Manchester November Handicap'. On returning to Workington, late at night, a Workington 'Cauliflower' was booked to take the front vehicles forward to Keswick, returning as empty stock in the early hours of the morning. Returning,the train crashed through the gates at Rakefoot crossing, the gatekeeper being asleep - and the driver too?

'The big engines'

It was reported that in 1936 a large tank engine of a highly competent class was run on the Keswick line – No.2313, once *The Prince*, a 2-6-4-T. The progressive bridge strengthening between Penrith and Keswick would be nearing completion at this time and this was probably some form of trial. The bridge-strengthening programme was never extended west of Keswick, but was finished thus far by 1938, when '4F' 0-6-0 engines were authorised to run

Left: 'The big engines' are here represented by No. 45559 *British Columbia*, a '5X' three-cylinder 4-6-0, described by the photographer as *toiling* up the 1 in 70 gradient past Blencow station; this is not surprising-with 10 vehicles of mostly BR Mk 1 stock. The train is the Newcastle-Keswick, June 23 1957. *Robert Leslie.*

Right: Examples of the LMS family of large passenger tank engines also worked on the Keswick road in later years. This is Stanier 2-6-4T No. 42594 climbing the gradient over Mosedale viaduct, with 'The Lakes Express' of Saturday 19 August 1961. *Robert Leslie.*

to Keswick. The first example arrived on the London (Euston)-Keswick Convention special working of July 15 1938. Incidentally, a '4F' would be a doubtful advance on a 'Cauliflower' in good order. A driver who endeavoured to work a heavy wartime train for Roedean schoolgirls with a '4F' suffered tribulations, shortages of steam and stops to 'blow up' on the grades.

The new 60ft turntable at Keswick made possible the first working of a 'Black 5' 4-6-0, in the summer of 1939. During and after the 1939-45 war, a '5MT' very occasionally worked a Penrith-Keswick goods. More regular, after the war, was the summer Saturday morning working of the Keswick-Manchester train by a 2-6-4T from Oxenholme shed. It was

detached at Penrith and worked the Euston-bound 'Lakes Express', which had come from Workington behind one or two 'Cauliflowers', south to Oxenholme.

As the NER Redhills-Eamont link had disappeared, the strengthening to Keswick was mainly of value for the few heavy trains which travelled to and from Keswick, via Carlisle, principally the 'Newcastle' on summer Sundays. This train was usually worked by 'Black 5' 4-6-0s in pairs, or a '5MT' with a '5X', or possibly even a three-cylinder 'Royal Scot' 4-6-0. No. 46136 *The Border Regiment* was employed on Sundays August 11 and 18 and again on September 1 1957. By courtesy of Mr Hugh G. Ellison, three logs of runs from Keswick are reproduced here.

6.30pm KESWICK-NEWCASTLE
'ROYAL SCOT' CLASS 7P 4-6-0 No. 46136 *THE BORDER REGIMENT*
10 COACHES (327/345 TONS) Sunday August 18 1957.

MILES	TIMING POINT	SCHEDULE	ACTUAL	SPEED	
0.0	KESWICK	0	0.00		1min late
1.0	Briery Mill Halt		3.54	24	
2.0	Milepost 15		6.04	28	
3.0	Milepost 16		7.53	40	
3.5	Threlkeld	9	8.38	30*	
4.0	Milepost 17		9.49	28	
4.5	Milepost 17.50		10.53	27	
5.0	Milepost 18		11.55	31	
5.5	Milepost 18.50		13.05	26	
6.0	Milepost 19		14.11	28	
6.5	Milepost 19.50		15.15	29	
7.0	Milepost 20		16.18	27	
7.5	Milepost 20.50		17.24	26	
8.0	Milepost 21		18.29	27	
8.2	Troutbeck		19.00	31	
8.5	Milepost 21.50		19.32	28	
9.5	Milepost 22.50		20.59	54	
10.5	Penruddock	26	22.23	*25/34	
11.0	Milepost 24		23.18	31/50	
12.0	Milepost 25		24.41	47	
13.0	Flusco Siding		25.47	62	
14.4	Blencow	33	27.51	28*	
15.2	Catch points		28.54	48	
16.6	Rehills Junction		30.29	64	
17.8	Penrith No.1		32.27	20*	
18.2	PENRITH	39	33.24		

Maximum equivalent drawbar horsepower : 1635.

Log: Courtesy H.G. Ellison

6.30pm KESWICK-NEWCASTLE
CLASS 5 4-6-0s Nos. 45371 & 45494
9 COACHES (301/310 TONS) Sunday June 22 1958
CLASS 5s Nos. 45368 & 45451
10 COACHES (334/345 TONS) Sunday July 6 1958

MILES	TIMING POINT	SCHED	ACTUAL	SPEED	ACTUAL	SPEED
0.0	KESWICK	0	0.00		0.00	
1.0	Briery Mill Halt		3.43	28	3.12	26
2.0	Milepost 15		5.39	33	5.22	28
3.0	Milepost 16		7.25	37	7.22	36
3.3	Stop for pilotman		8.28			
	Single line wkg		8.54			
3.5	Threlkeld	9	10.31	10	8.03	32
4.0	Milepost 17		12.48	24	9.12	27
4.5	Milepost 17.50		13.54	28/31	10.17	26
5.0	Milepost 18		14.56	26	11.28	24
5.5	Milepost 18.50		16.00	30	12.49	22
6.0	Milepost 19		17.05	27	14.04	24
6.5	Milepost 19.50		18.09	28	15.16	25
7.0	Milepost 20		19.15	27	16.26	26
7.5	Milepost 20.50		20.22	26	17.34	27
8.0	Milepost 21		21.30	27	18.42	27
8.2	Troutbeck		22.03	30	19.14	31
8.5	Milepost 21.50		22.37	28	19.47	29
9.5	Milepost 22.50		24.11	47	21.21	47
10.5	Penruddock	26	25.45	*25/33	22.54	*25/32
11.0	Milepost 24		26.47	32/50	23.51	33/48
12.0	Milepost 25		28.05	50	25.13	48
13.0	Flusco Sidings		29.13	59	26.21	62
14.4	Blencow	33	31.28	15*	28.02	35*
15.2	Catch points		32.43	45	29.02	48
16.6	Redhills Junction		34.21	63	30.36	65
					sigs	15*
17.8	Penrith No1		sig stops		32.52	
18.2	PENRITH	39	46.15		34.00	
	Net		34		33.50	

Logs: Courtesy H.G. Ellison

North Eastern Railway locomotives on the Keswick road

Reference has already been made to the accommodation of NER locomotives at Penrith (where a passenger engine for the Eden Valley line was housed) and Cockermouth (where provision of stabling was in fact never achieved). 'Day return' excursions from distant NER stations to Keswick have been noticed: six-coupled engines of, nominally, 'goods' classes are believed to have worked such trips, with perhaps an occasional 2-4-0 passenger engine, like those used on the Stainmore route.

The daily operation of NER locomotives, back to 1866, was on mineral duties. Until the first decade of the 20th century, a near-monopoly was held by the 'long boiler' 0-6-0s of Stockton & Darlington Railway derivation, hence titled 'Quakers', collectively the '1001' class. Broadly, their wheels were of 5ft diameter, with inside cylinders (17in or 18in x 24in) and the weight of engine (not including tender) in working order was about 35 tons. 'Double loads' became normal by the 1880s-1890s, comprising around 28 coke wagons, each of 10 tons capacity, and two brake vans were worked by two 'Quakers.' This represented maybe 400 tons of train westbound, and with one engine moved to the rear for the climb from Redhills Junctions on the CKPR. Working from Shildon to Cockermouth and back in a single shift of 15-16 hours was typical, and a marathon undertaking for the men, taking in Stainmore (1,378ft) and Troutbeck (889ft), in both directions. As the length of the railwayman's working day was progressively curtailed, Kirkby Stephen became the normal staging point; thus, Kirkby Stephen engines and its men, worked from their home station to Cockermouth and back, turning their engine at the passenger station and taking a meal-time break while the traffic was dealt with at the lower yard.

From 1901, Wilson Worsdell of the NER designed and built the handsome 'T' and 'T1' 0-8-0 locomotives, for mineral traffic, with 4ft 7 1/4in diameter wheels, outside cylinders (20in x 26in), with an engine-only weight in working order rather of more than 58 tons. In February 1904, he suggested to the CKPR that these new engines be employed on the NER's Cockermouth coke duties, by implication taking double loads unaided. CKPR General Manager Peter Thompson and and Engineer John Wood visited Vincent Raven, Mr Worsdell's assistant, to learn more, but, as noted earlier no agreement to strengthen bridges was achieved. The subject went into abeyance, although in August 1906 Mr Wood presented costs for the strengthening of bridges to take 'T' engines, but his Board elected not to proceed. The LNWR was rebuffed by the CKPR when, in May 1917, it wished to introduce heavier goods locomotives on the line via Keswick, presumably visualising its own 0-8-0 engines.

Meanwhile, in July 1906, the CKPR agreed to accept the 'C' and 'C1' class 0-6-0 engines of the NER on their line. The 'C' was a two-cylinder compound locomotive and the 'C1'

Below: This picture superbly illustrates the classic 'Quaker' long-boiler 0-6-0 engines of the SDR/NER, for so long the motive power for the coke trains westward and (mainly) coke 'empties' returning to the County of Durham. No. 1184 is pausing, eastbound, at Keswick, against Latrigg in the background. Note the comparatively light permanent way and the lack of trees near the station - and the panama hat! No. 1184 was the locomotive involved in the westbound runaway early on January 16 1896, when the signalman derailed it to avoid a collision. *D.F. Tee Collection.*

was the non-compound version, with 5ft 1in diameter wheels (like the 'C') but with 18in x 24in cylinders and Joy's valvegear. The weight of the 'C1' engine in working order was about 41 1/2 tons. This decision followed a meeting at Penrith between Messrs Thompson and Wood for the CKPR and Messrs Smeddle (District Locomotive Superintendent, Darlington) and Bengough (Civil Engineer) of the NER.

The true Wilson Worsdell 0-6-0 mineral engines were the 4ft 7 1/4in -wheeled 'P' (built 1894-98) and 'P1' (1899-1902), with 18in x 24in and 18 1/4in x 26in inside cylinders (respectively). They had steam brakes on the engines but no continuous brake for the train and in due time the 'C1' type (which also worked passenger trains on the NER) and the 'P' or 'P1' classes (mineral-only engines) infiltrated the coke workings to Cockermouth.

An older class of 0-6-0, originating in the Fletcher period of locomotive design, between the SDR 'Quakers' and the Worsdell types, was the '398' family, typically with 5ft wheels, 17in x 24in cylinders and a weight of 35 tons; these engines came to be represented at Kirkby Stephen and shared the Cockermouth runs. An observer at Keswick in summer 1920 noted locomotives of 'C1' and '398 types', all identifiable with Kirkby Stephen shed, engaged on the coke duties. This was just about the end of the active years of coke traffic to Cockermouth.

The LNER employed Worsdell six-coupled locomotives on such traffic as survived into 1923-26 and 1928-29. It is not thought that the LNER, successors to the NER, ever worked passenger trains to Keswick with its own locomotives.

Above: This is the only locomotive ever owned by the CKPR. Discussed in the text, it was never permitted to work on the railway. It is seen here at Cockermouth. *L&GRP.*

And the CKPR had a locomotive of its own.....

In the week when the CKPR opened its line to passenger traffic (January 5 1865), its Works Committee was authorised to purchase a small locomotive for use on the line, if deemed necessary. On May 11 of that year, the Committee asked the Engineer to secure quotations for the supply of a tank engine; presumably the primary aim was to have a ballast engine but the Secretary was to check with the LNWR that, if purchased, the locomotive could be employed occasionally in CKPR service. No doubt the LNWR was discouraging, or worse; the subject was dropped.

Coming to March 1900, the CKPR placed contracts for doubling the formation and structures of its route from Troutbeck to Penruddock and from Blencow to Redhills Junction; the contractor was W. Grisenthwaite, of Penrith. The new lines were completed in June 1901, including laying of the extra tracks, accomplished under the arrangements of the Railway Company's own Engineer. *Contract Journal* of June 26 1901 shows Manning Wardle locomotive Works No. 1064 (an 0-6-0T) for sale by William Grisenthwaite, styled contractor. Mr Grisenthwaite was of Penrith and the sale was handled by A.T. & E. Crow, who were well known as auctioneers of contract plant in the north of England. It was reported to the CKPR Board on November 14 1901 that, since their meeting on 10 October 1901, a locomotive engine, the property of Mr W. Grisenthwaite, had been purchased at his plant sale, for the purpose of ballasting and repairs of the permanent way. It was resolved to purchase a suitable van to work with ballast trains and to erect a shed for the engine at Flusco Quarry, or other convenient place. One recalls later reference to 'the

engine shed' at Flusco ballast quarry, thereby giving credence to this move.

The locomotive had inside cylinders (13in x 18in) and 3ft diameter wheels and a weight in working order of 22 tons. There was a raised round-top firebox and a large cab, with rounded eaves. It was one of the relatively few of the maker's 'M' class to be built with side tanks: it was despatched new from the company's Leeds works in May 1888, with the name *Oldham,* to T.A. Walker, at Latchford. This was on the alignment of his linear contract between the Mersey estuary and Manchester Docks (to be) constructing the Manchester Ship Canal. Its disposal from the MSC job has not been recorded specifically, but would probably have occurred after the opening of the canal in 1894.

On coming to the CKPR, the locomotive carried the name *Strachan No. 7.* Contractors J. Strachan figure as owners in Mannings' records, but with no dates recorded. A likely place for its employment by them would have been on the construction of the LNWR Weaste branch (Eccles to the MSC Railway) 1894-95, and subsequently Strachan made a new link line for the LYR between Whitehouse West and North Junctions: the contract was placed in October 1898 and the curved line opened in July 1900, with Strachan's locomotive for sale at nearby Penwortham Junction on 20 June 1900. Here, Grisenthwaite could well have bought it, to haul 'fill' on his CKPR project. A copy of the CKPR minutes of November 14 1901 would go to Euston as a matter of course and in no time whatever a strong objection to the CKPR's new locomotive was on the desk of the General Manager at

Keswick - from LNWR General Manager Frederick Harrison. Mr MacInnes, Carlisle Director of the LNWR and also a member of the CKPR Board, was asked to speak with Mr Harrison and set his mind at rest. This was in vain and on March 6 1902, Messrs Marshall, Glasson and Cropper (Charles James Cropper, of Burnside and a member of LNWR and CKPR Boards) met with - or were arraigned before (!) - LNWR Chairman Lord Stalbridge and Fredrick Harrison, at Euston, to discuss *Strachan No.7*. The LNWR officers viewed this as a matter of principle at stake; it was agreed that the LNWR would supply engine power as and when required by the CKPR for maintenance of its permanent way, or like needs. It transpired that the CKPR had used NER engines for such purposes, for the provision of which they paid, but the practice had ceased 'for a long time'.

The Keswick Board resolved on May 8 1902 to sell their locomotive, "as soon as a favourable opportunity offers." Three years later, Mr Cropper drew attention to the locomotive still being unsold and the Directors reiterated their wish to sell - at over £300. The topic next figured in the Boardroom some eight years later, on July 5 1913, when the Secretary reported: "The Company's locomotive engine, which has stood for some time in the carriage shed at Cockermouth passenger station, has been sold for £100." Unfortunately, the purchaser was not named but a short account in *The Locomotive* of May 15 1926 states that it was sold in June 1913 (which reconciles) to Mr Isaac Miller, of Carlisle. The 1913 directories show only R. Miller, "old iron merchant," of 15a John street, but one Isaac Miller, machinery merchant, of the Currock district, advertised locomotives for sale in the early 1920s. William Firth (maybe of William Firth Ltd, Doncaster, who advertised engines for sale or hire in 1913-14) sold Manning Wardle No.1064 around November 1914 to Hudswell Clarke of Leeds (across the street from their contemporaries, Manning Wardle).

After repairs, it was resold by HC to Sir John Jackson, a public works contractor, and sent to Codford (between Salisbury and Westbury), and named *Prince Edward*. Jacksons' relevant bills were paid by the War Department ('Secretary of State for War' in Manning Wardle records) which thus acquired the locomotive. The last supply of spare parts by Manning Wardle was dated February 26 1917. The correspondents of *The Locomotive* did not mention Codford, but believed that the engine later worked in Galloway, south west Scotland, so perhaps that was also an assignment for the War Department.

The late Syd Ridley (who lived until recent years at Motherby, as the last known 'servant' of the CKPR, and with lively memory) vividly recalled that, around 1912-13 (when he would be seven or eight years old), he sometimes visited his elder brother, then employed at Cockermouth station. Syd and another boy liked to explore the recesses of the MCR carriage shed; there, they would mount and 'drive' a stored locomotive called *Strachan*. Mr Ridley associated it with the dozen (stated) ballast wagons of CKPR, which had wooden 'dumb' buffers. Incidentally, an addition of four vehicles to the Company's ballast wagon fleet had been authorised in 1892 and in July 1913 there was a proposal to adapt one or two of the wagons for use at the vehicle loading bank, at Keswick. It is believed that the ballast train wagons used in the later days of the CKPR were LNWR vehicles. Mr Ridley understood that *Strachan* had been bought from a Scottish colliery and eventually went back to Scotland; this could derive from the Strachan firm's origins and, subsequently, might associate with Galloway.

Information in this section derives mainly from: Syd Ridley; T.H. Braithwaite (of Workington) and F. Stanley (an accountant of the CK&P section of the LMS) published in 'The Locomotive' of May 15 1926 (ref also June 15 1926); J.B. Latham; Russell Wear; the records of Manning Wardle and Hudswell Clarke, of Leeds; and the photograph of the locomotive reproduced by W. McGowan Gradon and later listed by LGRP as No.12726 (reproduced opposite).

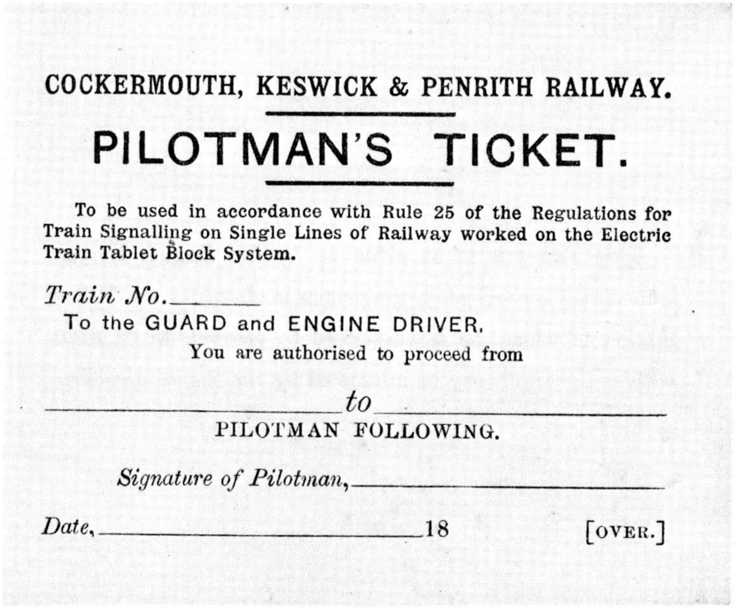

COCKERMOUTH, KESWICK & PENRITH RAILWAY.

PILOTMAN'S TICKET.

To be used in accordance with Rule 25 of the Regulations for Train Signalling on Single Lines of Railway worked on the Electric Train Tablet Block System.

*Train No.*_____
To the GUARD and ENGINE DRIVER.
You are authorised to proceed from

_____*to*_____
PILOTMAN FOLLOWING.

*Signature of Pilotman,*_____

*Date,*_____18   [OVER.]

SENIOR AND SPECIALIST STAFF

SENIOR AND SPECIALIST STAFF
THE COCKERMOUTH & WORKINGTON RAILWAY

Samuel Harford, Stationmaster at Masboro (Rotherham), Midland Railway, was appointed Secretary of the CWR but died on 24 March 1845, before he was due to move to Cockermouth. George H. Barnes, from the London, Brighton & South Coast Railway, was subsequently appointed in August 1845 but moved on in November 1846 to become Secretary of the MCR. His successor was Henry Jacob, from the East Lancashire Extension Railway (the line from near Ramsbottom to Colne) and he was styled Secretary & General Superintendent of the CWR. Within a few years, the chief officer was John Dodds, who served until his resignation wef 12 August 1856 - being by then 'Secretary, Engineer and Manager.' One gains the impression that he was latterly unpopular with his Board but he moved to Edinburgh and continued for a time to take a critical interest in the affairs of the Cockermouth company. Mr Tosh was temporarily Manager and Super-intendent, and, at the Board's request, he pre-pared an urgent report on the rundown condition of the locomotives. John Mayson was Secretary from August 1856 and shortly became Secretary & General Manager - appointments held for some ten years. Mr Tosh figured as Locomotive Superintendent and Thomas Drane, CE, was for a number of years the (civil) Engineer.

John Mayson was placed in charge of the LNWR's 'Whitehaven District', follow-ing its creation in 1866-67 from the acquired WJn and C&W Railways; he was (or soon became) 'District Manager'. He adopted the name 'J. Myson' to avoid confusion with Masons on the LNWR, but resigned around August 1869. G.P. Neele wrote, much later, that Mr Mayson's career with the LNWR was short and unsuccessful.

STAFF OF THE COCKERMOUTH, KESWICK & PENRITH RAILWAY

The chief officer of the Company was the Secretary & Manager (Secretary & General Manager from 1870) and,

effectively, there were only three successive incumbents, from 1861 to 1923. Henry Cattle was appointed on August 10 1861, at the first Board meeting. He had been chief clerk to A.C. Sheriff in the Hull District of the York & North Midland Railway. In 1864, he became the first representa-tive of the CKPR with the Railway Clearing House. He resigned in July 1870, moving to the Cambrian Railways' headquarters at Oswestry as their General Manager - or so it was understood in Keswick, although 'traffic manager' may have been more accurate. At least two of his best men soon followed him from Keswick.

Peter Thompson, previous-ly the Company's Accountant, was appointed 21 July 1870 and held the senior office on the CKPR until resign ing on March 1 1913, to take a seat on the Company Board.

John Clark, Traffic Superintendent, appears to have carried out all or most of the duties of Secretary & General Manager in 1913-14 and was formally appointed as such from July 1 1914; he carried these responsi bilities until the winding up of the Company in 1923. There had been a somewhat mysterious interregnum before John Clark was appointed. In anticipation of Peter Thompson's resigna tion, the office of Secretary & General Manager seems to have been advertised and A. Entwistle was appointed wef 1 March 1913. A personal letter from A. Entwistle, of 39 Dorset Square (near Marylebone station), London, to a director of the CKPR was dated February 25 1913 and expressed pleasure that the appointment would bring him back to old families and friends. There may be an implication that he had served the CKPR earlier in his career. Both the Company and personal files, so far as they exist, are silent until the minuting on July 4 1914 that Mr Entwistle had withdrawn his acceptance of office.

The Accountant

Peter Thompson (pictured inset, this page) was CKPR Accountant until 1870 and he may well earlier have been

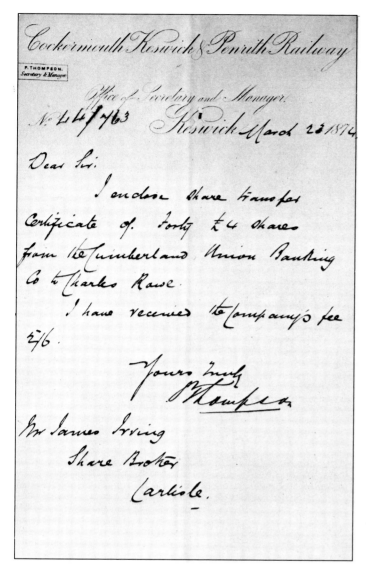

Facing page, inset: Peter Thompson probably joined the Cockermouth & Workington Railway in 1856. He progressed rapidly to be Secretary and General Manager of the Cockermouth, Keswick & Penrith Railway, from 1870 until 1913, and a Director from 1913 until his death in 1920.
Richard L. Pattinson/CRA.

Above: Here is a letter from Peter Thompson, written (to Mr James Irving, Share Broker, Carlisle) soon after he became Secretary & General Manager of the CKPR. It reads: " Dear Sir, I enclose share transfer certificate of forty £4 shares from the Cumberland Union Banking Co to Charles Rowe. I have received the Company's fee 2/6. Yours truly, P. Thompson." *Courtesy Derek Brough.*

the inspector of permanent way and mineral traffic engaged by the CWR in August 1856. He was succeeded as Accountant, in 1870, by Joseph Wales, previously Stationmaster at Cockermouth. An unhappy story ended in July 1885 with talk of criminal proceedings after defalcations of some £1,388 had allegedly been found in the Company's accounts.

John Postlethwaite, who had been Storekeeper & Chief Clerk, was made Accountant in May 1886, and resigned owing to poor health in June 1914. He was placed on pension and was among the people granted a gratuity in 1923. F. Stanley held the appointment from 1914 to 1923.

Traffic Superintendent

The first Traffic Superintendent was John Clark, who had been Chief Clerk in the Secretary's office from at least 1870 until 1886, when 'traffic' was added to his responsibilities - and in due course he was Traffic Superintendent', promoted in July 1914 to be the chief officer of the Company. John Robinson, previously cashier, was Traffic Superintendent from 1 July 1914 until 1923.

Engineer

The appointment of Thomas Bouch as Engineer was made at the first Board meeting, on August 10 1861, and he had overall responsibility for survey, design and construction of the railway and all its works. John Wood (CE by 1869; MInstCE by 1880) was resident engineer during construction (1862-64) and he was formally appointed Engineer of the Company by the Works Committee on October 6 1864, confirmed by the Board on January 5 1865, this appointment to be fully effective "when his arrangement with Mr Bouch terminates." John Wood was allowed private practice and he had a Carlisle address during many of his years with the CKPR. The doubling of sections of the line and the remodelling of Keswick station came within his province, regarding survey, design and execution. He was rewarded by significant gratuities on completion of these projects; note that the Company had been saved the engagement of a consulting engineer. When John Wood retired in November 1905, unanimous appreciation was expressed by Board members, including that "for ready assistance ever given in all circumstances of emergency and his soundness and wisdom in counsel on all occasions." In 1908, they invited him to join the Board, but he declined on health grounds.

A.M. Bristow was Engineer from December 1 1905 until August 1920, when he retired owing to poor health but was retained upon inside work; he died on October 23 1922. J.C.Boyd CE held the appointment from September 1 1920; he did not receive a gratuity in 1923 so perhaps he had moved to an appointment elsewhere towards that time.

The gratuities of March 10 1923, approved by the LMS, ranged from £1,000 to £30 and went to John Clark and other serving officers, senior head office clerks, stationmasters, the permanent way inspector and the former accountant.

Other appointments

Appointments in CKPR days included those of cashier, storekeeper, chief clerks and other clerks at Keswick head office, booking clerk at Keswick, goods clerk/agent at Keswick, notably Percy Sanderson, who joined the old Company in 1911 and served for both the LMS and BR at Keswick until 1958, in which time he also worked on behalf of staff and for the community as councillor and mayor. There was also the warehouseman at Keswick, the signal fitter and his assistant, (G.W. Carlton and Edward Elliott in 1913), a telegraph lineman and assistant, blacksmith, mason, joiner (R. Nichol in 1913), fencer (Nathan Routledge, c 1913-23), gardener (James Shrives, mentioned elsewhere), foreman of the labourers' gang, a timber loader and assistant with roving commission, and the policemen.

The Inspector of Permanent Way was a significant figure especially during the doubling works from the 1890s to 1902, and each track gang had its own Foreman Ganger and platelayers, with their 'length' to watch and maintain. The staff at Cockermouth were joint staff of the CKPR and CWR, and from 1866 to 1923 of the CKPR and LNWR.

THE BOARD OF DIRECTORS OF THE CWR

This company was formed by Act of Parliament of July 21 1845. Its initial Board of 12 members was elected on August 15 1845; the members in question were still on the Board in June 1847, a couple of months after the line opened. This record may omit some members of short tenure; it is not claimed as definitive in identifying the members of the Harris family ,who, with the Fletchers, were prominent in Cumberland coalmining.

John Wilson Fletcher: of Tarn Bank, Greysouthen had been on the provisional committee formed on July 26 1844 and was Chairman of the company from August 15 1845; he was a member of Board (and its Chairman) for many of the following years until his death in October 1857.

Joseph Harris: of Lorton, was on the provisional commitee, but it is unclear whether he was on the Board for a time.

Joseph Harris: of Greysouthen (sometimes described as of Brigham) was on the provisional committee, and on the Board, as Deputy Chairman from August 15 1845 until 1855. He would be the coalowner, of Greysouthen Colliery, who died on January 7 1860.

Jonathan Harris, Jnr CE: was on the Company board from August 15 1845 and probably throughout until his death - including a spell as Chairman circa 1853-56. This would be Capt. John Harris, CE, who succeeded as principal of Greysouthen Collieries and Brigham Limeworks and estates in January 1860, who died on January 251863. Many of the family's industrial interests were thereafter acquired by the Fletchers and so reached West Cumberland Hematite I&SCo Ltd and Allerdale Coal Company.

Joseph William Harris: probably of Papcastle was a member of the provisional committee but not the Company Board until its later years; he was certainly a member from 1856 to 1866. He is thought to be of W. Harris & Sons, the textile interests of the family, in Cockermouth.

John Charlton: of Workington served on the Board from August 15 1845 until about 1857.

George Cape: of Cockermouth was a member of the provisional committee and also the board from August 15 1845 until at least 1859. He provided office furniture in 1846 and looked after the brickwork of the foundations for Cockermouth station in 1856. In June 1857, he complained to the Secretary that he had visited the office and found no clerks present!

John Mordy & Abraham Robinson: Both were elected to the board 15/8/1845 and served through to 1847, but ceased to be members after the early years.

John Steel: of Derwent Bank, Cockermouth, served on the provisional committee and was a member of the Board from August 151845, through to the LNWR takeover in 1866. He was Chairman from November 17 1857 following the late J.W. Fletcher. He was the Company's solicitor, although not in his days as Chairman.

William Thornburn: of Papcastle was a member of the provisional committee and served the Company Board from

Above: Miles MacInnes, 1830-1909, of Carlisle, a thoughtful participant in Board deliberations at Euston, is seen as sketched by a fellow director of the LNWR, some six months before his death. He joined the LNWR and CKPR Boards in 1876 and was greatly respected and liked by colleagues and staff.
Courtesy Gurney MacInnes.

August 15 1845 until retirement on July 31 1856. He figured as a coalowner, shipping coals by way of the CWR and Workington Harbour. (Note also Wm Thornburn, Jnr).

Thomas Westray: of Kendal (later of Workington), was on the Board from August 15 1845 and in its early days. He resumed a seat in 1852 until retirement in July 1857.

John Whitwell: of Kendal, presumed to be the brewer, was a member of the board from August 15 1845 until 1852.

Jonathan Wood: of Cockermouth was on the provisional committee and on the board from August 15 1845 until retirement on July 31 1856.

Isaac Fisher: of Seaton joined the board in its early years but was not a member by the 1860-64 period.

George Castle: of Hensingham, Whitehaven joined the Board in its early years and was a member until his death circa December1856.

W. Wood: joined c1854 but dropped out by 1855-57.

Rev. Samuel Sherwin: of Dean probably joined the board in 1855-56 and attended a general meeting on January 31 1857 but attended no Board meetings of 1856-57 and he resigned in July1857.

Cockermouth, Keswick and Penrith Railway.

SECRETARY'S OFFICE,

KESWICK,

March 2nd, 1923.

We beg to inform you that a SPECIAL GENERAL MEETING of the Proprietors and the Debenture Stock-holders of the COCKERMOUTH, KESWICK & PENRITH RAILWAY COMPANY will, in accordance with the Railways Act, 1921, be held at the Keswick Hotel, Keswick, on Saturday, the 17th day of March, 1923, at 11-0 a.m. precisely, for the purpose of considering and, if so determined, of approving a preliminary Scheme in pursuance of the said Act for the absorption of the Cockermouth, Keswick & Penrith Railway Company by the London Midland & Scottish Railway Company.

We beg to forward you herewith a blank form of Proxy, with instructions for the use of the same in the event of your being unable to attend the Meeting, and if you desire to make use of the Proxy, a penny stamp must be affixed thereto previously to its being signed, and the Proxy, when filled up and signed, must be transmitted to the Secretary so that he may receive it not later than forty-eight hours before the time appointed for holding the Meeting.

JOHN WILLIAM PATTINSON, *Chairman.*

JOHN CLARK, *Secretary.*

Above: A special general meeting of the CKPR was held on March 17 1923, to formalise the Company's absorption into the London Midland & Scottish Railway, at the Grouping of January 1 1923. This was the letter sent to shareholders. *Harold D. Bowtell Collection.*

Edward Waugh: of Papcastle was Deputy Chairman of the Company in 1856-66 and continued as solicitor in succession to John Steel, through to the LNWR takeover. He was a promoter of the CKPR and for a long period its solicitor.

William Kitchen: of Whitehaven joined the Board on July 31 1856 but resigned in July 1857. However, he (or a son of the same name and town?) joined the Board on November 17 1857 – but then dropped out in the period 1860-64.

William Thornburn, Jnr: of Papcastle joined the Board on July 31 1856, in succession to William Thornburn (Snr). He resigned in June 1863, being then resident in London

Henry Fletcher: of Marsh Side, Workington joined the Board on December 16 1856 and continued until 1866. He

is believed to be a son of J.W. Fletcher, who died in October 1857 as Chairman of the CWR.

John Musgrave: of Whitehaven joined the Board on July 22 1857 and continued until 1866. He was a solicitor.

Isaac Fletcher: of Tarn Bank, Greysouthen joined the Board on November 17 1857, succeeding his late father J.W. Fletcher. He served until resigning on February 24 1863. He was appointed Chairman of the CKPR in 1867 and was MP for Cockermouth from 1868 to 1879, also a Director of the West Cumberland Hematite I.&S. Co. Ltd.

William Fletcher: of Brigham Hill, Brigham joined the Board on February 24 1863 and continued in office until 1866. He was a son of the late J.W. Fletcher and brother of

Above: The last meeting of the Directors and officials of the Cockermouth Keswick and Penrith Railway, was held on March 24 1923. The group is shown outside the Keswick Hotel.

Sitting (left-right): EDMUND RUSSBOROUGH TURTON MP, Upsall Castle, near Thirsk (Director) Nominated by the North Eastern Railway; CHRISTOPHER JOHN PARKER MFH,JP, The Laithes, near Penrith (Deputy Chairman); JOHN WILLIAM PATTINSON JP, Ravenstone, near Keswick (Chairman); JOHN CLARK (Secretary & General Manager); SIR JOHN SCURRAH RANDLES MP, Bristowe Hill, Keswick (Director).

Standing (left-right): F. STANLEY, (Accountant); The Hon. CHRISTOPHER W. LOWTHER MP, 14 Wilton Street, London, SW 1 (Director) Nominated by the North Eastern Railway; ROBERT JACKSON HOLDSWORTH, Seat How, Thonthwaite, near Keswick, (Director); J.C. BOYD (Engineer); ROBERT ERNEST HIGHTON JP, CC, Threlkeld Leys, near Cockermouth (Director); CHARLES JAMES CROPPER, Ellergreen, near Kendal (Director) Nominated by the London & North Western Railway; THOMAS WILLIAM MARK, Great Crosthwaite, Keswick, (Director); CHARLES HUGH PATTINSON, The Towers, Cockermouth (Auditor); J. ROBINSON (Traffic Superintendent)

Below, left: J.M. Cutts, Stationmaster at Troutbeck, 1912-c1926, is seen at his station in the era of the CKPR, wearing the Company's dignified atire for its Stationmasters. The raised letters 'CK&PR' appear on his hat, just below the brim. Note also the whistle. A 'buttonhole' is worn - and the bar and cross of St John Ambulance Association. It was Mr Cutts who first established a Sunday service in a room at Troutbeck station, a similar arrangement later being facilitated in a room on the Down side by Mr Cecil Oldfield, when he was Stationmaster, Threlkeld and Troutbeck. *Courtesy Ted Watson.*

Below, right: Uniform buttons in brass carry the monograms 'CKPR' and 'CJS' (Cockermouth Joint Station). Also illustrated are LMS and BR buttons (the LMS in silver finish, the BR in the aluminium/silver) and of the LNER. Note the unusual 'LMS & LNE' button, a style which suggests very early days after the 1923 railway Grouping and possibly worn by Penrith station staff. *From the collection of the late Syd Ridley, by courtesy of Mrs Ridley.*

Isaac Fletcher *(ante)*. He was appointed in August 1864 to the Cockermouth Joint Station Committee. He was a Director of the CKPR from its inception. He followed his brother as MP for Cockermouth, (1879-80) and was Chairman of the Cockermouth & Workington Junction Railway from 1880 to 1900. Later, he was Managing Director of the Allerdale Coal Company and he also established the Moresby Coal Company.

Isaac Gray Bass: The Crags, Broughton joined the board circa August 1861 and continued as a member until 1866.

James Dees: of Whitehaven joined the board around August 1863 and remained a member to 1866. He also served as: Engineer of the MCR (1850-59); Engineer to the Whitehaven Junction Railway by 1852 and until 1856; Engineer of the WC&ER, 1854-57. One notes also his report on the CWR line and its timber bridges in later 1856.

Robert Gibson: of Whitehaven joined the board circa September 9 1863 and continued as a member until 1866.

Note:
The nine members listed as continuing until 1866, relinquished their office on the transfer of the Company to the LNWR.

THE BOARD OF DIRECTORS OF THE COCKERMOUTH, KESWICK AND PENRITH RAILWAY

The Company was incorporated by Act of August 1 1861. When the first formal meeting of the Company was held on August 10 1861, at the Royal Oak, Keswick, the existing 'provisional committee' was superseded by a constituted Board of 12 members (15 members from August 31 1861). L.A. Hoskins was Chairman and Isaac Fletcher Deputy Chairman. Following the agreements negotiated with the LNWR and the SDR during February-September 1862, seven members (whose names were obtained by ballot) resigned their seats at February 28 1863 and two nominees of the LNWR were elected shortly after this.

The way was thus paved for a Board of 12 members, eight locally nominated, two nominated by the LNWR and two by the SDR/NER - a pattern which continued to the Grouping of 1923, when the Company passed out of existence, being absorbed into the newly-created London Midland & Scottish Railway Company. The seven members resigning on February 28 1863 were:- John Crozier, Arthur Dover, Isaac Gale and John Robinson (all elected 10/8/1861); Mark Cockbaine, William Fletcher and John Steel, MP (all elected August 31 1861.

There follows a statement of the eight 'survivors' of February 28 1863, followed by the four appointees of the larger Companies - and subsequent appointments down the years. Where members are designated with military rank, or as JP or MP, this does not necessarily apply throughout the period of Directorship. Dates of joining or leaving the board, where shown in month-and-year only, are to be taken as approximate.

Continued on page 191....

BOARD MEMBERS; COCKERMOUTH KESWICK & PENRITH RAILWAY

DATE JOINED	NAME (WITH RANK/APPOINTMENTS & ADDRESS)	COMPANY DUTIES/OTHER INTERESTS	LEFT THE BOARD
August 10 1861	Thomas Alison Hoskins JP Higham Hall (near Bassenthwaite Lake station).	Chairman from February 28 1863 to November 2 1867. He 'turned the first sod' on May 21 1862.	Retired November 2 1867
August 10 1861	Isaac Fletcher (1827-79) JP MP for Cockermouth. Elder son of John Wilson Fletcher, former CWR Chairman. Tarn Bank, Greysouthen	Deputy Chairman from February 28 1863 to November 1 1867. Chairman from November 2 circa April 1879. Also first Chairman of Keswick Hotel Company. Partner in family coalowners Isaac & William Fletcher & Co.	Died April 1879
August 10 1861	Isaac Gray Bass The Crags, Broughton (being north of the Derwent river)	Interested in coal and iron. When tendering resignation, he wrote from Aston Hall Colliery Hawarden (noted for early tramway); he was about to cease to live in Cumberland.	Retired April 26 1867
August 10 1861	John Jameson - JP Moorhouses, Penrith	Depy Chairman from November 2 1867. Chairman from April 1879, (but again depy from September 1879, at his wish)	Died October 1881
August 10 1861	Isaac Lowthian Penrith/by 1879: Chatsworth Square, Carlisle	Resignation due to continued ill health	Retired February 4 1880
August 10 1861	Thomas McGlasson, Penrith	Of Penrith brewers	Died August 1870
August 10 1861	John Simpson, Penrith		Died July 1872
August 10 1861	John James Spedding - Major, JP Greta Bank, Keswick, with lands above the station/later of Windebrowe	Depy Chairman from June 11 1879, Chairman from August 6 1879. The pulpit in Crosthwaite Church, Keswick is a memorial to him.	Died December 8 1909
March 28 1863	William Nicholson Hodgson - DL, JP MP for Carlisle/ East Cumberland (ranging 1847-76) Newby Grange, Crosby, Carlisle (and 33 Duke Street, St James's London)	Nominee of LNWR	Died November 1876
March 28 1863	Andrew Green Thompson - Major (later Colonel), JP. The Hollies Keswick (also of Bridekirk, near Cockermouth)	Nominee of LNWR. Interested in W. Cumberland iron and steel industry	Retired (?) 1882
April 25 1863	Henry Pease - MP Pierremont, Darlington	Nominee of SDR/NER and chairman of SDR/director of NER, Tees Valley Rly, Eden Valley Rly, SDLUR	Died August 1881
April 25 1863	Isaac Wilson - JP Nunthorpe Hall, Middlesbrough	Nominee of SDR/NER and director of SDR/NER, EVR, SDLUR, etc; a figure in the Teesside iron industry.	Retired August 1879
May 11 1867	Henry Gandy - Capt, DL, JP, - son of John Gandy, of Oakland, Windermere. Became High Sheriff of Westmorland. Eden Grove, Penrith/Castle Bank, Appleby/ Skirgill Park, Penrith (bought 1879, sold by his son in 1925).		Died June 1888
November 2 1867	Arthur Dover Skiddaw Bank, Keswick	Had also been a Board member, 1861-63	Died January 1874
cAugust 1870	C.H. Wake - Lt. Colonel Ormathwaite House, Keswick		Died February 1872

BOARD MEMBERS;
COCKERMOUTH KESWICK & PENRITH RAILWAY *(Continued...)*

DATE JOINED	NAME (WITH RANK/APPOINTMENTS & ADDRESS)	COMPANY DUTIES/OTHER INTERESTS	LEFT THE BOARD
February 24 1872	Hon Percy S. Wyndham - MP Cockermouth Castle/Isell Hall (Leconfield Estates)	An infrequent attender at board meetings	Retired June 1876
July 27 1872	William Harrison, Penrith		Died June 1878
February 7 1874	William McGlasson The Close, Embleton.	Farmer and Landowner. He was brother of Thomas who died 1870 *(ante)*	Died July 1890
June 14 1876	Henry Charles Howard (1850-1914) - DL, BA, JP, High Sheriff of Cumberland 1879 MP, for Penrith, 1885-86. Greystoke castle - inherited Greystoke estates but not the associated Dukedom.	Depy Chairman from November 8 1906 Chairman from January 13 1910	Died August 1914
November 29 1876	Miles MacInnes (1830-1909) - BA, MA, JP, Eldest Son of General John MacInnes (D 1859) of Fern Lodge, Hampstead. Became alderman and Vice Chairman of Cumberland CC, and Depy. Lieut. MP (Lib) for Hexham, 1885-95 West Heath, Hampstead, but soon moving to Rickerby house, Carlisle (to which he succeeded 1876 under will of George Head Head, of Head's Bank, Carlisle). Rickerby House was retained in the family until 1914.	Simultaneously joined LNWR Board and (as LNWR nominee) CKPR Board in 1876, as successor to W.N. Hodgson, also of Carlisle. On his death, it was written by the secretary of the LNWR Temperance Union, Carlisle: 'We have lost our very best friend, on whom railwaymen on the LNWR line have looked for help when in trouble and also in our Christian and temperance work'.	Died October 1909
	The name 'Miles MacInnes' was carried by locomotive LNWR 2507/LMS 5335, during 1910-35, this being a 4-4-0 of the classic 'George the Fifth' class.		
August 7 1878	Sir Henry Ralph Fletcher-Vane, Bart (1830-1908) - DL, JP. Hutton-in-the-Forest (from 1964, William Morgan Fletcher-Vane was created Baron Inglewood)	Depy chairman from August 27 1881 until October 4 1906, when he relinquished this appointment but remained on the Board.	Died June 1908
June 11 1879	Edward Waugh - MP from August 1881 Cockermouth - a prominent figure in the town	He had been on the Board of the CWR and a promoter of the CKPR. He served the CKPR as a solicitor from its formation until June 1879 (Edward Lamb Waugh was then appointed)	Died March 1891
August 1879	Alfred Kitching, Elmfield, Darlington	A nominee of NER. Presumed to be Alfred Kitching (1808-82), partner in William & Alfred Kitching of Hope Town Foundry, Darlington (cf. locos built 1846-47 for CWR)	Died February 13 1882
February 14 1880	Thomas Altham, Penrith	cf. the foundry and ironmongery business of Penrith in 1880s, and indeed in 1980s.	Died August 14 1900
August 19 1881	David Dale (becoming Sir David Dale, Bart) West Lodge, Darlington.	A nominee of the NER - with SDR and Consett Iron Company links.	Died April 1906
October 5 1881	John Pattinson, Vale View, St Bees/Greenbank, Whitehaven	Principal of the family flourmills, adjoining Whitehaven harbour and Bransty station (See also J.W. Pattinson, below)	Died March 1903
August 9 1882	James Cropper - MP for Kendal for 15 Years Chairman of Westmorland CC from 1888. Ellergreen, Burneside, Kendal	A nominee of the LNWR. Principal of the paper mills: James Cropper & Co., Burneside (see also Charles James Cropper, below)	Died October 16 1900
1882	Sir Henry M. Meysey-Thompson, Bart - MP (later: Lord Knaresborough), Kirkby Hall, York.	A Nominee of NER. A very infrequent attender at Keswick. Note that his father Sir Harry S. Meysey-Thompson, Bart had been Chairmen, YNMR, 1849-54 and on NER board 1855-74.	Retired May 1901

Table continued overleaf.....

BOARD MEMBERS;
COCKERMOUTH KESWICK & PENRITH RAILWAY (*Continued...*)

DATE JOINED	NAME (WITH RANK/APPOINTMENTS & ADDRESS)	COMPANY DUTIES/OTHER INTERESTS	LEFT THE BOARD
July 11 1888	Reginald Dykes Marshall (1832-1913) - DL, JP Castlerigg Manor, Keswick. He was grandson of John Marshall, of Patterdale Hall, and son of John Marshall (1797-1836), MP for Leeds, who purchased the family estates near Derwentwater in 1832 and put in hand building of St John's Church, Keswick.	A very active Director throuout the years 1888-1913. Depy Chairman from January 13 1910.	Died October 1913
August 9 1890	Thomas Glasson (of the McGlasson family - son of Thomas, who died 1870, *ante*) Castle Bank, Penrith (and later quoted as Barco, Penrith)	Penrith brewer, also (by 1910-11) chairman of Threlkeld Granite Co. The CKPR passed through his lands in the Redhills-Stainton vicinity.	Died July 1912
May 9 1891	Hamlet Riley (1851-1922) - Major, DL, LLB, JP. High Sheriff of Cumberland, 1901. Ennim, Blencow	Depy Chairman from December 1913. Chairman from August 1914	Died October 14 1922
August 25 1900	John Watson Nelson, Eden Bank, Langwathby		Died September 1913
November 16 1900	Charles James Cropper, Ellergreen, Burneside, Kendal. The name 'Charles J. Cropper' was carried by locomotive LNWR 1567/LMS 5917, during 1914-34; it was a 4-6-0 of the 'Claughton 'class the premier express locomotive type on the LNWR.	Nominee of LNWR on death of James Cropper. Chairman of James Cropper & Co. Ltd.	March 1923
May 17 1901	The Hon Cecil Duncombe (of The Fevershams, of Duncombe Park, Helmsley) Newton Grange,York.	A Nominee of the NER. He attended a Keswick meeting on July 11 1901 but seemingly no further meetings of the board.	Died May 20 1902
August 1 1902	Harry Tennant (sometimes Henry Tennant, as beneath his portrait in the NER Boardroom) Holgate Hill House, York.	A Nominee of the NER. He was on the NER board 1891-1910 and depy chairman of NER 1905-10. He attended at Keswick August 30 1902 but next on April 12 1906 (when a NER item was on the board agenda).	Died October 1910
May 14 1903	John William Pattinson (1871-1931) Richmond Hill, Whitehaven (to 1914)/Bolton Hall, Gosforth (1914-19)/Ravenstone, Bassenthwaite (1919-26).	Principal of the millers at Whitehaven. He followed his father, John Pattinson, on the CKPR board and was a regular attender. Chairman from November 1922. Other directorial interests included Threlkeld Granite Co. Ltd and at one time the Keswick Hotel Company.	March 1923
May 28 1906	Arthur Francis Pease. Hummersknott, Darlington.	A nominee of NER, Believed never to have attended at Keswick board meetings	Retired June 1907.
July 12 1907	Edmund Russborough Turton - MP Upsall Castle, Thirsk.	A nominee of the NER. He attended at Keswick August 31 1907, and then intermittently. He served as chairman of the RCH, in addition to NER and other Railway Company directorships.	March 1923
August 13 1908	Christopher John Parker (1859-1932) - DL, JP. The Laithes Skelton, Penrith (a property which he bought). A number of other Parker family houses and estates in Penrith and CKPR territory included Lathendales at Greystoke, now well known as a Quaker guest house.	Depy Chairman from 1922	March 1923
February 3 1910	Fredrick William Chance (1852-1932) (becoming Sir F.W. Chance, KBE). MP for Carlisle, 1905-09 and Mayor, 1907. High Sheriff of Cumberland 1915. Morton, Carlisle.	A nominee of the LNWR. The family were notable in Carlisle and district, as also before and after his time. He was a director of Ferguson Brothers, cotton manufactuers, of Holme Head,Carlisle.	March 1923

DATE JOINED	NAME (WITH RANK/APPOINTMENTS & ADDRESS)	COMPANY DUTIES/OTHER INTERESTS	LEFT THE BOARD
February 10 1910	John S. Randles (1857-1945) (becoming Sir John in 1913). MP (Con) for Cockermouth, 1900-06 and 1906-10 and Manchester NW 1912-18 and Manchester Exchange 1918-22. Brostowe Hill, Keswick.	He joined the board of Moss Bay H.I. & S Co. Ltd in 1890 and was appointed Chairman of Workington I&S Co. Ltd. on its formation in 1909. He was also a Director of the FR, 1911-23.	March 1923
	John S. Randles was son of the Rev. Marshall Randles, DD (1826-1904), Professor of theology in Wesleyan college, Didsbury. Sir John and Lady Randles (the latter nee Elia Hartley Spencer) spent the winter 1913-14 in India and he addressed Wesleyan missions in that country.		
October 13 1910	Sir Walter Richard Plummer - member of Cumberland C.C. 4 Queen's Square, Newcastle upon Tyne.	A nominee of the NER. He attended occasionally at Keswick.	Died December 10 1917
March 1 1913	Peter Thompson, Mellan, Keswick.	He had been on the staff of the CKPR before its opening in 1865; secretary and manager from July 21 1870. Giving up these offices in 1913 to join the board.	Died August 29 1920
December 6 1913	Robert Jackson Holdsworth. 110 Chorley New Road, Bolton/ Seat How(e),Thornthwaite from 1925 - of Wood End, Thornthwaite	A cotton spinner and hence Bolton associations. Also a director of Cumberland Granite Co, of Embleton, and later of Keswick Granite Co. Ltd.	March 1923
December 6 1913	Thomas William Mark. Great Crosthwaite, Keswick.		March 1923
November 7 1914	Robert Ernest Highton (1858-1931). Mayor of Workington, 1902-05. and 1910-14. A Cumberland County Councillor. Newlands,Workington/Threlkeld Leys, nr Cockermouth.	He was general manager of Moss Bay H. I. & S. Co. Ltd and had other interests in iron and steel.	March 1923
February 1918	Hon C.W. Lowther - Major, MP. He was son of James Lowther the first Lord Ullswater. 14 Wilton Street, London SW1/Westwood, Mayfield, Sussex.	A nominee of the NER	March 1923

The equanimity of the members of the Board was threatened in February 1913, when, at the shareholders' meeting, there was apparently an attempt not to re-elect Christopher Parker, of Penrith, a member since 1908. However, at an adjourned meeting on March 29 1913 he was re-appointed by a majority of 673 votes (perhaps implying that shares counted as votes) - and he continued as a member right through to the last meeting, on March 24 1923. Also in February 1913, John Randles, of Keswick, confided to J.W. Pattinson that: "Mr. Mark is very determined to clear Howard out and says that Howard ought to come home and fight." Henry C. Howard, of Greystoke Castle, had been a Board member for 37 years and was Chairman of the Company. Doubtless the reference is to Thomas W. Mark, of Keswick, presumably an influential shareholder who felt strongly that the Chairman was ineffective. In the event, T.W. Mark was himself elected to the Board in December of that year (1913) and Henry Howard died in August 1914, still as Chairman, and succeeded by Major Hamlet Riley. Mr Mark served until 1923.

From the time of completion of the station buildings at Keswick, in the early days of the CKPR Company, Board meetings were held in the Boardroom. On March 24 1923, the final meeting was attended by eight members, namely six local directors and the two NER nominees. The two members who died in 1920 and 1922 had not been replaced and the two LNWR nominees did not attend. This was probably out of courtesy, in view of their association with the Company 'taking over', but Charles James Cropper joined his colleagues for the group photograph (see page 186) in front of the Keswick Hotel and would presumably be present at a final luncheon.

Below: This group of railwaymen, seen at Troutbeck in CKPR days, comprises: Richard Hebson (left) and Joseph Watson (right), at the time senior and second signalmen; Tom Mitchinson is seated (right), the ganger in charge of the length. His colleagues of the gang are: Mark Cockbain (seated, left) Chapelhow and William Bainbridge (standing, second and third from the left) and T. Thwaite (the tall figure) the assistant timber loader, who moved to Australia. James Postlethwaite, the CKPR's timber loader, took the photograph.

Dick Hebson has 'CKP' tabs on his jacket collar. Joe Watson and T. Thwaite are wearing the CKPR company's green corduroy uniform. *Courtesy: Ted Watson.*

Below: The staff at Cockermouth station are gathered in the entrance. A proclamation is glimpsed beyond - perhaps the Armistice of 1918 - siginificantly, a member of staff killed in this war does not appear. The folk shown are: standing (L-R) An unidentified tall figure wearing traditional CKPR jacket and green corduroy trousers, and prominent CJS (Cockermouth Joint Station) lapel badges; an S&T inspector (with bowler); T. Armstrong (porter, from 1901); John Vickers (in service since 1900); Robert Little (Stationmaster, 1891-1921); a tall porter; Mark Allinson (signalman); Thomas Arthur Ridley (elder brother of Syd); Jack Stanley (signalman). Kneeling (L-R): Son of Reg Litt, Reg Litt; Billy Hartley and Percy Sanderson (Clerk). *Courtesy: Syd Ridley Jnr.*

Chapter 11

THE GLORY OF LAKELAND'S NORTHERN RAILWAY

A happy tribute, with a tinge of sadness......

Railwaymen and travellers prefer to forget the truncated decline of 1966-72 and remember the Keswick line's full 40 miles of active service to the community, in its magnificent setting. So, in this final pictorial chapter we will celebrate this marvellous country railway, which was once such an important part of Lakeland life.

The pictures have been chosen to illustrate the splendid surroundings, the characteristic motive power and distinctive traffic. Admirers of this railway paid their last respects to the entire through route on April 2 1966, a fortnight before closure west of Keswick, when the Stephenson Locomotive Society's North Western Area, jointly with the Manchester Locomotive Society, arranged the *Lakes and Fells* railtour. Scenes from that memorable day are presented

Above: A quite mgnificent picture which superbly captures the spirit of Lakeland's northern railway. On Whit Monday in 1963, a Carlisle-Keswick train is seen approaching Keswick in the charge of a pair of Ivatt '2MT' 2-6-0s. The train is just crossing one of the distinctive bowstring girder bridges which helped give the route its special character. *Stephen Crook.*

as a tribute to the railway and its people. The train originated in Manchester and travelled north via the Settle & Carlisle route and Carlisle Upperby to reach Penrith. Appropriately, Ivatt Class 2MT 2-6-0s Nos. 46458 and 46466 took over at this point, from LNER Class A3 'Pacific' No. 4472 *Flying Scotsman* at Penrith's Up main line platform, to take the train forward to Workington.

The weather was crisp and cold, with a good deal of snow. It was a splendid day, albeit tinged with sadness.....

Above: A final reminder of the industrial western end of the route, on which its foundations and early prosperity had been built. A 'Cauliflower' 0-6-0 is rounding the sharply curving approach to Derwent Junction, Workington, with a short freight train from Cockermouth. The locomotive is carrying a shedplate bearing the 12D - used by Workington in LMS days after 1935. By 1985, the terraced cottages in the background had also disappeared, along with the railway, which closed between Keswick and Workington in 1966. Note the signal on the single track which crossed the coastal main line (off left) to the docks. *Richard L. Pattinson/CRA.*

Above: On September 4 1954, Ivatt '2MT' 2-6-0 No. 46459 pauses at Keswick with the day's Down *Lakes Express*, bound for Workington. The train had been worked into Penrith by Stanier 'Princess Coronation' 4-6-2 No. 46236 *City of Bradford*. The beauti- ful light of this September evening illuminates to advantage the glazed screens and roof of the attractive buildings. Travellers from the south are dispersing to their homes and holiday haunts. *Harold D. Bowtell.*

Below: A pleasant scene at Keswick after 1955, when the first green-liveried DMUs were introduced into service between Workington and Penrith. The detail of the cast iron canopy is interesting to note, and a painted notice (P-3-52) on the saw-tooth valancing seems to indicate that the station was last painted in March 1952. This train was heading for Workington, and the car nearest the camera is No. M79017. *Ivor Nicholas.*

Left: Coming down the bank towards Penrith No. 1 box is 'Mickey Mouse' 2-6-0 No. 46458, heading a goods train from the limeworks at Blencow, on July 26 1962. *Derek Cross.*

Above: The line's premier pasenger duty was *The Lakes Express*, which linked Workington, via Keswick and Penrith, with London Euston. Here, very clean Ivatt 2-6-0 No. 46491, a stalwart of the line, climbs past Penrith No. 1 box and onto the CKPR line with the Down 'Lakes' during 1962. The leading coaches are LMS vehicles. *Derek Cross.*

Right: On April 2 1966, the joint SLS/MLS *Lakes and Fells* railtour ran over the entire 40 miles or so between Penrith and Workington, just a couple of weeks before the section west of Keswick closed. Here, the train is awaiting departure from Penrith's Down main line platform after the detaching of No. 4472 *Flying Scotsman* in favour of 'Mickey Mouse' 2-6-0s Nos. 46458 and 46426 for the onward journey through Lakeland. *Harold D. Bowtell.*

Above: There was snow in the fells on the April 2 1966, and between from Workington and Cockermouth, '2MT' No. 46432 had been out with staff clearing snow from points and other problem areas. The locomotive is seen at Cockermouth returning tender first to Workington. *Ian S. Carr.*

Left: The *Lakes and Fells* train is approaching Blencow, on the initial climb, from Penrith. Single line tokens had to be exchanged in passing through the station, of which the buildings are seen ahead.
Harold D. Bowtell.

Top: The only halt for the *Lakes and Fells* railtour was at Keswick, remarkably smart and tidy at this time, despite its imminent loss of through station status. *Harold D. Bowtell*

Above: With snow-capped peaks in the background, the railtour is seen hastening beside Bassenthwaite Lake, nearing Hursthole Point and Beck Wythop cottages. *Derek Cross.*

Above: Easing to run cautiously past Cockermouth signalbox, the token authorising travel from Bassenthwaite Lake station is about to be passed out to the signalman by the fireman aboard No. 46426. *Ian S. Carr.*

Left: .... the changeover has been effected and the new token authorising onward running to Brigham is checked by the enginemen as they accelerate through Cockermouth's platforms before carefully descending the bank to the old Cockermouth Junction and the 'C&W' section. Compare this picture with that taken earlier in the day, reproduced on page 198 - the bright sun had completely thawed the snow which had prompted line clearance operations!

Beyond Workington, this railtour ran south over the former - Furness main line, to Hellifield and Manchester with a complement of travellers from many parts of Britain. *Flying Scotsman* took over the train again at Arnside, that evening. *Ian S. Carr.*

ACKNOWLEDGMENTS

It has been a pleasure and privilege to enjoy the co-operation of many old and new friends in course of my research and in furthering the presentation of the story of the cross-country railway through Lakeland. The archives staff at Carlisle Castle have been ever-patient and the WCML has become well-worn in course of 'day trips' of more than 500 miles between Oxenholme and Kew Gardens, for delvings in the Public Record Office. Above all, I thank the many folk who devoted their working lives to the railway concerned, or lived and maybe farmed beside it and then talked with me; clarity of recollection provides a wonderful perspective for the historian. I thank, among others:

Jim Airey and Mrs. Airey, Frank Alcock, Roy Anderson, Doctor Michael Andrews, G.J. Aston, Nancy Banks-Smith, Mrs. Bennett, J.S. Berry, Ian Bishop (and Trust House Forte, for whom he is a manager), Robert Bond, George Bott, W.E. Boyd, J. Bernard Bradbury, Henry and Mrs. Briggs, Derek J.W. Brough, Joe W. Brownrigg, Dorothy Butcher, Ian S. Carr, Joseph C. Carruthers and Mrs. Elizabeth Carruthers (nee Longcake), Oliver F. Carter, John McG.Charters, Les G. Charlton, Frank Clarkson, J.G. Coates, Edgar Corless, Elizabeth Cook, Mary Cowperthwaite, Bert and Mrs. Cowperthwaite, Derek Cross, E. Lloyd Daniels (and the Derwent Railway Society), J.D. Darby, W.B. Darnell, John Dawson, Alan G. Dunbar, John Duncan, Hugh G. Ellison, John Farrer, Gordon and Mrs. Ferries, Neville Fields, Edward Foster, Richard D. Foster, E.H. Fowkes, Gregory R. Fox, Mrs. Emily Gates, Gordon Graham, Jack Hall, John M. Hammond, Eric W. Hannan, Kenneth Harper, Stanley and Mrs. Harrison, Tom W. Hartley, William and Mrs. Hebson, Major J.W.B. Hext, J.D. Hinde, Robert Hodgson, Peter Holmes, Geoffrey O. Holt, Kenneth Hoole, Geoffrey Horsman, Philip Houldershaw, the Reverend Rodney Hughes, Roy V. Hughes MBE, T.A. Hughes, Harry Jack, Tom W. Jackson and Mrs. Jackson, Mrs. Mary Johnston, William and Mrs. Kelt, Jack Y. Lancaster, Robert Leslie, Lance Laverick, Geoffrey Lord, Peter and Ann Los, John McCallum, R.B. Hasell McCosh, Gurney MacInnes, John Mandale, Thomas Murray, Charles Neele, Edwin K. Nelson, Gordon Nichol, Kenneth J. Norman, Cecil and Mrs. Oldfield, Barbara M. Patterson, John and Mrs. Pattinson, Clive Pattinson, Derek A. Pattinson, George H. Pattinson, Michael Peascod, J.D. Petty, Ronald N. Redman, Syd and Mrs. Ridley, John E. Roberts, Peter W. Robinson, Miss Mary Routledge, Eric S. Russell, Ian G. Sadler, Percy and Mrs. Sanderson, Carol Sarsfield-Hall, Mr. and Mrs. Scott, James L. Slater, David L. Smith, H.R. Stones, D.H. Stuart, Ted Talbot, Richard Tangye, Thomas Taylor, David F. Tee, Albert Tims, John Tinkler, Thomas Tinkler, Joseph and Mrs. Tinnion, Ron Tinnion, Jessie Titterington, Edwin and Marina Thompson, Oswald W. Todhunter, Jack Tyson, Phoebe Wallace, A. St.G. Walsh, Edward Watson, Joseph K. Watson, Joseph Watson (of Workington), D.R. Wattleworth, David R. Webb, G.D. Whitworth, James Willan, J. Banks Wivell and Mrs. Wivell (nee Philipson), Bob Wren, William Young and Mrs. Young (formerly Hughes).

Special thanks are due to Arthur Chambers for his encouragement, and various cartography; to Doug Rendell for his extensive and professional photographic copying and other work on my behalf; and to Ken Norman for his enthusiastic pilotage in the Richard Pattinson collection (which is in the care of the Cumbrian Railways Association). Photographers and sources of illustrations are acknowledged individually, where known to me. Friends who have read critically and most helpfully through drafts of various parts of the work are: Richard Foster, John Hammond, Kenneth Hoole, Roy Hughes, David Tee, Albert Tims and Dudley Whitworth.

Authorities consulted include the Public Record Office, Kew; the National Railway Museum Library, York (with a special word of thanks for John Edgington) the Cumbria County Record Office, Carlisle Castle (Bruce Jones and colleagues); Abbot Hall Art Gallery and Museum, Kendal (Miss Mary Burkitt and colleagues); the Fitz Museum, Keswick (Norman Gandy); Manchester Central Library (and notably Harry Horton); Tullie House Library, Carlisle (Mr. Wilkinson and Mr. White); the library of the Institution of Civil Engineers; Cumbria County Council (Bridges Department); the Keswick Convention (Maurice Rowlandson and colleagues) British Railways – several departments, including; Robert H. Blyth and colleagues of Manchester, on signalling; the Chief Civil Engineer, LMR and his colleagues at Preston; and Messrs Nicholson and Copeland at Workington. John Hurst and colleagues at the *Cumberland and Westmorland Herald*, Penrith, also readily offered the hospitality of their archives.

WORKS OF REFERENCE:

The Iron and Steel Industry of West Cumberland (J.Y. Lancaster & D.R. Wattleworth, 1977).
Railway Reminiscences (G.P. Neele, 1904).
A History of the Cockermouth, Keswick and Penrith Railway (W. McGowan Gradon, 1948)
The Cockermouth, Keswick and Penrith Railway - In Memoriaum (J.M. Hammond, 1972).
Forgotten Railways of North West England (John Marshall, 1981).
A Regional History of the Railways: the Lake Counties (David Joy, 1983).
The North Eastern Railway (W.W. Tomlinson, 1914).
The Stainmore Railway (K. Hoole, 1973)
History of Cockermouth (J. Bernard Bradbury).
Threlkeld, Cumbria; Glimpses of Village History (J.H. Vine Hall, Threlkeld, 1977).
Diary of George Schollick, 1893-1928.
The Chronicles of Boulton's Siding (Alfred Rosling Bennett, 1927), ref pp 46-47 and 264.
Cumbrian Families and Heraldry (Roy Huddleston & R.S Boumphrey).
Notable Cumbrians (Chance).
Westmorland and Cumberland Leaders (Ernest Gaskell).
The Impact of the Railway on the development of Keswick as a tourist resort, 1860-1914 (Dissertation by Paul Richard McGloin, University of Lancaster).
Register of closed Passenger and Goods Stations (C.R. Clinker, 1978, and supplements).

A Biographical Dictionary of Railway Engineers (John Marshall, 1978).
The Railway Magazine, 1897-1984, and in particular; *1907* (first part) : J. Thornton Burge on pp 372-373; and year *1921* (second part) Cecil J. Allen on pp73-80.
Trains Illustrated, year *1961*; Cecil J. Allen on pp 598-604 & 629.
Cumbria: December 1966 pp 432-5 and February 1973 (W.R. Mitchell on Threlkeld).
Newsletter of the Cumbrian Railways Association including -
E. Craven on locomotives of the CWR, in *February 1978 p9* and *Oct 1978 pp 2-5*;
P.W. Robinson on the CK&PR until 1866, in *July 1979 pp 5-7*;
G. Thomlinson on early days, in *August 1984 pp 41-46*.;
Newsletter of the National Trust - on Canon Rawnsley.
Journal of the Stephenson Locomotive Society, especially on LNWR engine sheds and *J.W. Armstrong on Tebay* (the latter in *1953, pp 161-2*).
The Railway Observer (RCTS), particularly in the later 1930s and subsequently on renumbering of motive power depots.
Railway Junction Diagrams (of the Railway Clearing House).
Ordnance Survey map sheets to 25in scale, various editions.
Bradshaw's Railway Timetables and *Bradshaw's Manual*, various years.

Harold D. Bowtell,
Kendal,
Westmorland
January 1989,